WONDERS
OF THE WORLD

Lionel Grigson
Foreword by Cliff Michelmore

GALLERY BOOKS
An Imprint of W. H. Smith Publishers Inc.
112 Madison Avenue
New York City 10016

Page 1: The snow-covered summit of Mount Fuji, Japan.

Title pages: The glow of sunset behind the San Francisco-Oakland Bay Bridge and the San Francisco city skyline.

Page 6: The Grand Canal, Venice, with the Palazzo Cavalli Franchetti left and the church of Santa Maria della Salute in the distance.

Introduction by Eric Inglefield.
Essays on Mount Etna, the Colosseum,
the Terracotta Warriors of Xi'an and the
Rocky Mountains by Eric Inglefield.

First published in Great Britain in 1985 by
The Hamlyn Publishing Group Limited

This edition published in 1989 by
Gallery Books
an imprint of W.H. Smith Publishers Inc.
112 Madison Avenue, New York City 10016

Copyright © 1985 The Hamlyn Publishing Group Limited

ISBN 0-8317-9495-X

Printed in Spain

Contents

Foreword

A Spanish writer and philosopher wrote that 'To be surprised, to wonder, is to begin to understand'. I think that travellers, be they international jet-setters or those who prefer their armchairs, should always pack in their knapsacks those two essential items – 'wonder' and 'surprise'. They are always 'Wanted on Voyage'. Apart from anything else they always provide adequate compensation for that most unwelcome and miserable of travelling companions, 'disappointment'. If a place fails to live up to expectations or reputation, our luggage seems to get heavier. So the delight of experiencing surprise and wonder with

enthusiasm is absolutely necessary for any successful, enlightening trip. Those of us who travel for a living, taking in the sights of the world as we go, are constantly envied by those who are forced to stay at home. The annual foray on holiday is not the same thing. They seem to imagine that our lives are one long voyage of discovery like some latter-day Marco Polo or Captain Cook.

It is no use explaining that whilst we are being carried off to far-away places with strange sounding names we are working, that there is nothing glamorous about the actual travelling and

that there are times when we end up in far-from-romantic destinations. Experience teaches you not to dwell on the fact that the words 'travel' and 'travail' come from the same etymological root, but to remember that you are lucky to be there and that you have brought with you the ability to be surprised.

I wonder if those travellers of old were envied as they struck out from their home shores motivated, as most were, either by acquisitiveness or religious zeal? As they crusaded, campaigned and conquered were they filled with surprise when they first set eyes upon myth-laden temples, historic buildings and the great riches of the Orient? I do not doubt that they were as intrigued as we are to this day at the glories of nature and the wonders of the ancient world. They were the first to bring back incontrovertible accounts of their discoveries, the first eye-witness reports of new lands, people and hitherto unseen masterpieces of man and nature. There is no doubt that, like the painters and writers, the travellers and merchants who have followed their tread, they often exaggerated what they saw or experienced.

All of us travel for our own reasons with our own motivations. We are all on our own voyage of reconnaisance or exploration, whether we do the actual travelling or let our imaginations fly by leafing through a book such as this most attractive and informative one – *The Wonders of the World*. In it you will I hope find wonders – both man-made and natural – that will surprise you and help your understanding.

Television, magazines, films and books all open up this wonderful world of ours for us. Once travellers were carried across the Alps by elephants or into Samarkand in sedan chairs; others took the Grand Tour or went on *voyages philosophiques*. Today jet aircraft, international telephones, satellites and computers which talk to each other may have reduced our time scales. What none has done is to reduce the beauty and glory of the Taj Mahal, the Valley of the Kings at Luxor or the sight of the setting sun in the Grand Canyon. There are many extraordinary wonders in this world, ancient and modern. I hope that you enjoy the fine selection within this book.

Introduction

'How great is the wonder of heavenly and earthly things!' Cicero, *De Natura Deorum*.

Anyone who has ever gazed up at the sky on a clear, dark night and tried to grasp the significance of the millions of stars in the vastness of space has surely felt that strange mixture of emotions that we call wonder. Even with all the advances of modern science, which have given us radio telescopes and space probes, we are really little further forward in discovering the true nature and meaning of the universe than was the Roman writer and thinker Cicero in the first century BC. The heavens are still something which we can only perceive, with our limited understanding, as the creation of some divine being, before which we feel admiration, fear and respect. As the nineteenth-century Scottish thinker Thomas Carlyle observed in one of his essays, 'wonder is the basis of worship'.

In the same way, many of the seemingly inexplicable and awe-inspiring phenomena of nature that we can observe all around us can most conveniently be explained away as the visible proof of the creative hand of God. It has been so since time began. When the great Italian poet Dante declared that 'Nature is the art of God', he was simply expressing an age-old belief held not only by primitive peoples everywhere but also by the great civilizations of history. Whenever natural phenomena could not be accounted for by rational explanation, religious myths based on the machinations of the gods provided suitable answers (because they were man-made) and offered comfort from the terrors of the real world. Every natural wonder had its attendant deity.

For primitive peoples, such frightening natural occurrences as thunder and lightning could only sensibly be interpreted as expressions of divine wrath. So when Kiowa Indians on the Great Plains of North America heard thunder crashing around that tall pillar of rock known as the Devil's Tower, they were convinced that the Great Spirit was using its flat summit as a drum upon which to vent his fury. It is thus easy to see how, because thunder and lightning were common events in the earth's mountainous regions, areas which were largely inaccessible to mere mortals, the loftiest peaks came to be regarded as the dwelling-places of the gods and therefore objects of wonder and awe. Thus the ancient Greeks considered cloud-mantled Mount Olympus as the abode of Zeus and other mythical deities, and Mount Etna, an unpredictable and violent volcano in Sicily, as one

of the subterranean forges of Hephaistos, the god of fire. Awe, respect and fear, in varying degrees, were the emotional responses to divine manifestations such as these which people believed they detected in nature.

There were in ancient times, however, scholars such as Aristotle and Pliny the Elder who attempted to investigate more deeply the wonders of the natural world, and their observations, though now found to contain many factual inaccuracies, were a stimulus for many later European thinkers. While Pliny was the accepted authority on all scientific matters until the Middle Ages, Aristotle and other Greek philosophers had to wait until their rediscovery during the Renaissance for their work to be given serious analysis. But it was the rationalism of the seventeenth and eighteenth centuries – the Age of Reason– that gave rise to the fundamental scientific investigation of natural phenomena through such new intellectual disciplines as geology. The earth's wonders were now being coaxed to give up their secrets.

It was at this time that reports by European travellers and explorers of unusual land features in far-away places encouraged the growing curiosity of the public about the world. Sometimes the stories filtering back were accepted at face value. In the early nineteenth century, for example, the American explorer Zebulon Pike's mistaken contention that the Great Plains of the West – now

Above right: elegant columns stand amid the ruins of the once-magnificent Roman Temple of Jupiter at Baalbek in present-day Lebanon. They are an eloquent reminder of the many architectural wonders created in ancient times throughout the world.

Right: The awesome Devils Tower, one of America's natural wonders, rises abruptly into the sky 865 feet (264 metres) above the rolling plains of Wyoming. This eerie column of volcanic rock is enshrouded in the myths and legends of the Indians, and has also featured as a mysterious presence in the space film 'Close Encounters of the Third Kind.'

vast wheatlands and cattle ranches – were 'incapable of cultivation' created the myth of the 'Great American Desert' that lingered on for years. No one, however, believed the apparently incredible tales that the rugged fur-trapper John Colter brought back from a trip to the Rocky Mountains in the winter of 1807–8. Colter spoke of a snow-covered forested land where boiling water shot into the sky in great jets and gurgled out of mineral-encrusted springs, where the air was laden with sulphurous fumes and clouds of steam that hissed from deep gashes in the ground, and where forest clearings were filled with cauldrons of bubbling hot mud. What his contemporaries laughingly dubbed 'Colter's Hell' we now know was that astonishing area of volcanic activity designated as Yellowstone National Park, one of the most fascinating of the earth's natural wonders.

With the exploration of the world's more remote areas in the last two centuries, countless spectacular sights, including mountains, rivers, lakes, waterfalls, rock formations and caves, have been added to its catalogue of natural wonders, many of them described in this book. Among North America's many spectacles are Carlsbad Caverns, Crater Lake, the Grand Canyon, Niagara Falls and Yosemite National Park. South America boasts Angel Falls, Lake Titicaca, Sugar Loaf Mountain and the vast Amazon River Basin among its special wonders. Elsewhere are such splendours as the

Great Rift Valley, River Nile, Sahara Desert and Victoria Falls of Africa; the Dead Sea, Mount Everest and Mount Fuji of Asia; and Ayers Rock and the Great Barrier Reef of Australia. In Europe there are sights that have been known for centuries, among them Mount Etna, the Norwegian fjords, the volcanoes of Iceland and the Dolomites of Italy. Many of the world's most spectacular natural wonders are now protected as national parks and are popular places of pilgrimage both for sightseers and scientists.

In addition to such natural wonders, our planet has a rich store of magnificent architectural and engineering masterpieces created by mankind over thousands of years. When contemplating these creations, we are filled with admiration and astonishment at our own genius rather than with any sense of humility or awe before the evidence of some God-given gift of creativity. Yet there is also a certain amount of deference in our reactions, for undoubtedly many of the world's great buildings – royal palaces, great cathedrals, mighty castles and even city halls – were deliberately intended to impress either by size or the richness of their decoration, or both, and to inspire a degree of awe before the superior human power that they represented. Those man-made structures considered to be sufficiently splendid to be named as a wonder also have another quality: a universality of appeal that gives them a special status in any period of time in any part of the world. Such were the lovely buildings constructed on the Acropolis in Athens in the fifth century BC, which, in the words written by the Greek essayist Plutarch some five hundred years later, 'were created in a short time for all time'.

Long before Plutarch, in the second century BC, the Greek poet Antipater of Sidon had drawn up a selection of what he considered to be the greatest architectural and engineering monuments then known, the so-called 'Seven Wonders of the World'. From his list only the Pyramids of Egypt – probably the world's most famous buildings – are still standing. His other choices were the Hanging Gardens of Babylon, the statue of Zeus at Olympia, the Temple of Artemis (or Diana) at Ephesus, the Mausoleum at Halicarnassus, the Colossus of Rhodes and the Pharos of Alexandria, all of which are described in The Seven Wonders of Antiquity. From the evidence later investigations have been able to uncover, all of these structures were truly impressive feats of creation.

It is curious to note that many of the outstanding buildings of the past which most people would include in a list of all-time wonders have been subjected during their history to vicissitudes and dangers not compatible with their aesthetic value.

The Parthenon, one of the buildings on the Acropolis of Athens, for example, was used as a gunpowder store in the seventeenth century, and in January 1985 part of the magnificent temple of Borobudur was blown up in an act of terrorism. The Colosseum in Rome was plundered for building stone by Popes building splendid palaces during the Renaissance. Indeed, the Renaissance, with its idealization of classical Greek and Roman culture, was more concerned with discussing the abstract 'idea' of the perfect Utopian civilization than with studying and preserving the rich heritage of ancient monuments which it actually possessed. So the Roman Forum was to remain half-buried in the mud for many years to come.

It was only when travellers in the seventeenth and eighteenth centuries described the ruins of ancient cities they had seen in various parts of the world that a real desire to investigate and document them was awakened, and aristocratic gentlemen began the Grand Tour round the most fashionable sites. One of the most influential of these travellers was French-born Jean Chardin,

whose descriptions of the amazing ruins at Persepolis, made on visits to Persia in the 1660s and 1670s, were published in 1711. Soon afterwards, excavations at the Roman cities of Herculaneum and Pompeii and the decipherment of the Egyptian hieroglyphics on the famous Rosetta Stone by Jean François Champollion captured the imagination of Europe and gave added stimulus to the study of the ancient civilizations. What had been until then virtually treasure hunts mounted by aristocratic collectors in search of valuable antiquities was now turning into proper scientific investigation. The new science of archaeology had been born. In the course of the nineteenth century, many relics from the great civilizations of the world came under close scrutiny, and the ruins at such sites as Baalbek, Petra, Chichén Itzá, Machu Picchu and Angkor Wat came to be recognized as some of mankind's greatest architectural achievements.

Scattered throughout the world there is also a rich legacy of treasures whose good state of preservation has not called for rediscovery by the archaeologists. Among these are the Japanese temples at Nara, the mosques of Isfahan, the Taj Mahal and rock-cut temples of Ellura and Ajanta in India, and a host of castles, palaces and cathedrals in Europe such as the Moorish palace of the Alhambra in Spain, Neuschwanstein Castle in Bavaria, the palace of Versailles in France and the awesome Tower of London. There are also many great cities around the world that can be considered in their entirety as man-made wonders for the cultural heritage they represent – such cities as Jerusalem, Venice, Leningrad, New York City and Brasília.

Governments around the world are becoming increasingly aware of the value of the natural and man-made wonders that they have in their charge, and many are ensuring that their treasures are properly protected and preserved for the benefit and enjoyment of future generations.

The dramatic peaks of the Dolomites in northern Italy (below left) are among Europe's most spectacular natural wonders. Equally impressive are the towering skyscrapers of New York, which create one of the world's finest skylines (below right).

Seven Wonders
of Antiquity

The Pyramids at Giza, Egypt

The Colossus of Rhodes

Rhodes, the chief island of the Dodecanese and 12 miles (19 kilometres) from the coast of Turkey, has had as long and varied a history as almost any island in the Mediterranean. A Greek island now, as it was in ancient times, Rhodes also experienced rule by the Romans, Persians, Arabs, Venetians, Genoese, the crusading Knights of St John, and the Turks. Much of this chequered past is revealed in the rich architectural heritage of the city of Rhodes. But only two simple pillars in the harbour mark the presumed site of Rhodes' most famous monument – the Colossus.

In 312 BC Rhodes decided to join King Ptolemy of Egypt in his war against Antigonus of Macedon, and greatly contributed to Ptolemy's success. Smarting for revenge, the Macedonians returned to punish Rhodes a few years later and besieged the city with a vast force of men and ships. Though they were greatly outnumbered, the Rhodians managed to beat back the Macedonian attacks for a whole year until Ptolemy of Egypt finally sailed to their rescue.

Among the defenders of Rhodes had been a sculptor, Chares of Lindus. To commemorate their deliverance from the Macedonians the jubilant Rhodians commissioned Chares to create a huge bronze sculpture in honour of the island's patron deity, the sun god Helios, or Apollo. As an additional memorial to the great siege, the Colossus was to be cast entirely from metal taken from the war engines abandoned by the Macedonians.

The task took Chares twelve years, from 292 to 280 BC. According to one story, when the statue was all but complete Chares found that he had made a mistake in his calculations and killed himself. If this is true, it amounted to history's greatest piece of self-criticism. The Colossus was hailed as the most perfect representation of the human form ever achieved, and was immediately declared to be one of the wonders of the world.

The Colossus is thought to have been 105 feet (32 metres) high and to have weighed about 295 tons (300 tonnes). It stood near the harbour, but exactly where is not known. According to some accounts, ships sailed between its legs, and a large mirror set in its chest was so brilliant that it could be seen by ships leaving Egypt.

But the Colossus was to be the most short-lived of the ancient world's wonders. Only fifty-six years after it was put up, an earthquake brought the Colossus crashing down on to the harbour rocks, where it lay broken into many pieces. The pieces were still there in the first century AD, when the Roman historian Pliny described them: 'Few men can clasp the thumb in their arms, and the fingers are larger than most statues. Where the limbs are broken asunder, vast caverns are seen yawning in the interior . . .'

When the Arabs captured Rhodes in the seventh century AD, the mighty statue's remains suffered the final indignity of being sold to a Jewish merchant for scrap. Nine trips each by a hundred camels were needed to carry the pieces away.

Right: The harbour at Rhodes, the main town on the Aegean Island of the same name, was the site of the huge monument known as the Colossus in the third century BC.

Below: The great Colossus of Rhodes, according to some accounts, once stood astride the entrance to the island's port, so high that ships could sail between its legs.

The Hanging Gardens of Babylon

All that remains today of the once mighty city of Babylon are a few ruins by the River Euphrates in Iraq. Nearly four thousand years ago Babylon was already the capital of one of the world's first great empires, Old Babylonia. Eventually, Babylonia was defeated by the rival empire of Assyria. But in 626 BC an alliance between the Chaldeans of southern Babylonia and the Medes of Persia defeated Assyria, and the Chaldean ruler Nabopolassar made himself king of Babylon.

During the reigns of Nabopolassar and his son Nebuchadnezzar II (605–561 BC) Babylon regained and even exceeded its old glory. Nabopolassar built mighty walls around the city and Nebuchadnezzar continued this work, throwing up fortresses and strongpoints along the walls. A great bridge was built across the Euphrates, and a splendid fortified royal palace rose above the city.

Near to the palace, by the banks of the Euphrates, Nebuchadnezzar built the famous Hanging Gardens which were regarded as one of the wonders of the ancient world. Nebuchadnezzar's queen was a princess of his father's allies, the Medes, whose armies had helped defeat the Assyrians. According to legend this queen, Semiramis, missed the hills of her Persian homeland and disliked Babylon's flatness. So Nebuchadnezzar decided to please her by building a man-made hill in the form of terraced gardens.

The Hanging Gardens rose to a height of about 328 feet (100 metres) – nearly three-quarters of the height of the Great Pyramid – and were surrounded by a reinforcing wall 23-feet (seven metres) thick. Wide marble staircases connected the terraces, which were supported by rows of arches. Stone flowerbeds, lined with lead and filled with soil, lay along each terrace and were filled with a profusion of exotic trees, shrubs, flowers and creepers.

On the top terrace a series of cisterns fed the fountains, waterfalls and streams which kept the Hanging Gardens watered. The water was raised from the Euphrates by pumps, probably Archimedian screws, worked by slaves.

While we can spare a thought for the slaves whose non-stop labour irrigated them, there can be no doubt that the Hanging Gardens of Babylon must have been one of the most beautiful sights in the ancient world. Equally, they must have been a prodigious feat of architecture and hydraulic engineering, since considerable skill and ingenuity would have been needed to prevent the masonry from being undermined and weakened by the water which kept the gardens lush.

For all its splendour, the new Babylonian empire was short-lived. Only twenty-two years after Nebuchadnezzar's death, it fell to the Persian emperor Cyrus the Great, whose army entered the city without a struggle. The Hanging Gardens may have survived until the third century BC, when they were described by a Babylonian priest, Berossus. But today all that is left of them is the remains of a well and one or two arches.

Right: The famous Hanging Gardens of Babylon were built in the sixth century BC by Nebuchadnezzar II to please his home-sick queen, Semiramis. Although less impressive than this somewhat romantic artist's impression, the gardens were a remarkable feat of water engineering.

Below: A lion finely modelled in relief once decorated the magnificent glazed brick walls of the throne room in Nebuchadnezzar's splendid palace in Babylon.

The Pharos at Alexandria

Founded by Alexander the Great after he conquered Egypt in 332 BC, Alexandria became Egypt's chief port and one of the great centres of culture during the Hellenistic age.

For a good part of its history, Alexandria had an appropriate beacon in the remarkable lighthouse which stood by the harbour on the island of Pharos. Built in white marble in about 270 BC, during the reign of King Ptolemy II of Egypt, the lighthouse was designed by the Greek architect Sostratos. According to some accounts it stood 440 feet (134 metres) high, with a square bottom section, an octagonal middle section and a circular top section. Other historians say that it was built in eight or four towers, one above the other and each smaller than the one below.

In the topmost section or tower stood a vast brazier which was kept burning day and night to provide a beacon. The beacon was visible to ships more than 25 miles (40 kilometres) out in the Mediterranean. On the summit of the lighthouse was a huge mirror. In this mirror, according to legend, it was possible to see everything that was happening in Constantinople – right across the eastern Mediterranean and Asia Minor! It was also said that the mirror could be used like a burning glass to focus the sun's rays on hostile ships far out at sea and burn them.

Allowing for such exaggeration, the lighthouse at Alexandria must have deserved to be ranked among the wonders of the ancient world. Though it was not the first lighthouse in the Mediterranean, it was certainly the largest. The island on which it stood soon gave its name to the lighthouse itself, and so the word Pharos came to be used in many languages for any lighthouse.

The Pharos continued to light ships to Alexandria for nearly nine hundred years, until the Arabs captured the city and half dismantled the great lighthouse. It is said that the caliph al-Walid was tricked into doing this by a spy sent by the emperor of Constantinople, who wanted to prevent the Pharos being used to benefit Muslim shipping. The spy claimed that a fabulous treasure was buried underneath the Pharos. Only when the lighthouse was beyond reconstruction did the caliph realize the trick. By then, too, the great mirror had fallen and shattered to smithereens.

What was left of Pharos survived until 1375, when an earthquake shook Alexandria and hurled the remains of the ancient lighthouse into the harbour, where some of its once white marble stones still lie.

The great Pharos at Alexandria, Egypt, was a famous landmark for seafarers for nine hundred years until dismantled by the Arabs.

The Pyramids of Giza

The pyramids of Egypt are without doubt the most famous structures ever built. Of the seventy-odd pyramids built over a thousand years, the three at Giza, the gigantic tombs of the pharaohs Cheops, Chephren and Mycerinus, are by far the largest. Built 4600 years ago during the Fourth Dynasty, the Giza Pyramids came to be considered the greatest of the Seven Wonders of the Ancient World, and they are the only ones still standing.

The largest of the three Giza Pyramids is the Pyramid of Cheops, often called the Great Pyramid. In its base area of about 570000 square feet (53000 square metres) it would be possible to fit comfortably St Paul's Cathedral and Westminster Abbey, St Peter's in Rome and the Cathedrals of Milan and Florence. The Great Pyramid is estimated to contain some 2300000 limestone blocks, each weighing 2.5 tons (2.5 tonnes) and measuring about three feet (a metre) in each direction.

As astonishing as the size of the Great Pyramid is the accuracy of its construction. At the base the average length of the four sides is 755 feet (230.12 metres); the difference between the longest and shortest baseline is just eight inches (20 centimetres), and the four corners make almost perfect rightangles to within fractions of one degree. By observing the stars, the builders of the Great Pyramid were able to align its sides to face the cardinal points of the compass, also to within fractions of a degree. With an angle of elevation of 52° the Great Pyramid rises to a height of nearly 490 feet (150 metres).

Nobody knows how many people worked on the Great Pyramid or exactly how it was built. Vast numbers were certainly necessary: Sir Flinders Petrie, the great archaeologist, calculated that 100000 men transported the blocks to the site and another 4000 worked on the actual construction.

The first task was levelling the Pyramid's bedrock foundation. This was done by surrounding the base area with mud and filling it with water. Trenches were dug in the rock floor at equal depths from the water's surface. Then the water was run off and the rock chipped away to the level of the trenches. In this way the foun-

Right: The famous Sphinx, cut out of solid rock near the pyramids of Giza more than 4500 years ago, bears the weather-worn portrait head of the pharaoh Chephren on the body of a lion.

Below: The Pyramid of Mycerinus, the smallest of the three great pyramids at Giza, was once faced in granite and limestone, but now bares the rough stones of its core to the elements of weathering.

dation was levelled to an accuracy of within half an inch (nearly 13 millimetres) at the outside edge.

After being quarried in the Mokkatam Hills the limestone blocks were brought to the site by sledge and barge. The Egyptians had no pulleys, so the only way to raise the blocks to the height necessary to fit them into the Pyramid would have been an inclined plane – a long ramp built to cover one side of the Pyramid.

How the inside of the Pyramid was built is unknown, but it may have been around a vertical core of masonry, as in earlier pyramids. The core would have been cased with limestone blocks to give a stepped effect. The steps were then filled in with 'packing blocks' and lastly the sides were dressed with smooth facing stones.

In the centre of the Great Pyramid lies Cheops' burial chamber. Built of granite, it measures 34 by 17 feet (10.5 by 5.3 metres) and is 19 feet (5.8 metres) high. The king's granite sarcophagus still lies in the room's west side. From the entrance on the north face of the Pyramid, a corridor descended into the foundation rock, leading to an uncompleted burial chamber. About 66 feet (20 metres) from the entrance, the original corridor connected with a second corridor which ascends for about 131 feet (40 metres) before levelling off and leading to a second uncompleted tomb chamber. This continues into a wide ascending passage, called the Grand Gallery, at the top of which is the king's burial chamber.

Cheops' Pyramid is surrounded by rows of low, flat tombs called mastabas and three small pyramids in which his family and high officials were buried. By the south wall is an underground chamber, discovered in 1954, which contained Cheops' funeral ship, untouched since being placed there 4600 years before.

The second Giza Pyramid, the Pyramid of Chephren, lies to the south-west of the Great Pyramid, and is only slightly smaller – 460 feet (140 metres) high and 709 feet (216 metres) square, with a slightly steeper angle of elevation. The top quarter of this pyramid has its original white limestone facing, unlike Cheops' Pyramid which has been completely stripped of its facing. The Pyramid of Mycerinus, the third and smallest Giza Pyramid, lies south-west of Chephren. It is 354 feet square (108 metres square) and 230 feet (70 metres) high, and contains less than a tenth of the limestone built into each of the other two pyramids. It was faced in pink granite and limestone.

Apart from its pyramids, the most famous feature of Giza is the Sphinx, carved out of living rock in the form of a human-headed lion. A portrait of Chephren, it was later worshipped as a sun god. This colossus, 66 feet (20 metres) high and 240 feet (73 metres) long, guards the causeway which leads to the Pyramid of Chephren.

The evolution of the pyramid form is probably connected with early Egyptian sun worship. A pyramidal stone, the *benben*, symbolized the sun god, its slanting sides representing the sun's rays. So the pyramid itself may simply have been an enlarged form of this symbol. At certain times, especially when afternoon clouds form in winter, the sun's rays break through at exactly the angle of the sides of the Giza Pyramids. It is easy to see why the Egyptians regarded a pyramid as 'a

staircase to heaven being laid for the king'.

The five largest pyramids, including the Giza Pyramids, seem to have been built in a single century, and at an early stage of Egyptian history. They were much larger than subsequent pyramids and one interesting explanation of this puzzle is that the early pyramids were undertaken less for their end result than as a scheme of public works. This would have had the double advantage of employing thousands of peasants during the slack season, when the yearly Nile flood made farming impossible, as well as involving them in a great collective project to develop a sense of nationhood.

The famous pyramids at Giza still stand as a monument to the great civilization of the Egyptian pharaohs many centuries ago. Built to contain and conceal the tombs and treasures of the pharaohs Cheops, Chephren and Mycerinus, the pyramids are masterpieces of geometrical precision. Their simple, clean lines, devoid of any decorative features, have an impressive and haunting beauty. Seen from the south, the Pyramid of Mycerinus (left), flanked by the smaller pyramids of his three queens, is overshadowed by the much larger Pyramid of Chephren (centre), with its distinctive surviving cap of limestone, and the Great Pyramid of Cheops (right).

The Olympian Zeus

The gods of the ancient Greeks were not very god-like, for although they were immortal and had superhuman powers, in every other way they were like men and women, with human failings, jealousies and rivalries. Perhaps this is why the Greeks were so attached to them. The mightiest of their gods was Zeus, son of the titans Cronos and Rhea. He was regarded as the king and father of gods and men, with power over all other deities except the Fates. Despite his marriage to his sister Hero, or Juno, Zeus was always having affairs with other goddesses and with ordinary mortals, introducing himself to Leda as a swan and to Europa as a bull. However, the Greeks still worshipped Zeus with great solemnity.

Mount Olympus, in north-east Greece, was the home of the gods. But one of the main centres for their worship was the Plain of Olympia in the Peloponnesus of southern Greece. Here, from 776 BC, the great festival of the Olympic games was held every fourth year in honour of Zeus. In the fifth century BC, the Greeks decided to build a temple to Zeus, with a magnificent image of the god, in the sacred grove of Olympia.

When the temple was finished, Pheidias, one of the greatest Greek sculptors, was asked to make the statue of Zeus. But it was years before Pheidias, who was supervising the building of the Parthenon in Athens, could come to Olympia to begin work.

When the Olympian Zeus was finally completed, in about 435 BC, it was universally agreed that Pheidias had produced a masterpiece. Like the Athena statue he had made for the Parthenon, the Zeus was a chryselephantine (gold and ivory) work. The flesh parts were carved from ivory mounted on a wood or stone core, and the draperies and other ornaments were cast from gold. The figure of Zeus was crowned with a carved olive wreath and seated in a magnificent cedarwood throne, adorned with gold, ivory, ebony, precious stones and paintings of beasts and other images. In his right hand Zeus held a winged statue of the goddess Victory, also of ivory and gold; in his left hand he carried a sceptre topped with an eagle. About eight times larger than a man, the statue reached nearly 59 feet (18 metres) to the ceiling of the temple.

From ancient coins on which it was depicted, we know that the Olympian Zeus had long hair, a bushy beard and a moustache with long ends. Seated at the far end of the temple, the colossal figure must have been an impressive sight.

The Romans adopted Zeus, under the name of Jupiter. It is said that the emperor Caligula (who fancied himself as a god) wanted to take the Olympian Zeus to Rome and have its head replaced with a carving of his own head. But when his workmen came to take the Zeus, they were driven out of the temple by spine-chilling peals of laughter.

Finally, however, the Olympian Zeus was removed to Constantinople by the emperor Theodorus I, where it was destroyed by a fire in AD 475. But the ruins of the temple can still be seen at Olympia, and the moulds in which Pheidias cast the gold parts of his great statue have recently been discovered.

Right: The Olympian Zeus, an impressive statue of the father of the ancient Greek gods, once sat at one end of the temple built in his honour in the sacred grove at Olympia during the fifth century BC. The awesome gold and ivory figure was the creation of the great sculptor Pheidias.

Below: The site of the Great Temple of Zeus, amid the trees at Olympia, is today marked only by a few remaining blocks of stone. Magnificent sculptures from the building, however, are preserved in the Olympia Museum.

The Temple of Artemis at Ephesus

Near the village of Aya Soluk in modern Turkey, not far from the Aegean coast, are the ruins of the ancient Greek city of Ephesus, the most important of the twelve Ionian cities of Asia Minor.

From early times Ephesus was a centre of worship of the goddess Artemis, or Diana. The daughter of Zeus and twin sister of the sun god Apollo, Artemis was the goddess of chastity and hunters. But at Ephesus, her characteristics were different: she was worshipped as a goddess of fertility. Her statue there, which was believed to have fallen from heaven, was a many-breasted idol, symbolizing the productive forces of nature.

Artemis was so important to the Ephesians that they built for her a temple which by all accounts must have been the finest in the ancient world. One writer put it at the top of the list of the world's wonders: 'I have seen the walls and hanging gardens of old Babylon, the statue of Olympian Jove [Zeus], the Colossus of Rhodes, the great labour of the lofty Pyramids, and the ancient tomb of Mausolus, but when I beheld the temple at Ephesus towering to the clouds, all these other marvels were eclipsed'. And according to another ancient writer the temple 'surpasses every structure raised by human hands'.

The great temple of Artemis was rebuilt several times. The first version was built in the sixth century BC by the architect Chersiphron and his son Metagenes. Croesus, the last king of Lydia, is said to have contributed some of his legendary wealth to the building.

In 356 BC the temple was burnt down by one Herostratus, an Ephesian citizen who wanted to immortalize himself. The rebuilding was carried out by the joint efforts of all the Ionian cities of Asia Minor; ladies sold their jewels to defray the cost, and kings presented replacement columns. The new temple was completed in about 323 BC. With an estimated size of 341 feet (104 metres) by 164 feet (50 metres), and one hundred and twenty-seven marble columns more than 60 feet (18 metres) high, it easily excelled the Parthenon of Athens.

One of the temple's greatest admirers was the young conqueror Alexander the Great, who by coincidence had been born on the night of the old temple's destruction. He offered to reimburse the Ephesians for the entire cost of the rebuilding if they would inscribe his name on the temple as its dedicator. They tactfully refused, saying that it was not right for one god to make dedications to

23

An artist's impression of the immense Temple of Artemis at Ephesus (above) captures the serene beauty of one of the ancient world's finest wonders. The exquisitely carved base of a column in the British Museum (right) is one of the few remaining fragments of this architectural masterpiece.

another. To further smooth Alexander's feelings, a painting of him on his horse was commissioned from the artist Apelles and hung in the temple. It is said that Alexander did not think the picture lifelike, but changed his mind when his horse neighed at the horse in the painting.

A great advantage for the Ephesians in having this glorious temple was that admirers of Artemis from many countries deposited their wealth there, so that it became, as one writer noted, 'a common treasury for all Asia'.

The temple was finally destroyed when the Goths sacked Ephesus in AD 262. This time it was not to be rebuilt, and its ruins were cannibalized for stone for other buildings. Finally the site was buried by the changing course of a river. All that is left of the temple that 'surpassed every structure raised by human hands' is a few fragments of its columns in the British Museum.

The Mausoleum at Halicarnassus

The stiffest test of a 'wonder of the world' is whether its particular name passes into general use as the term for everything of the same type. The best example of this is the word 'mausoleum', which we apply to any ornate tomb (or sometimes, in a derogatory sense, to a grandiose but lifeless building). The original mausoleum was the famous tomb of King Mausolus at Halicarnassus (now the Turkish city of Bodrum) in Asia Minor.

During the fourth century BC Mausolus was the satrap or ruler of Caria, a province of the Persian empire. When he died in 353 BC his queen, Artemisia, who was also his sister, was so grief-struck that she mixed his ashes with her drink. To perpetuate his memory she decided to build the most splended tomb possible.

Artemisia sent to Greece for a team of outstanding artists and craftsmen, including the architects Pythios and Satyros, and the sculptors Scopas, Bryaxis, Leochares and Timotheos. When Artemisia died in 350 BC, only three years after Mausolus, the work on the tomb was nowhere near completion. But the artists went ahead and finished it as a record of their skill and for their own fame. Their effort was not wasted, because the completed tomb was soon hailed as one of the

most magnificent wonders of the world.

The Mausoleum was built to a square plan, with sculpted friezes around all four sides. Above the base, a colonnade of thirty-six slender marble columns held up a massive stepped pyramid, which seemed to float in the air. On the summit of the pyramid stood a carving of a horse-drawn chariot which probably contained standing statues of Mausolus and Artemisia. The whole structure was about 141 feet (43 metres) high.

The Mausoleum survived until the fourteenth century AD, when it was destroyed by an earthquake. Early in the fifteenth century, the Knights of Rhodes captured Halicarnassus and used most of the remains of the Mausoleum as building stone for a castle. Today, only a few fragments of the Mausoleum are preserved in the British Museum, but the word survives as testimony to the splendour of the world's greatest tomb.

The elaborate tomb built for the Persian ruler Mausolus at Halicarnassus in present-day Turkey (above) stood for a thousand years after its completion in the fourth century BC. A colossal statue of Mausolus found among the ruins (left) is now preserved in the British Museum, London.

25

Africa

Mount Kilimanjaro, Tanzania

The Nile

The cradles of most ancient civilizations were the fertile plains of great rivers: the Tigris and Euphrates in South-west Asia, the Yangtze in China and the Indus in the Indian subcontinent. But nowhere has there been such a close and dramatic association between a river and a civilization as between the Nile and Egypt. With its yearly flood, rich in the reddish-grey silt which it deposited in the Nile Delta to form Africa's most fertile soil, the Egyptians could scarcely fail to be conscious that they owed everything to the Nile, and they revered the river accordingly.

From its furthest source, the Kagera River in Burundi, east-central Africa, to its Mediterranean mouths, the Nile flows northwards for about 4131 miles (6648 kilometres), making it the world's longest river (beating the Amazon by about 93 miles [150 kilometres]). Draining about one tenth of Africa, the Nile's drainage basin is also the world's longest, but its area of some 293150 square miles (3349000 square kilometres) is less than those of the Amazon or Zaire basins.

The Kagera River flows from the highlands of Burundi across Rwanda and Tanzania to enter the huge but shallow Lake Victoria, from which the Nile proper rises. At its outlet from Victoria near Jinja in Uganda the Nile is about 1312 feet (400 metres) wide. From here the river is known by various names as it flows through Lakes Kyoga and Mobutu Sese Seko (formerly Lake Albert) and on into the Sudanese plain. Here, flowing slowly, the river divides into many meandering branches and channels which form the huge swampy area called the Sudd. Masses of swamp vegetation, including grasses and reeds, form floating islands which block the river's channels.

At Lake No, in south-central Sudan, the Mountain Nile is joined by the Bahr el-Ghazāl from the south-west, and becomes the White Nile.

At Khartoum the White Nile is joined by the river's greatest tributary, the Blue Nile, which drains from the high Ethiopian mountains to the south-east. Rising in Lake Tana, northwestern Ethiopia, at an altitude of 5905 feet (1800 metres), the Blue Nile is about 850 miles (1368 kilometres) long. About 199 miles (320 kilometres) north of Khartoum, the united Nile is joined by another eastern tributary, the Atbara, which rises near Lake Tana. It is the Blue Nile and the Atbara which are mainly responsible for the Nile's flood. Both rivers are swollen annually from June to September by the summer monsoon rains and the melting snows of the Ethiopian Highlands. It is estimated that at this time the Blue Nile supplies about two thirds of the Nile's waters.

After joining the Atbara the Nile flows through the arid Nubian desert for 1678 miles (2700 kilometres), making a big S-shaped bend before reaching the borders of Egypt. From Khartoum to Aswan, in southern Egypt, the Nile occupies a narrow valley with little flood plain for cultivation. Continuous navigation is hindered by a number of cataracts. There were six of these rapids, but the second cataract has been submerged by the water trapped behind the Aswan High Dam.

Begun in 1960, the dam is 364 feet (111 metres) high and 2 miles (3.2 kilometres) across. Behind it is Lake Nasser, the world's largest man-made lake, nearly 298 miles (480 kilometres) long and reaching into northern Sudan. Many archaeological sites were permanently flooded by the rise of Lake Nasser. But some, including the famous temple of Abu Simbel, have been moved to new positions above the level of the lake.

From Aswan the river enters the Nile Valley proper, where its flood plain varies from eight to ten miles (16 kilometres) in width. In Egypt the Nile is lined with famous structures and ruins of ancient dynasties, as at Luxor and Karnak (the site of ancient Thebes), Memphis and Giza. Below Cairo the river enters the triangular lowland which forms the Nile Delta. About 99 miles (160 kilometres) from south to north and with a coastline of 49 miles (240 kilometres). In ancient times the

Below left: The swollen waters of the Blue Nile thunder over impressive falls before joining the White Nile at Khartoum in Sudan.

Below: The stupendous rock-cut temple of the pharaoh Ramses II at Abu Simbel was saved from permanent submersion when the Aswan High Dam was built.

delta had seven branches; now there are two main mouths, the Rosetta in the west and the Damietta in the east.

The earliest use of the Nile for irrigation began with the planting of seeds in the mud after the annual floodwaters receded. In time, the traditional method of basin irrigation developed, by which the floodwater was run into large basins divided by earth banks, and allowed to drain away after two months, leaving its silt behind. But this method allowed only one crop a year. Over the last one hundred and fifty years, various barrages and dams (of which the Aswan High Dam is the most ambitious) have been built to retain the Nile's floodwater for year-round or perennial irrigation.

The source of the Nile was a matter of mystery and legend for many centuries. Ptolemy, in the second century AD, believed it to be 'twin lakes', fed by the fabled Mountains of the Moon. The truth was pieced together by several nineteenth-century explorers: John Hanning Speke, who discovered Lake Victoria in 1858 and later (1861–2) identified it with the Nile; Samuel Baker, who discovered Lake Mobutu Sese Seko; and H.M. Stanley, who in two journeys discovered Lake Edward and the Ruwenzori Mountains. These discoveries proved that the White Nile has two main sources of supply, Lake Victoria, and Lakes Edward and Mobutu Sese Seko, joined by the Semliki River.

A band of green irrigated farmland borders the Nile as it flows through Egypt, contrasting with the desert that stretches to the horizon on both sides.

The Sahara Desert

The Sahara, with an area of 3320000 square miles (8600000 square kilometres), is the world's largest desert. As large as the whole of the United States of America, it covers almost all of North Africa, and is part of a still larger desert chain – the Afro-Asian desert zone, which includes the Arabian Desert.

Bordered by the Mediterranean Sea and the Atlas Mountains to the north, the Atlantic Ocean to the west and the Red Sea to the east, the Sahara has a 3200-mile (5150-kilometre) coastline. Both in the north and south the desert has no sharp borderline, but there are border zones about 62 miles (100 kilometres) wide where the land gradually shades into desert. The southern transitional zone, between the Sahara and the savanna grassland of Africa's Sudan region, is called the Sahel.

The Sahara mainly consists of a series of plains, ranging from 590 to 1181 feet (180 to 360 metres) above sea level, and lowlands and depressions. The largest, the Qattara Depression, is 436 feet (133 metres) below sea level. On the whole, the Sahara is much lower than the rest of Africa. It has only two mountain chains: the Ahaggar Mountains, rising to 9852 feet (3003 metres), and the Tibesti Mountains, rising to 11204 feet (3415 metres).

The name Sahara comes from the plural of the Arabic word for desert, and many parts of the desert have their own separate names – for instance, the Tanezrouft in south-west Algeria and north-east Mali, an exceptionally barren part of the Sahara forming a 'desert within a desert'; and the Ténéré, or Land of Fear, in the eastern Sahara. The desert is divided between ten countries: Morocco, Algeria, Tunisia, Libya and Egypt in the north; and Mauritania, Mali, Niger, Chad and Sudan in the south. An eleventh territory, the former Spanish Sahara, is disputed between Mauritania and Morocco.

Most people think of the Sahara as an endless sea of sand, swept into dunes by the wind. In fact, sand, or *erg*, takes up only about a fifth of the desert; the two other main surfaces are *hamada*, consisting of jagged boulder fragments, and *reg*, or gravel.

Nevertheless, it is the shifting, wind-swept sand dunes which provide the Sahara's most beautiful landscapes. Reaching heights of 755 feet (230 metres) they form characteristic shapes: long, narrow dunes called *sif*, and crescent-shaped dunes or *barchan*.

The Sahara is hot. In fact, daytime temperatures can reach an unbelievable 183°F (84°C) – more than twice as hot as the hottest summer day in temperate regions. The warmest months are July and August in the northern Sahara and May and June in the southern part. On the other hand, the

Endless seas of wind-swept sand dunes extend across the immense Sahara, the world's largest desert.

temperature drops dramatically at night, and frost and ice can occur in the north and at high altitudes. In the Tibesti Mountains, the temperature can fall to 5°F (−15°C).

Apart from the burning sun, the most constant feature of the Sahara's climate is the wind, which blows every day, often carrying sand and dust. Some places have sandstorms for seventy days of the year. The hot, dry south winds which bring these sandstorms have various Arabic names; one of the best-known is the *khamsin*.

For all its dryness, the Sahara is not without rain. The tropic or mid-Saharan region may go for years without a single drop, but in the north there is winter rainfall and in the southern Sahara there is fairly regular summer rain. Often, however, the ground is so hot that the rain evaporates before it reaches it.

Nor is the Sahara without life. The main groups of plants which manage to sustain a foothold in the desert are grasses and members of the pea, goosefoot and sunflower families. Desert trees include date palms in the north, doom palms in the south and several species of tamarisk and

Left: The Tuareg are a nomadic people who herd goats, sheep and camels in the inhospitable hot wastelands of the western Sahara. Wind-breaks erected round their encampments and veils worn across the face protect them from the sharp flying sand.

Right: Great expanses of jagged boulder fragments emphasize the harshness of the terrain in the central Sahara. Here the rugged forms of the Ahaggar Mountains loom above the surrounding plateau, their hard, ancient rocks resisting weathering by the elements.

acacia. But the most fertile spots are the oases, dotted about the desert, which are fed by underground water.

The commonest desert animals are burrowing insects and rodents, such as the kangaroo-like jerbil. Larger animals include the gazelle, which is one of several animals found on the plateaux of the Sahara.

The Sahara was not always a desert. There have been several alternations of wet and dry periods in its climatic history, and the transition to the present dry period began only in about 3000 BC. In prehistoric times the Sahara was more widely occupied than it is now: archaeological evidence shows the presence of man and big game including buffalo, giraffe, elephants and even hippopotamuses.

The modern Saharans roughly belong to four groups, all mainly of Berber descent: the Arab-Berber peoples of the north; the less Arabized Moors of the west; the Tuareg of the south-central mountains; and the Teda of the Tibesti Mountains and southern Sahara.

In former times the Saharan peoples were mainly pastoral, herding camels, sheep and goats. The larger groups dominated the desert, controlling the oases which linked the caravan routes that criss-crossed the Sahara. The veiled Tuareg were particularly renowned for their warlike qualities and fierce independence.

For many centuries the trans-Sahara routes linked the peoples of black Africa with the cities and ports of the North African coast, carrying a rich trade in gold, ivory, slaves and salt. This, the old Saharan trade, with its stately processions of laden camels gliding over the desert, is a thing of the past. But the Sahara perhaps is gaining new importance as a possible source of minerals. In the meantime, the world's greatest desert retains its strange, romantic appeal.

Great Zimbabwe Ruins

The Great Zimbabwe Ruins, which rise among the granite hills and rich savanna of the edge of Mashonaland in southern Africa, have given their name to the country of Zimbabwe.

These ruins are the largest and most impressive ancient site in Africa south of the Sahara. Until recently they were also the most mysterious, as they had been abandoned for centuries and their origins and purpose could only be guessed at. Many colonial Europeans were reluctant to believe that Africans built Great Zimbabwe. But archaeological work at the site has shown that it was indeed built by Africans, who had occupied it for some five hundred years until the middle of the fifteenth century.

Great Zimbabwe is basically a series of massive stone walls, built from small granite blocks laid in courses like brickwork, but without mortar. Rising starkly and unexpectedly in a countryside where until recently the only other buildings were grass-roofed huts, the walls form what appear to be dense mazes spread over 99 acres (40 hectares) of hill and valley.

In fact the mazes are walled enclosures of various shapes and sizes, each with doorways which are sometimes stepped. Inside the enclosures are many more short lengths of wall, some curved and some straight. At first sight they seem to start and stop without reason. But it has been shown that these internal walls once connected up numbers of round houses in each enclosure, making a separate courtyard for each house. The houses were made of a gravelly clay called *daga*. After Zimbabwe was abandoned, they gradually collapsed, leaving their courtyard walls standing.

The Zimbabwe enclosures are in two main groups. One group, the Hill Ruin, stands on a boulder-strewn granite hill to the north. The other group lies on a granite shelf on the opposite side of a shallow valley to the south of the hill. In the valley between the two main groups are several more smaller enclosures.

The largest of the enclosures is the Elliptical Building, at the southern end of the group opposite the Hill Ruin. Its outer wall forms a rough ellipse with a circumference of 800 feet (244 metres). This wall is the largest single prehistoric structure in sub-Saharan Africa. As it curves from the north-west it gradually becomes taller and wider until at the east end it reaches nearly 33 feet (ten metres) high and more than 16 feet (five metres) thick. This part of the wall has the most regular stonework of Great Zimbabwe, and is capped with a patterned frieze.

Just inside the east end of the Elliptical Building is a solid, circular tower of stonework, the Conical Tower, which provides the focus to the whole building. It is 30 feet (9.1 metres) high and 18 feet (5.5 metres) round. Possibly the Conical Tower symbolized the tribute due to a king or chief. It is similarly shaped to grain bins formerly used by the local Karanga people, and grain was a common tribute to Karanga chiefs. It is fairly certain that the Elliptical Building was a royal enclosure.

A combination of modern archaeology and oral traditions has made it possible to piece together the history of Great Zimbabwe. The ancestors of its builders are thought to have settled at the site in the tenth or eleventh centuries. By the early fourteenth century it had become a wealthy centre of trade with the Swahili towns on the coast and also an important centre of religion. Then, in the middle of the fifteenth century Great Zimbabwe was abandoned when its trade was disrupted, and its people moved northwards to re-establish themselves in the Zambezi Valley. But the buildings have survived, to become an important reminder of past African achievements – and a symbol of future hopes.

Below: The mysterious stone-built enclosures of the Great Zimbabwe ruins in southern Africa were built between the tenth and fourteenth centuries.

The Great Rift Valley

Above: The Conical Tower, one of the best-known features of the Great Zimbabwe ruins, displays the early craftsmen's skill in building without mortar.

The fissure in the earth's crust known as the Great Rift Valley stretches nearly 6214 miles (10000 kilometres) from the Lebanon in south-west Asia to Mozambique in south-east Africa. As well as crossing East Africa, this colossal rift forms the Red Sea and continues towards the Mediterranean as the Jordan Valley. In all, it takes up about a sixth of the earth's circumference, and is easily visible from the moon.

Geologists think that the Rift was formed as a result of the process by which the original super-continent, Gondwanaland, separated into the present continents and the gaps between them were filled by oceans. When the Indian Ocean was created, molten rock poured from beneath East Africa, causing parts of its crust to subside. This weakness eventually developed into a connected series of earth movements in which the Rift Valley floor sank beneath parallel fault lines. The main phase of faulting happened quite recently in geological time, about eleven million years ago. In the last three million years, more faulting has taken place along the valley floor and the valley's shoulders have been thrust upwards. By forcing molten rock up at the sides, the sinking valley floor caused intense volcanic activity. Today, about thirty active or semi-active volcanoes and many boiling springs are evidence that rifting is still going on.

The most dramatic part of the Great Rift Valley stretches about 1490 miles (2400 kilometres) from Ethiopia's Red Sea coast to Lake Manyara in north-east Tanzania. For most of this distance the valley is about 30 miles (48 kilometres) across, widening to about 300 miles (480 kilometres) in the Danakil Desert of Ethiopia.

The southern apex of the Danakil triangle is formed by the narrowing of the Rift Valley as it enters the Ethiopian Highlands. Leading southwards to Kenya, the line of the Rift is marked by a chain of lakes: Zwai, Langana, Abiata, Shala, Awausa, Abaya and Stefanie. Beginning with Lake Turkana, the largest Rift lake, the chain continues through Kenya to north-east Tanzania. Only two of the Rift Valley's lakes, Barringo and Naivasha in Kenya, are completely fresh. All the rest are either slightly or very tainted with soda, which bubbles up with the Rift's hot springs and volcanoes and finds its way into the lakes. The Rift's soda lakes, especially Nakuru in Kenya, are the home of the world's greatest concentration of flamingoes – about three million from a world population of five million.

The less alkaline Rift lakes include Turkana in northern Kenya and Shala and Abiata in the Ethiopian Rift Valley. These support fish populations and a varied fauna ranging from hippos to crocodiles and hundreds of waterbird species including pelicans, kingfishers, herons, fish eagles and cormorants. Lake Turkana is estimated to hold twelve thousand crocodiles. They feed mainly on the lake's abundant supply of Nile perch, the largest fish found in the Rift Valley.

The Rift's savanna plains contain some of Africa's last herds of big game. At Lake Manyara National Park in Tanzania is Africa's highest elephant population, averaging twelve animals per square mile (five per square kilometre). South of Lake Naivasha, in Kenya, the narrow, twisting pass called Hell's Gate contains a cross-section of the Rift Valley's wildlife: reedbuck, duikers, dik-diks and other antelopes, zebra herds, ostriches, leopards, jackals and hyenas, and baboons. At an altitude of 6200 feet (1890 metres), the freshwater lake itself is the highest and one of the most beautiful of the Rift lakes. A vast population of fish eagles feeds on the tilapia and black bass which flourish in the lake. The rich birdlife of Naivasha also includes starlings, woodpeckers, kingfishers, herons, egrets and wagtails.

Much of the Rift Valley, even where it is most inhospitable, has supported many different tribes for many thousands of years. Some are hunters, others are farmers, and many of them are nomadic pastoralists, supported by their wandering flocks of cattle or goats. Along the Rift in southern Kenya and Tanzania live the famous Masai. Around Lake Turkana are scattered several tribes whose way of life is little changed from the Stone Age. The Turkana, who live on the western shore, were nomadic grazers of cattle, camels and goats. Increasing pressure on the land has hemmed them into a territory which is too small for their needs. Some Turkana have become fishermen, using methods such as gill-netting. The El Molo tribe, who live at the southern end of Lake Turkana, have always lived as fishermen, spearing or netting fish from their palm-log rafts.

The unique geology of the Rift Valley makes it rich in fossil remains, and it seems likely that the earliest human beings evolved in this region.

Above: The burning salt flats of the Danakil Desert, in Ethiopia, mark the northern end of the Great Rift Valley before it enters the Red Sea. This is the homeland of the Danakil nomads.

Opposite page, top: Lake Nakuru, one of the lakes in the Rift Valley of Kenya, is the home of millions of flamingoes and other birds, which gather there to feed in its soda-rich waters.

Right: Escarpments mark the edge of Kenya's Rift Valley, offering superb panoramas of the valley floor below. This part of Africa's vast grassland region supports many wild animals.

Kilimanjaro

Kilimanjaro, Africa's highest mountain, stands in northern Tanzania, touching the border with Kenya. The first European to see Kilimanjaro, in 1848, was a German missionary, Johannes Rebmann. His reports of a snow-covered mountain near the equator were greeted with derision by armchair theorists in Europe, who insisted that such a thing was impossible. But there is no arguing with facts, especially when they are as substantial and majestic as Kilimanjaro, which at 19340 feet (5895 metres) easily outstrips any peak in the European Alps or American Rockies.

About 99 miles (160 kilometres) south of the Rift Valley, Kilimanjaro is a volanic massif, stretching east-west for 50 miles (80 kilometres). The massif includes three main volcanoes, all virtually extinct. The youngest and tallest, Kibo, is joined by a seven-mile (11.2-kilometre) saddle to Mawenzi (17552 feet/5350 metres), the remaining core of what was formerly Kilimanjaro's summit. The third volcano, Shira (12387 feet/3775 metres), is a ridge-shaped remnant of an earlier crater.

Kibo appears as a smooth, snow-capped dome, but it contains a vast crater or caldera nearly one mile (two kilometres) across and, on its south side, about 984 feet (300 metres) deep. On the rim of the crater is Uhuru Point, the summit of all Africa. In the depression of the crater is a smaller ash cone, which shows signs of residual volcanic activity, and isolated thick glaciers. Outside the crater, glaciers descend to 14000 feet (4260 metres) on Kibo's south-western slopes, but on the northern side they reach only a little way below the summit.

In contrast to Kibo, Kilimanjaro's subsidiary peak, Mawenzi, is jagged and much eroded. It is split from east to west by the Barrancos gorges. There is no permanent ice, and only a few snow patches.

The well-watered, fertile southern slopes of Kilimanjaro are the homeland of one of Tanzania's most interesting tribes, the Chagga, who keep cattle and grow bananas and coffee. Although there is plenty of rain, it is very unevenly distributed through the year, so in order to water their land during dry periods the Chagga have

Right: The last rays of sunset tint the snow-clad summit of the volcano Kilimanjaro, Africa's highest peak, which towers above the grasslands of Tanzania.

Below: When seen from the air, the dark, gaping crater of Kibo, Kilimanjaro's main summit, is an awesome spectacle outlined by snow.

developed an amazingly complex system of irrigation channels. This has helped them to become East Africa's most efficient coffee producers.

Above the 5900-foot (1800-metre) contour line all of Kilimanjaro is a nature reserve. The lowest part of the reserve consists of Chagga shambas (farms), but above this there is a zone of dense cloud forest with plenty of animals. The most striking are colobus monkeys, with their beautiful, long black and white coats and harsh cry. They make huge leaps from branch to branch, and seem to use their long coats as a sort of parachute or gliding device. Kilimanjaro's rarest animal is the Abbot's duiker, only found in the mountain forests of northern Tanzania. Reddish-brown, it is about 30 inches (75 centimetres) high at the shoulder. Being nocturnal, it is hardly ever seen. Unlike the mountains of Kenya or the Ruwenzori, Kilimanjaro has no bamboo zone, and the forest merges first into scrub and then into open moorland.

The Victoria Falls

The Victoria Falls, on the Zambezi River, are Africa's mightiest waterfall and one of the world's most impressive natural spectacles. Only Angel Falls and Niagara Falls rival them for splendour, but the Victoria Falls are about one and a half times as wide and twice as high as Niagara.

The 2175-mile (3500-kilometre) Zambezi River, Africa's fourth longest river, rises in north-west Zambia and flows southwards through Angola and Zambia. Curving eastwards, the river tumbles abruptly over the Victoria Falls to enter its mid-course, forming the border between Zambia to the north and Zimbabwe to the south. For about 124 miles (200 kilometres) above the falls, the Zambezi flows through a wide, shallow valley. As the river widens, the number of islands in it increases, some of them thickly forested. Nothing in the river's leisurely pace suggests the approach of the Victoria Falls. However, the great cloud thrown up by the falls can sometimes be seen from 37 miles (60 kilo-

metres) away, and, as they are neared, the sound of the falls builds up to a deafening roar.

The waters of the Victoria Falls do not descend into a pool, as in most great waterfalls, but into a deep, narrow fissure which extends 5577 feet (1700 metres) across the Zambezi at one of the river's widest points. This chasm has a maximum depth of 354 feet (108 metres) and varies between about 79 and 240 feet (24 and 73 metres) in width. The greatest volume of the falls, in the flood season from March to May, is some 270156 cubic feet (7650 cubic metres) per second. This drops to as little as 33176 cubic feet (935 cubic metres) per second in the dry season during October and November. The annual average is some 38846 cubic feet (1100 cubic metres) per second.

Among the local Kalolo-Lozi tribes, the African name for the falls is *Mosi-oa-tunya* – Smoke-that-thunders. Air currents force the mist and spray upwards to form huge clouds over the falls, reaching over 1000 feet (300 metres) high. In the mist, beautiful rainbows form and during each new moon, the mist even reflects a lunar rainbow.

The crest of the falls is divided into several sections. The wide Eastern Cataract, which is often dry in the low-water season, extends from the eastern shore. Its western limit is formed by a deep pool called the Armchair Depression. Beyond this, two promontories form the Rainbow and Horseshoe Falls. Then comes Namkabwa (formerly Livingstone) Island. Between this and Cataract (formerly Boarunka) Island are the Main Falls, which are split by a fissure. Between Cataract Island and the western shore is the narrow precipice of the Devil's Cataract.

Along the edge of the cliff facing the falls is the famous Rain Forest, a densely wooded strip of land which is constantly watered by the falls' spray and stays an intense green all the year round.

The outlet of the Victoria Falls is a narrow gorge

The Victoria Falls are most spectacular in the early part of the year, when the swollen waters of the Zambezi River plunge into a great chasm amid clouds of mist (below). In the dry season, the falls are reduced to a comparative trickle (opposite page).

about 1680 feet (512 metres) from the eastern side. Only 210 feet (64 metres) wide and 387 feet (118 metres) long, this gorge channels the entire Zambezi River to a fearful whirlpool called the Boiling Pot. From here the river passes into 45 miles (72 kilometres) of steep-sided, zig-zagging gorges forming the Grand Canyon of the Zambezi.

Close to the falls, the canyon is spanned by a 656-foot (200-metre) long road-rail cantilever bridge, completed in 1905. The bridge gives a superb view of the falls, which spray passing trains. A 2000-kilowatt hydroelectric plant, completed in 1938, harnesses the energy of the falls to provide power for the region.

For centuries before the arrival of Europeans, the Smoke-that-thunders was well known to the African tribes who lived in the vicinity. They considered that such a stupendous example of the powers of nature was well worthy of worship. The first European to see the falls was David Livingstone. He discovered them during his descent of the Zambezi in 1855, and named them after Queen Victoria.

The Americas

The Rocky Mountains near Aspen, Colorado, U.S.A.

Niagara Falls

The Niagara Falls, shared by the United States of America and Canada, are one of the world's most famous natural spectacles. There are more beautiful waterfalls, such as the Angel Falls of Venezuela or Yosemite Falls in California; and higher ones, such as the Victoria Falls of the Zambezi River or the Iguassu Falls in South America. But for sheer vastness and volume of water the Falls of Niagara are unmatched.

The Niagara River, only some 36 miles (58 kilometres) long, flows northwards to connect Lake Erie to Lake Ontario and forms the boundary between Canada and the United States. The Falls occur about halfway between the two lakes. They are divided by the forested Goat Island into the Horseshoe, or Canadian Falls, which is 157 feet (48 metres) high with a crest 3008 feet (917 metres) wide, sweeping round in a great semicircle; and the American Falls, 167 feet (51 metres) high with a crest 1060 feet (323 metres) wide. The boundary line passes through a corner of the Horseshoe Falls, leaving Goat Island, which is a reservation, entirely in the United States. About six per cent of the Niagara's water passes over the American Falls, while ninety-four per cent passes over the Horseshoe Falls. At the foot of the American Falls is the Cave of the Winds, a rocky chamber 98 feet (30 metres) by 75 feet (23 metres) formed by erosion. Below the Falls, the Niagara rushes between steep, perpendicular walls through a series of rapids which culminate in the Whirlpool Rapids.

Connected by two bridges over the rapids, two cities both named Niagara Falls, one Canadian and the other American, flank the Falls. Queen Victoria Park, in the Canadian city, gives the finest view

of the Falls; the best view from the American side is from Prospect Point on Goat Island, on the brink of the ledge overlooking the river. There are also panoramic views from the New York State Observation Tower and from three Canadian towers – the Skylon, Kodak and Minolta. From Canada's Queen Victoria Park gigantic searchlights illuminate the Falls at night with changing colours.

Since 1829, when a certain Sam Patch successfully 'swam' over them twice, the Niagara Falls have been a magnet for death-defying stunts. Women as well as men have shot the Falls in barrels, or in protective swathes of automobile tyres; some people have survived the descent. In 1859 and again in 1860, the great Blondin was the first to cross the Falls on a tight-rope.

The Niagara Falls were known to many North American Indian tribes long before the arrival of the Europeans. The first Europeans to see the Falls were members of the French explorer Robert de La Salle's expedition in 1678, including Father Louis Hennepin, who revisited and described the Falls in 1683. During the eighteenth century the Falls were in the centre of a region of trading posts and frontier forts; several battles were fought in the vicinity during the War of 1812. Bridge builders first spanned the river in 1835. Since the late nineteenth century, when the waters were first harnessed for generating electrical power, the Niagara Falls have become one of the world's greatest hydroelectric centres.

But it is for the awe-inspiring sight – and sound – of the Niagara's waters, plunging into their turbulent rapids, that the Falls are justly famed.

The two main sections of the Niagara Falls are the aptly named Horseshoe Falls (below) and the smaller American Falls (opposite page).

New York City

Paris and France; Rome and Italy; London and England; New York and the United States ... Which is the odd pair out? The last, since New York is not the capital of the United States of America, nor even of New York State. But for most people this vast, crowded metropolis on America's eastern seaboard is the very symbol of the United States, summing up the strengths (and weaknesses) of the world's richest and most powerful nation.

Foreigners have always been aware of New York City because of its position as the Atlantic gateway to the continental United States. For some, New York has been the jumping-off point, and, for others, the fulfilment of the American Dream. During the last half of the nineteenth century New York and its Statue of Liberty were a beacon to immigrants. Between 1865 and 1900 no less than 13260000 foreigners entered the United States of America, mostly through New York Harbour. As a result, New York is not just a national but an international metropolis, with its population of

nearly eight million descended from most of the world's nations and races. Equally, 'The Big Apple' has long been a magnet for ambitious Americans of all kinds, from businessmen, lawyers and politicians to writers, artists and jazz musicians hoping to try their luck against the world's best.

Lying at the mouth of the Hudson River in the south-east tip of New York State, the city covers about 365 square miles (945 square kilometres), of which about 168 are inland water. It is divided into five boroughs: Manhattan, the Bronx, Queens, Brooklyn and Staten Island. The Bronx is the only mainland borough, stretching along between the Hudson and East Rivers. Queens and Brooklyn lie south-west of the Bronx, occupying the western end of Long Island. To the west of Brooklyn is Staten Island in Upper and Lower New York Bays.

One of the finest views of Manhattan's famous skyline is from Upper New York Bay (below), where the Statue of Liberty (left) greets ships entering the harbur. An exciting and captivating city, New York is also a thriving cultural centre that boasts such outstanding institutions as the Guggenheim Museum (far left).

But it is Manhattan, with its famous skyline of skyscrapers, which is the heart and symbol of New York. Surrounded by the Hudson River on the west, the Harlem River to the north and northeast, the East River to the east and Upper New York Bay (the Hudson mouth) on the south, Manhattan Island is the smallest and most densely populated New York borough, with more than a million and a half people in its 22 square miles (58 square kilometres).

Here, in this microcosm of the United States, are Times Square and Broadway, centre of the world's most famous theatre district; Fifth Avenue, with its superb shopping promenade; Greenwich Village, with its artists and writers; Wall Street, financial centre of the United States, home of the ticker-tape welcome for returning heroes and epicentre of history's most celebrated financial crash; and many other landmarks. Much of Manhattan is covered with asphalt and concrete, but in the middle is the refreshing greenness of Central Park, with its 840 acres (340 hectares) of grass and trees.

Firmly anchored into the solid rock beneath Manhattan are the thousands of skyscrapers which give New York its futuristic look and make the streets seem like deep canyons. Today, the city can only lay claim to the world's second and third tallest buildings (both in Manhattan): the 110 storey World Trade Centre (1348 feet/411 metres) and the 102 storey Empire State Building (1250 feet/381 metres without mast). Manhattan's profile is constantly changing as magnificent new buildings soar into the sky among such older landmarks as the Chrysler Building with its Art Deco spire. Some of the newer structures, such as the Trump Tower, are dramatically clad in reflecting glass; others, among them the A.T. & T. Building, have

Below: Throughout the year Central Park is a popular place of escape from the bustle of Manhattan's crowded streets.

Below right: Framed by the Queensborough Bridge, which spans the East River, Manhattan's skyline features the Empire State and Chrysler Buildings.

strikingly designed tops that give the skyline additional visual impact.

Above all, New York is a city of extremes and contrasts. In climate it is stiflingly hot and humid in summer and bitterly cold in winter. Socially, it is home to some of the world's wealthiest people, while many others live on welfare in slums.

With its grid-plan layout and numbered streets, New York is no different from many other American cities, but its cultural wealth is almost unmatched. Among its most famous museums are the Metropolitan Museum of Art, the American Museum of Natural History, the Museum of Modern Art, the Frick Collection, the Guggenheim Museum and the Brooklyn Museum. The most spectacular cultural institution is the Lincoln Center for the Performing Arts: its buildings, surrounding a lagoon and a fountain, house the Metropolitan Opera, the New York City Opera, the New York Philharmonic and the New York City Ballet.

To the outsider, New York is an undifferentiated megalopolis; in reality its patchwork of national and ethnic groups, each in its own district, gives much of the city a parochial atmosphere rather like a series of villages.

One of the world's youngest great cities, New York was founded by the Dutch as New Amsterdam after Henry Hudson's discovery of the Hudson River in 1609. In 1664 it was captured by the British and renamed New York in honour of Charles II's brother the Duke of York. From 1785 to 1790 the city was briefly the capital of the United States. New York's trade and industry sharply increased after the Erie Canal was opened in 1825, but the city's most rapid expansion took place after the American Civil War, coinciding with the great flood of immigrants in the later nineteenth century. New York has lurched through a series of financial crises as many citizens have moved beyond the city limits, taking their taxes with them. But, for all its problems, New York retains its unique character as probably the world's most exciting and varied city.

Yellowstone National Park

In the heart of the 'wild' west, Yellowstone National Park is the oldest, largest and in many ways the most impressive of the national parks of the United States of America. Its 3472 square miles (8992 square kilometres) take up the north-west corner of Wyoming and overlap into Idaho and Montana. The rugged, mountainous terrain is alternately inviting and frightening. In some parts, Yellowstone resembles the surface of a hot, inhospitable alien planet, with boiling sulphur pools, bubbling mud pools and geysers hissing and exploding.

A series of plateaux – Central, Pitchstone, Madison and Mirror – between 6995 feet (2132 metres) and 8494 feet (2589 metres) above sea level, make up the park. These in turn are enclosed by ridges and peaks rising from 9993 feet to 11991 feet (3046 to 3655 metres). The Continental Divide crosses the park, and the area is segmented by lakes, creeks and rivers, of which the largest is the Yellowstone. The Yellowstone River has cut the huge gash of the Grand Canyon (not to be confused with the Grand Canyon of the Colorado River) 20 miles (32 kilometres) long, 1598 feet (487 metres) wide and 1198 feet (365 metres) deep. The Yellowstone Lake, through which the river flows from south to north, is about 20 miles (32 kilometres) long. At an elevation of 7733 feet (2357 metres) and with an area of 139 square miles (360 square kilometres), this beautiful lake is the largest body of water in the United States at so high an altitude. Also in the park are the spectacular, two-stage Yellowstone Falls; the Lower Fall, at 308 feet (94 metres), is nearly twice the height of the Niagara Falls, while the Upper Fall is 108 feet (33 metres) high. Another major feature in the park is the series of beautiful natural limestone terraces that have been built up by hot water deposits at Mammoth Hot Springs.

Three Indian tribes, the Sioux, Algonquins and Shoshones, originated near the sources of the

Yellowstone River, but they regarded the geysers and other geothermal peculiarities of the region with great circumspection and gave them a wide berth. Even the reports of John Colter, a member of Lewis and Clark's expedition who was the first European to explore the region in 1807–8, were dismissed as tall stories. Over the next sixty years hunters, trappers and traders brought back accounts of Yellowstone which were greeted with similar scepticism. After the American Civil War, however, the area was mapped, and in 1872 an Act of Congress established Yellowstone as the United States' first national park.

Today, Yellowstone Park is one of America's leading tourist areas. Among the 3000-odd geysers, pools and springs the star is 'Old Faithful', the geyser which hurls a jet of near-boiling water more than fifty metres into the air more or less every sixty-five minutes. Each year growing numbers of tourists brave summer temperatures of 89°F (32°C) to camp, explore and fish; and intense winter cold to ski and snowshoe.

The streams abound with fish – cutthroat, Mackinaw and eastern brook trout, chub, grayling and even Loch Leven trout imported from Scotland. Though fish can be caught without a licence in season, the park's abundant game is protected. American bison roam the eastern ranges, mountain goats spring along the high slopes, and the park's forests and meadows teem with black and grizzly bears, deer, elk and antelope. Eagles, hawks, geese, ducks and the rare trumpeter swans breed in Yellowstone. The floors of the deciduous forests are carpeted with hundreds of species of wild flowers.

Below left: The curious Minerva Terrace, at Mammoth Hot Springs, is one of Yellowstone National Park's most famous attractions. Here hot water welling up from deep below ground has built up step-like deposits of soft travertine rock.

Below: At the northern edge of Yellowstone National Park the Yellowstone River plunges over its spectacular Lower Falls into a deep gorge. The yellow-tinted rocks here have given the park its name.

Modern hotels and cafeterias, chalets and holidaymakers cannot disperse the wild and sometimes forbidding spell of Yellowstone with its other-worldly atmosphere engendered by the bright midday vision of the Grand Canyon, the sun glistening on the yellow stone which gives the park its name, a silent hawk circling high above, and the silver thread of the river far below.

The geyser Old Faithful, Yellowstone National Park's most popular attraction, never fails to draw crowds to see its spectacular eruptions of hot water, which occur at regular intervals of just over an hour. Other geysers nearby, including the Beehive, Giantess, Lone Star and Riverside geysers, are characterized by eruptions of varying height, duration and timing, but are equally fascinating.

Brasília

The simple but splendid goal of Brasília was to plant a new and ultra-modern city as capital in the middle of Brazil. This, it was hoped, would be a symbol of Brazil's determination to overcome its most vexing contradiction: that after 400 years the bulk of the population was still concentrated in the narrow coastal region, while the enormous potential wealth of the interior was still largely untapped.

The proposal that the capital should be in Brazil's Central Plateau dated back to 1789, and after Brazilian independence in 1822 government after government pledged itself to move the capital from Rio de Janeiro. The decision finally to realize this pipe-dream was at last taken by President Juscelino Kubitschek on his election in 1956. In less than three years, the site had been chosen, a master plan selected, building was underway and the government was ready to move from Rio.

The master plan for Brasília was chosen in a competition open to all architects in Brazil, with a selection committee which included architects and city planners from Britain, France and the United States of America as well as Brazil. The first prize went to Lúcio Costa, who had entered the competition late and reluctantly, submitting a design sketched with twenty-five cents' worth of paper and pencils. Costa's disciple, the world-famous architect Oscar Niemeyer, who helped design the United Nations building in New York, designed Brasília's public buildings.

Brasília's setting is the Federal District of 2260 square miles (5853 square kilometres) carved out of the vast cattle and diamond state of Goiás, on the 3497-foot-high (1066-metre) Central Plateau. Costa's basically simple, but imaginative and revolutionary plan, sets the city along two axes crossing at right angles. One, the north-south axis, is curved, so that when seen from above Brasília's shape is like a swept-wing aircraft. An almost 19-mile-long (thirty-one kilometre) man-made lake surrounds the city on three sides.

Along Brasília's seven-mile-long (eleven-kilometre) east-west axis (the fuselage of the aircraft) are ranged government and public buildings. The nose of the aircraft is formed by a vast triangular esplanade, the Plaza of the Three Powers, with the buildings of the Congress, Supreme Court and

Bold, sculptural shapes characterize Niemeyer's ultramodern Congress Building in Brasília.

Executive. Behind the plaza are the ten-storey ministries.

The aircraft's wings are an eight-mile (thirteen-kilometre) residential arc of houses and super-blocks. Most of the superblocks comprise from ten to sixteen apartment buildings six storeys high. They are screened by trees and surrounded by playgrounds and gardens. Each superblock has its own primary school and shops.

Downtown Brasília is at the crossing of the two axes, with hotels, shopping, banking, cultural and recreation districts. Thanks to generous parking space, there are no traffic jams at the centre. All through Brasília overpasses and underpasses criss-cross so that traffic lights are not needed on the city's main arteries.

The overwhelming impression created by Brasília is a sense of scale and space, in which geometrical uniformity is avoided by setting curved against straight vistas. Niemeyer's build-ings, in sweeping concrete and glass, re-echo this futuristic interplay of lines and curves. The Presi-dential Palace, on the outskirts of the city beyond the Plaza of the Three Powers, is surrounded with curved, flat pillars like paper cut-outs. Another of Niemeyer's imaginative designs is Our Lady of Fatima Chapel. With its swooping roof, supported by curved supports, the building seems divorced from the ground, with an appearance of weight-

Brasília is a bold concept incorporating superb modern architecture. Among the many fine buildings in this striking city are (opposite, left) the Ministry of Justice, which has artificial cascades between its columns; (above) the Palace of the Planalto, the President's offices facing the vast Plaza of the Three Powers, with its steel Monument to the Warriors: and (left) the Church of Dom Bosco, with its beautiful stained glass windows, fine crystal lamps and enormous wooden Crucifix.

lessness. This and many other buildings and open spaces in the city have provided scope for superb work by Brazil's best sculptors and artists.

Today, Brasília has about 200000 inhabitants, and is building up towards its projected population of half a million. Rio de Janeiro, 600 miles (965 kilometres) to the south-east, with over three million people, has not yet been supplanted as Brazil's cultural and economic capital. It would be more accurate to say that a division of labour has taken place between Rio and Brasília, with Brasília growing into its role as political capital.

A city is a highly complex organism which needs generations, even centuries, in which to grow and develop. It is perhaps still too early to tell if Brasília will succeed as a new centre of gravity for Brazil. But if inspired planning and architecture are any guarantee, it stands every chance.

The Petrified Forest, Arizona

From a distance, Arizona's famous Petrified Forest does not seem very like a forest at all. No trees stand in this 146 square mile (378-square-kilometre) region of high, desert plateau in north-east Arizona. The main vegetation is cacti and yucca growing among the buttes and low mesas which bake under the ferocious sun.

However, once in the Petrified Forest it is obvious that one is in the presence of a unique natural phenomenon: the mineralized, rock-solid remains of thousands of trees lying on their sides, forming the richest collection of petrified wood known. Ranging in size from giant trunks to small pieces, these bizarre remains glint and glow in almost every imaginable colour – oranges, reds, yellows and rusts, whites, greys and tans, purples, blacks and blues. Only the green of living chlorophyll is missing. Heightening the impression of a natural Aladdin's Cave are brilliant chips of agate, onyx, jasper and carnelian in the desert sand.

Originally, the Petrified Forest was an actual living forest. Some two hundred million years ago, in what is now high, arid desert was a low, swampy basin thickly covered with trees, ferns and mosses, overlooked by groves of conifers on the hills and ridges above the swamp. Over many millenia, the trees were toppled by natural forces and carried by floods to the centre of the basin. There they were gradually buried beneath thousands of metres of sand, mud and mineral-rich ash left by earlier volcanic activity.

The fossilized remains of once-mighty trees that lived millions of years ago litter the desert in the Petrified Forest National Park, Arizona (below). The brilliantly coloured glassy deposits in the rock logs reveal the presence of mineral oxides (left).

Right: Northern Arizona's Painted Desert unfolds a strange landscape of arid, rounded badlands tinted with horizontal bands of pink, brown and white.

The tissues of the buried wood were impregnated with mineral solutions of silica, iron and manganese which filled in each cell, retaining its imprint so that the exact detail of the wood was reproduced in mineral form.

Once formed, the multicoloured, petrified logs might have lain below the surface for ever. But about seventy million years ago, during a mountain building period, the strata carrying the logs were thrust high above sea level and the Petrified Forest was exposed through gradual erosion.

In all, the region actually contains six forests, the most beautifully coloured of which is the Rainbow Forest with many trunks more than 98 feet (30 metres) long. Overlooking Long Logs, where trunks are piled up on each other, is an old Indian pueblo built of pieces of petrified wood. Agate Bridge, one of the region's most interesting features, is a huge single log forming a bridge more than 98 feet (30 metres) long with both ends buried in sandstone.

At the northern end of the Petrified Forest is another extraordinary natural feature of Arizona, the Painted Desert. Here, the colours of the Petrified Forest reappear in intricately sculpted layers of sandstone, shale and clay. The colours and shapes of the Painted Desert change constantly with the direction of the sun; they are at their most dramatic in the sharp shadows of early morning and late afternoon.

With their strange and harsh beauty, the Petrified Forest and Painted Desert are among nature's greatest displays of virtuosity.

Sugar Loaf Mountain

In January 1502, the Portuguese explorer Gonzalo Coelho discovered what he thought was a great river mouth on the coast of southern Brazil, and named it Rio de Janeiro – River of January. However, he had discovered a bay, so its name was transferred to the military settlement that was founded on its shores in 1565, and the bay was renamed Guanabara. In time, the settlement named after a non-existent river grew to become both Brazil's and South America's second largest city.

Rio de Janeiro's setting, between forested mountains and the sparkling waters of Guanabara Bay and the Atlantic Ocean, is one of the finest in the world, rivalled only by San Francisco Bay and Sydney Harbour. One of the best vantage points from which to appreciate Rio's scenic splendour is from the summit of the city's famous natural landmark, Pão de Azucar – the Sugar Loaf Mountain.

Standing on a peninsula overlooking the entrance to the bay, the Sugar Loaf is a massive granite outcrop 1325 feet (404 metres) high, at the end of a short mountain range between Rio and the Atlantic Ocean. It is aptly named for its smoothly rounded, conical shape, which exactly resembles one of the loaves in which sugar used to be sold before it came in packets.

As one enters Guanabara Bay through the Laje Channel from the Atlantic, the Sugar Loaf presents its most benign aspect. Sloping to the sea, its right flank looks gentle enough to walk up. In fact, it is a very tough rock climb, and no one managed, or saw the need, perhaps, to scale the Sugar Loaf until the middle of the nineteenth century, when a British sailor on shore leave scrambled up. Today, a cablecar takes visitors to the top, via the flat summit of the adjacent Urca Hill. The more adventurous can chimney up through a 797-foot (243-metre) cleft in the rock.

From the summit of the Sugar Loaf a superb vista stretches in every direction, from the fabulous Itaipu Beach on the Atlantic to the bay and city,

rimmed by the famous Copacabana Beach with its elegant hotels. Bounded by the Atlantic shore on the south and Guanabara Bay to the east, the teeming city of Rio is built on and between a series of steep hills backed by mountains in the north-west. On the highest of these, Corcovado, is the huge statue of Christ the Redeemer.

Perhaps the most exciting time to be on the Sugar Loaf is when the annual pre-Carnival Ball is held on the summit to kick off the four days of Rio's famous carnival, before Lent. But a stranger spectacle is to be seen on New Year's Eve, when, from the Sugar Loaf, the beaches of Rio appear to have been invaded by myriad fireflies. The fireflies are, in fact, the candles held by thousands of black and white followers of the Afro-Brazilian religion Macumba, as they honour the sea goddess Iemanjá.

The unmistakable shape of Sugar Loaf Mountain dominates the magnificent natural harbour of Rio de Janeiro. Tall modern hotels line the superb beaches that fringe the smaller bays at its foot, among which is the world-famous Copacabana Beach.

The Rocky Mountains

The Rocky Mountains, North America's highest and most spectacular mountain range, popularly known as the Rockies, stretch for 3200 miles (5100 kilometres) down the western side of the continent from Alaska to New Mexico. They, in turn, are part of a series of ranges and high plateaux that together form the great highland barrier known as the North American Cordillera. This is itself the northern section of the extensive chain of mountains that continues southward through Mexico into the mighty Andes of South America. The Rockies contain some of the most magnificent mountain scenery in the world, and each year thousands of visitors come to marvel at their breathtaking beauty.

Along their entire length, the Rockies are broken up into numerous local ranges that for the most part continue the general north-south trend. The width of the system consequently varies between 100 and 400 miles (160 and 640 kilometres). Snaking its way along the crests of the ranges is the Continental Divide, the watershed separating rivers that flow westward into the Pacific Ocean from those that drain the eastern slopes into the Arctic Ocean or Gulf of Mexico, notably the Mackenzie and Missouri rivers and their tributaries.

For convenience the Rockies are often divided into four main sections from north to south. In the far north, the Arctic Rockies extend from the remote wilderness of the Brooks Range, an east–west chain of mountains in northern Alaska, through a series of ranges that arc across north-western Canada. The highest peaks here rise above 7000 feet (2135 metres), with Mount Sir James McBrien in the Mackenzie Mountains soaring to 9040 feet (2760 metres).

South of the Liard River, in northern British Columbia, the Northern Rockies continue beyond the Canada–United States border into Idaho and Montana. Lofty peaks climbing to nearly 13000 feet (3965 metres), immense dazzling icefields, plunging valleys clothed in thick forests, and ice-cold sparkling lakes mark this section of the Rockies as a region of outstanding natural beauty. Many of its scenic wonders are enclosed in several national parks: Jasper, Banff, Yoho and Waterton Lakes in Canada, and Glacier in the United States. A curious geological feature here is the Rocky Mountain Trench, a long stretch of flat land, river valleys and low hills that runs along the western flank of the mountains from the Yukon to Montana.

Further south the Middle Rockies seem to disintegrate into several widely spaced ranges separ-

59

ated by vast flat basins as they pass through Wyoming. The north-western part of the state contains the wonders of Yellowstone National Park, a land of open grasslands, thick forests, lakes, waterfalls and river gorges teeming with wildlife, but better known for its hot mineral springs, spectacular geysers, bubbling mud pools and other curious volcanic features. To the south the horizon is pierced by the jagged summits of the Grand Tetons, a majestic block of mountains, now designated as a national park, that rise abruptly from the flat expanse of the valley of Jackson Hole. The highest point of the Middle Rockies, however, is Gannet Peak, a 13785-foot (4204-metre) mountain in the Wind River Range.

The Southern Rockies, which extend from southern Wyoming into Utah and through Colorado into New Mexico, contain the highest peaks in the whole Rocky Mountain system. In Colorado more than 50 peaks tower above 14000 feet (4267 metres) amid landscapes of stunning beauty, the highest of them, Mount Elbert, reaching 14331 feet (4371 metres). In the Front Range, which rises steeply from the Great Plains in Colorado, is Rocky Mountain National Park, an area of outstanding scenery encompassing magnificent snow-mantled peaks, immense glaciers, lakes and forests.

The Rocky Mountains were created during an intense period of upheavals in the earth's crust

between 85 and 65 million years ago. The surface layers of rocks were folded or faulted (cracked) into blocks by movements of the great plates that make up the crust, and molten rock welled up from deep below ground. More recently, immense glaciers and the forces of erosion have worn down the surface rocks to shape the magnificent scenery we see today.

Among the scenic highlights of the Canadian Rockies is Jasper National Park (below right and left), one of several national parks along the border between Alberta and British Columbia. Rugged mountain peaks, dazzling glaciers, ice-cold lakes, rushing torrents and dark green forest contribute to the scenic grandeur of this part of Canada.

Large areas of the Rockies are clothed in forests of pine, spruce, fir, aspen and other trees. The tree line, the altitude above which trees do not thrive, varies from about 12000 feet (3660 metres) in New Mexico to only 2500 feet (762 metres) in the bleak mountains of the Arctic. On the higher slopes alpine meadows dotted with colourful wild flowers gradually give way to the rocky crags and screes of the summits, where only lichens, low-growing plants and scrubby bushes can survive the extreme cold and deep snows of the winter months. In the dry plateau regions of the Middle and Southern Rockies, sagebrush and other tough, drought-resistant plants are the dominant vegetation, with cottonwoods and other water-loving trees forming

roamed the area and left such artifacts as pottery, stone tools and arrowheads, rock carvings and paintings, and cliff-side dwellings such as those at Mesa Verde in Colorado.

The first white people to cross the Rockies were Sir Alexander Mackenzie in 1793 and the expedition of Meriwether Lewis and William Clark in 1804–6. They were followed by a host of doughty explorers, fur traders, trappers and mountain men, many of whose names are immortalised on the history of the West, among them Simon Fraser, Jedediah Smith, Jim Bridger and John Fremont. During the great gold rushes of the late 1850s prospectors and miners flooded into the Rockies to seek their fortune. Many of the riproaring boom towns they threw up were later abandoned as the ores ran out, their decaying remains now serving as ghostly reminders of those exciting pioneer days.

Mining is still a major industry of the Rocky Mountains region. There are large quantities of copper, iron, gold, silver, lead, zinc and other metals, in addition to coal, oil shale, petrolium, natural gas and uranium. Tourism is increasing in importance. For many people, however, the Rockies simply offer an opportunity to escape from the pressures of modern life amid scenery of staggering natural beauty. As the naturalist Enos Mills, who himself was mainly reponsible for the setting up of Rocky Mountain National Park, once wrote, 'He who feels the spell of the wild, the rhythmic melody of falling water, the echoes among the crags, the bird songs, the wind in the pines . . . is in tune with the universe'.

lush strips of green along the banks of rivers and creeks.

From the Arctic to New Mexico the Rockies abound in wildlife, the wide range of animals that thrive in its remote wildernesses including the caribou, moose, deer, elk, bighorn sheep, mountain goat, grizzly and black bear, puma (or mountain lion), bobcat, coyote and beaver. Evidence of human habitation in this wild region dates from a thousand or more years ago, when Indian peoples

Top left: Jagged peaks in Wyoming's Grand Teton Mountains create one of the most beautiful and spectacular sections of America's Rocky Mountains.

Bottom left: Scenery of exceptional beauty is enclosed in the Rocky Mountain National Park, in Colorado. Hallett Peak (left) is just one of many peaks here that soar above 12000 feet (3600 metres).

Right: The Old Trail Town in Cody, Wyoming, has a collection of old cabins and other buildings used by pioneer settlers in this part of the Rocky Mountains long ago.

63

Carlsbad Caverns

To see the first of the many phenomena associated with Carlsbad Caverns, in New Mexico, it is not even necessary to enter this vast system of limestone caves. Seated in a specially-built amphitheatre at the cave mouth, at sunset on any night from May to October, tourists can witness – and hear – the extraordinary spectacle of Bat Flight, as thousands upon thousands of bats whirr and spiral their way out of their subterranean home in search of their evening meal.

Carlsbad Caverns, made into a national park in 1930, is in the south-eastern corner of New Mexico, 15 miles (twenty-four kilometres) from the Texan border to the south and 27 miles (forty-three kilometres) from the town of Carlsbad to the northeast. Approaching the caverns across the Chihuahua Desert, the monotony of the flat, undulating terrain begins to be broken by the rise of the foothills of the Guadalupe Mountains which are a few kilometres into Texas. But there is nothing to indicate that beneath 73 square miles (189 square kilometres) of this hilly, desert country, covered with cacti, there is one of the world's most intricately beautiful cave networks.

More than two hundred million years ago, the entire area of Carlsbad Caverns was covered by an inland sea, at the edge of which coral polyps built up a massive limestone reef. Eventually the sea dried up and the reef became buried under thousands of metres of sediment. Then, some twenty million years ago, a huge geological fault split the reef and thrust mountains upwards. The thick sedimentary strata above the reef began to erode, and ground water containing carbon dioxide began to seep down into the limestone mass, creating hollow spaces as the limestone was changed into soluble calcium bicarbonate. As the water table gradually lowered, the hollows became huge cavities; these became even larger as massive, porous blocks of rock, no longer supported by water, collapsed. The seepage of surface water continued, carrying dissolved limestone on to the walls of the caves, which gradually solidified to create myriad limestone formations: icicle-like stalactites hanging from the ceilings, stalagmites growing up from the floor, monumental pillars where stalactites and stalagmites met and fused, limestone domes and a multitude of other shapes.

From the entrance to the caverns, an imposing natural arch 89 feet (twenty-seven metres) wide and 39 feet (twelve metres) high, a steep, switch-

back path leads downwards to the main corridor at a depth of 828 feet (252.5 metres). The corridor leads through a series of astonishing chambers: the King's Palace, a circular cave with elaborate limestone ornamentation and draperies of sparkling cave onyx; the Queen's Chamber, with delicately-shaped 'elephant ear' formations; and the Papoose Room with its low, stalactite-packed ceiling. Finally there is the magnificent Big Room, a massive subterranean cathedral with a ceiling of 256 feet (seventy-eight metres). About half a mile (0.8 kilometres) long and 400 feet (122 metres) across at its widest, this main cavern, with its constantly varied patterns of stalactite and stalagmite formations, is among the world's most striking examples of natural architecture.

Below left: Dramatic lighting illuminates the weird clusters of dripping stalactites in the Papoose Room, one of the fascinating underground chambers in the Carlsbad Caverns of New Mexico.

Below: Many of the rock features in Carlsbad Caverns have identifying names, such as the famous Totem Pole. This curious rock column is a stalagmite formed by water dripping rapidly from the cave roof and is 38 feet (11.5 metres) long.

San Francisco

There could be no greater contrast to New York, the low, rocky and barren coasts of New England and the grey-green swell of the Atlantic Ocean, than San Francisco with its azure Pacific setting and Californian cliffs changing colour through gold, red or blue depending on the time of day. Two such different cities could only be on opposite sides of a continent.

Built on the northern tip of the peninsula enclosing San Francisco Bay, the city has a perfect natural setting: to the west, the limitless expanse of the Pacific Ocean; to the east, the bay, forming a wide and magnificent natural harbour; and to the north, the Golden Gate Strait, connecting the ocean to the bay and spanned by probably the world's most famous suspension bridge. Apart from the frequent, mysterious fog which rolls in from the Pacific, and occasional smog, San Francisco enjoys a nearly ideal climate, rarely hotter than 69°F (21°C) or colder than 30°F (−1°C).

More than five million people live in the nine counties of the Bay Area, with about 705000 in the compact, 47-square-mile (120-square-kilometre) area of the city of San Francisco.

Not least of San Francisco's charms is its hills: it is built on and round more than forty of them. The downtown area in the north-east, in particular, is like a switchback, with some of the world's steepest streets. One of the city's most famous features, a unique cable-car system, was designed to cope with the steep gradients. The cars run on rails like trams, but are pulled along by a moving cable beneath the street.

Another special attraction of this beautiful city is its legacy of Victorian houses, many well-preserved examples of which line the streets of the Mission District and the area around Union Street known as Cow Hollow. There is also much fine modern architecture, among which the spectacular St Mary's Cathedral is an outstanding landmark.

Market Street, with its department stores and shops, is the main downtown street, not too different from the hustle and noise of any American main street. Just to the north of Market Street is the impressive Civic Centre, including City Hall, the San Francisco Museum of Modern Art and the Performing Arts Center. Nob Hill, to the north-east, is one of the city's highest points, with luxury houses and hotels.

East of Nob Hill is San Francisco's famous China-town, the world's largest Chinese community outside Asia. Although much Americanized, this is still a quarter of Chinese and Chinese speech, with buildings painted green for long life and red for vitality, in the Chinese tradition. Not far away is Union Square, the heart of the downtown hotel and shopping area.

The 'Wall Street of the West', San Francisco's financial district, centres on Montgomery Street, east of Chinatown. Here, two of the most prominent landmarks are the 853-foot (260-metre) Transamerica Pyramid, a white office building rising like a slender, gleaming pyramid, and the fifty-two-storey Bank of America nearby, the world's largest commercial bank. A recent addition to this area is the spectacular Embarcadero Center, a complex of office and hotel towers incorporating landscaped plazas and three levels of shops and restaurants. South of the financial district is the new Moscone Convention Center, which provides excellent facilities for business conventions, trade shows and other events.

Cutting a broad swathe from the middle of the city to the Pacific shore is Golden Gate Park, with its glades and gardens, where jewel-like humming-birds dart and hover in front of fuchsia blossoms, and the air is scented with pine trees. Among the park's special features are outstanding art and science museums and the famous Japanese Tea Garden. From Lincoln Park, where there is an oceanic golf course among eucalyptus trees, the cliffs of the Golden Gate can be seen opening out to the blue Pacific.

Left: San Francisco's Chinatown is a piece of the Orient transported to America's west coast. Centred on Grant Avenue, this busy, atmospheric district contains the largest Chinese community in the United States.

Below left: On summer mornings the Golden Gate Bridge, at the entrance to San Francisco Bay, is often engulfed in banks of fog which roll in from the Pacific Ocean.

Below: An impressive span of the San Francisco-Oakland Bay Bridge leaps across the Bay from Yerba Buena Island to merge with San Francisco's busy financial district. Here, towering skyscrapers, including the distinctive Transamerica Pyramid, create an enchanting skyline.

The port of San Francisco borders the bay, which forms the world's largest landlocked harbour. Running along the shore is the wide, long street of the Embarcadero. At the middle of the port is the Ferry Building with its famous clock tower, a distinctive landmark. Fisherman's Wharf, at the northern end of the Embarcadero, is famous for its seafood restaurants; it used to harbour a huge fleet of colourful fishing boats. Alcatraz Island, in the bay, was a famous, escape-proof federal prison from 1933 to 1963; today, it is a tourist attraction. Other highlights of the waterfront area are the shopping and entertainment complex of Pier 39, the collection of old ships moored at Hyde Street Pier, and the shopping meccas of The Anchorage, The Cannery and Ghirardelli Square.

Two spectacular bridges link San Francisco to other parts of the Bay Area. The San Francisco-Oakland Bay Bridge, one of the world's longest bridges over navigable water, is more than 8 miles (13 kilometres) long including its approaches. Opened in 1936, it cost more than $76 million. Really a series of bridges, it links San Francisco to Yerba Buena Island in the bay by two suspension spans. From Yerba Buena, the bridge crosses to Oakland and Berkeley. The Golden Gate Bridge, one of the world's largest and most dramatically situated suspension bridges, spans the Golden Gate Strait, connecting north California to the San

Francisco Peninsula. Designed by Joseph Strauss, it was completed in 1937 at a cost of $35.5 million. The magnificent sweep of the Golden Gate Bridge is the first structure seen by ships as they approach San Francisco. The span between the bridge's two towers is 4199 feet (1280 metres).

The first Europeans to settle the San Francisco Peninsula were the Spanish, who founded a fort and mission there in 1776. The settlement by the mission was named Pueblo de San Francisco, but the port and town which grew up in the early nineteenth century, when California was a Mexican possession, was known as Yerba Buena (meaning 'good herb') from an abundance of wild mint. During the Mexican War in 1846 the Americans captured Yerba Buena and renamed it San Francisco. With the California gold rush of 1848 the town grew like wildfire, and continued to expand as the supply centre for a series of mining booms. Most of San Francisco, however, was ruined in an earthquake in 1906, which killed seven hundred people and made 300000 homeless, through the earthquake itself and the ensueing fires. Movement in the San Andreas Fault in the earth's crust was the cause. But the city was rapidly rebuilt, and continued to grow in the twentieth century, although Los Angeles and Oakland were challenging it as the leading Pacific port. During World War II, San Francisco became a leading ship-building centre. The 1960s and 1970s saw large-scale urban renewal.

Today San Francisco, like most other great cities, has its share of problems. But it remains one of America's most beautiful places as well as being, with Los Angeles, the commercial, intellectual and artistic centre of the western United States.

Left: Like other American cities, San Francisco has a regular grid pattern of streets, with low-rise buildings and houses in the outer areas and a cluster of prestigious modern office and hotel towers in the central business district.

Right: San Francisco's beloved cable cars clatter up and down the city's many hills, powered by a moving steel cable that runs beneath the street. At the end of the line, such as the terminus at Powell and Market Streets, the cars are turned round on revolving turntables, ready for the journey back.

Yosemite National Park

Yosemite National Park, in the Sierra Nevada mountains of east central California, embraces an area of superb natural beauty which has held visitors spellbound since its discovery in the middle of the nineteenth century.

The region's most spectacular scenery is in the Yosemite Valley in the heart of the park, at an altitude of 3937 feet (1200 metres). An expedition led by Joseph Walker may have come to the edge of the valley in 1833; but the members of James D. Savage's expedition, sent in 1851 to pacify the Yosemite Indians, seem to have been the first Europeans to actually enter it. The expedition was a failure, but one of its members, a young soldier named Lafayette Bunnell, was so enchanted by the valley's High Sierra scenery that he risked Indian ambushes to explore the area singlehanded. The Scots naturalist John Muir, who reached Yosemite in 1868, became its greatest devotee. He wrote to Ralph Waldo Emerson inviting him to join him there. Though by then he was an old man, Emerson took up Muir's invitation, and wrote in his journal that the grandeur of the Yosemite mountains was perhaps unmatched in the world.

The high valley which so thrilled Bunnell, Muir

*Right: Fed by melting snows
the spectacular Yosemite
Falls take two tremendous
leaps down sheer rock walls
into the Yosemite Valley.*

*Below: The stunningly
beautiful Merced River
valley, the heart of Yosemite
National Park, is overlooked
by towering granite peaks
and precipitous rock faces,
such as Half Dome (right).*

and Emerson was carved by the westward-flowing Merced River. The action of glaciers ground the Merced Canyon into a smooth, U-shaped valley nearly one mile (1.6 kilometres) wide and deep. These glaciers 'sheared off' the shallower canyons of tributary streams flowing into the Merced to form hanging valleys or natural water spouts. The result was the world's greatest natural display of waterfalls cascading into Yosemite Valley.

The Yosemite Falls are formed by Yosemite Creek leaping from its hanging valley 2425 feet (739 metres) above the valley floor. The Upper Falls are 1430 feet (436 metres) and the Lower Falls are 322 feet (98 metres) high; their combined height is more than ten times the height of Niagara Falls. Bridalveil Falls make their descent of 620 feet (189 metres) from the valley's southern wall, while Vernal and Nevada Falls cascade over giant glacier-formed granite steps. The 318-foot (97-metre) Vernal Falls are famous for the rainbows which form in the mist at their base. Some of the valley's falls only appear during the spring high water season, such as Ribbon Falls (1611 feet/491 metres), the world's highest free-leap fall; Sentinel Falls (2001 feet/610 metres); and Silver Strand Falls (1171 feet/357 metres).

Other scenic features of the valley include Mirror Lake, with its crystal-clear smoothness reflecting its jagged surroundings; Tenaya Canyon (named after the Indian chief whom Savage was sent to capture); and granite crags such as the sheer, slab-sided El Capitan and the Half Dome, a near-precipice rising 3996 feet (1218 metres) above the valley floor.

Over sixty different animals, including two species of bear, cacomistle, wolverine and mountain lion, and two hundred bird species ranging from golden eagles to Red Anna humming birds, are found in the forests and on the mountain slopes of the Yosemite region. There are three groves of *Sequoiadendron giganteum* trees, the world's largest and oldest living organisms. The most famous is the Mariposa Grove 35 miles (56 kilometres) south of Yosemite Valley; it includes one of the biggest trees in the world, the Grizzly Giant with its base 33 feet (ten metres) in diameter.

It was in 1890 that Yosemite was demarcated as the second of the great national parks of the United States; its area today is 60890 acres (307932 hectares). The park is criss-crossed by 684 miles (1100 kilometres) of trails, with hotels, restaurants and 'scenic points'. Glacier Point, for instance, with its hotel and view point, hangs 3248 feet (990 metres) above the valley. No doubt John Muir would have been dubious about all this, but the beauty and serene grandeur of Yosemite effortlessly dominate such signs of human presence.

Angel Falls

Rising from the dense jungle in the Gran Sabana region of eastern Venezuela are a series of massive tablelands or *mesas*, some more than three kilometres high, with their sides and flat tops eroded to strange and bizarre shapes – a remote, outlandish setting in which it would not be too surprising to come across Sir Arthur Conan Doyle's *Lost World*. Here, spurting from the side of the great mesa known as Auyán-tepuí or Devil Mountain, is Angel Falls, the world's highest waterfall, fifteen times higher than Niagara Falls.

Apart from their extraordinary height, Angel Falls have the distinction of being the most recently discovered of the world's great natural spectacles. They are also one of the most inaccessible. The discovery of Angel Falls in 1935, by the aviator and prospector James Angel, had all the qualities of an adventure story. Angel had spent years flying around Central and South America searching for a lost river deposit of gold nuggets, to which he claimed an old prospector once led him on a mystery flight. Flying over Auyán-tepuí, Angel saw the mighty falls which were to be named after him. In 1937, he and two companions crash-landed their plane in a boulder-strewn swamp on top of the mesa, but they were unable to reach the falls. It was not until 1949 that an American-led expedition succeeded in reaching the foot of Angel Falls and made an accurate survey to confirm that they were indeed the world's highest waterfall.

Auyán-tepuí, like the other great plateaux and escarpments of South America and Africa, was raised in the later Tertiary Period (two and a half to sixty-five million years ago). Many millenia of erosion have dug out huge crevices and fissures on Auyán-tepuí's flat top, which trap the heavy tropical rainfall of the Gran Sabana. The waters of Angel Falls burst out of Auyán-tepuí between 197 feet and 295 feet (sixty and ninety metres) below the edge of the sheer cliff overlooking the Churún River. The first straight drop is 2646 feet (806.6 metres) (more than twice the height of the Eiffel Tower), and the remaining falls are 564 feet (171.8 metres), totalling 3210 feet (978.4 metres). About 500 feet (152 metres) wide at their base, the falls form a huge pool, darkened by spray, which drains into the Churún, a tributary of the Caroní River. Behind the waterfall is a huge, natural amphitheatre.

Angel Falls, the world's highest waterfall, are hidden in the remote forests of Venezuela and can only be seen in their entirety from the air.

The Galápagos Islands

Among the strangest places on the earth's surface are the Galápagos Islands, a remote Pacific archipelago which straddles the equator about 600 miles (965 kilometres) from South America. To the west there is no land for nearly 3107 miles (5000 kilometres). The Galápagos are also known as the 'Enchanted Isles', but their enchantment is very different from that of the typical Pacific islands of popular imagination. Far from being palm-fringed coral atolls, the Galápagos are a series of harsh and forbidding volcanic peaks which boiled up from the Pacific floor in a series of eruptions in geologically recent times. The archipelago includes many small islands and about fifteen larger ones. The largest, Isabela (Albemarle) is about 80 miles (129 kilometres) long and rises about 5597 feet (1706 metres) above the sea. A number of other islands are between 10 and 20 miles (16 and 32 kilometres) long, with peaks rising above 2952 feet (900 metres). Some of the older islands, such as San Cristóbal (Chatham), have been eroded to fairly gentle contours. But several of the younger islands, such as Fernandina (Narborough), are still volcanically active and have jagged profiles.

These desolate, fantastic islands were discovered in 1535 by Fray Tomas de Berlanga, Bishop of Panama. They looked to him 'as though God had caused it to rain stones'; and he called them *Islas de los Galápagos* – Tortoise Islands – because of the giant tortoises which crawl over the sharp, sun-baked lava. Though the Galápagos can be drenched with rain from December to March, there is of no permanent water because the porous lava and pumice of the islands absorbs nearly all the rainfall, leaving only temporary pools.

The visitor's first sight of the Galápagos Islands is of low, rocky coastal cliffs and shores of black lava. Thousands of scuttling, vividly scarlet crabs contrast with their surroundings. Here, too, is found a species of lizard unique to the Galápagos, the giant marine iguana, which dives into the sea to munch seaweed among the surf. Two kinds of seabird which live only on the shores of these islands are the Galápagos cormorant and penguin. Because it has no predators and therefore no need to fly, the Galápagos cormorant's wings are reduced to ragged stumps that act only as balancers. The Galápagos penguin is a cold-water species but it can live in the Galápagos because the cold Humboldt Current washes the islands.

Behind the shores are arid lowlands of glassy volcanic grit which abound with tall tree cacti and prickly pears, sometimes combining with thorny acacias to form impassable barriers. Feeding on the prickly pears, juicy pads, thorns and all, are giant

74

land iguanas.

Higher up, where there is more moisture, the scenery changes. Even outside the rainy months, the island peaks may be cloaked by damp mists brought by the South-east Trade Winds. As a result, parts of the higher slopes are covered with quite lush forest. Draped with mosses and lichens, the trees are interspersed with clumps of tall grasses and tree ferns. Above the forests and up to the rims of the volcano craters is grassland with ferns, liverworts and mosses.

Despite their desolate appearance, the Galápagos are no desert. But the islands are strange not only because many of the odd animals and plants are unlike those of anywhere else, but also because, compared with the nearest mainland, South America, there are many missing species. For instance, there are no herbivorous mammals native to the Galápagos, and only a few species of land birds: cuckoos, hawks, flycatchers, mockingbirds and finches.

It was these peculiarities which attracted the attention of the most famous visitor to the Galápagos, Charles Darwin, and prompted him to formulate one of the greatest revolutions in the history of ideas – the theory of evolution by natural selection.

In 1835, HMS *Beagle*, with Darwin aboard as ship's naturalist, made a routine stop at the Galá-pagos. During the *Beagle's* short stay, Darwin observed and collected all the wildlife he could. He was particularly puzzled by two questions: why it was that the animals and plants of the Galápagos should differ so much from those of South America and all other island groups, and why even the same species seemed to differ from island to island within the Galápagos. Darwin concluded that the number of species was not fixed and immutable, but was constantly changing in response to the opportunities offered by the environment.

The real enchantment of the Galápagos Islands, then, is that their remoteness has made them a unique natural laboratory, offering an unrivalled glimpse of the workings of the evolutionary process.

The unique wildlife of the Galapagos Islands, in the Pacific Ocean off the coast of South America, is one of the wonders of the natural world. It inspired the nineteenth-century naturalist Charles Darwin to work out his revolutionary theory of evolution by natural selection. Among the many captivating creatures to be seen on these craggy volcanic islands are the blue-footed booby (far left) and such unusual animals as the fearsome-looking marine iguana (below left) and the giant tortoise (below).

Chichén Itzá

One of the most sophisticated civilizations of the New World was developed by the Maya people of the Yucatán Peninsula of Mexico and Central America. During their period of highest development, before AD 1000, the Maya, unlike the Inca and Aztec peoples, did not evolve an empire but were divided into city states. Although they had no writing, did not use the wheel and knew little of metals, the Maya were well advanced in art, architecture, mathematics, engineering and astronomy. They developed the concept of zero, a number system based on twenty and a calendar more accurate than the Julian calendar. Their temples and other important buildings were made of stone and mortar and faced with carved stone.

Probably the finest of the cities built by the Maya was Chichén Itzá, in the Yucatán Peninsula. Finally abandoned after a civil war in the middle of the fifteenth century, the massive limestone structures of the city became completely overgrown by a jungle of low yic-yac trees until the middle of the nineteenth century, when the American explorer John L. Stevens began to excavate them.

A religious centre which was ruled by priest-politicians, Chichén Itzá is remarkable for the careful mathematical proportions of its ruins. One of the most famous buildings is the lofty, sun pyramid of Kukulcan 197 feet (sixty metres) high, with its crowning temple of sacrifice. The steep steps up the side of the pyramid were designed to become gradually wider, so that as one climbs them, perspective is defied and the steps seem to continue endlessly.

Another finely proportioned structure, on the outskirts of the city, is the so-called Ball Court, with fine temples at either end. Here, two parallel walls 262 feet (eighty metres) long and 121 feet (thirty-seven metres) apart form the sides of a court in which the Maya played a ritual game called *tlachtli* – a kind of basketball with a rubber ball (the use of rubber was a discovery of the Pre-Columbian Indians).

Leaving the Ball Court, one passes reclining blocks of carved limestone which are surprisingly like twentieth-century sculpture. They represent the Mayan rain god, Chac-Mol, but all their features have been weathered away. To the Maya, water supplies were the critical factor in locating their cities, especially in Yucatán, where the soft limestone absorbed rain as soon as it fell. Chichén Itzá's two great natural wells gave the city its name: Chichén means 'mouth of the wells', and the Itzá were the Maya people who founded the city.

A path through the jungle leads to one of these wells, the Cenote or Sacred Well, 59 feet (eighteen metres) in diameter, which breaks through the

Right: Adjoining the Temple of the Warriors at Chichén Itzá (top) is the remarkable Court of the Thousand Columns, once covered by a vaulted roof. The entrance to the temple (bottom) is flanked by pillars embellished with fierce serpent heads. In front is the reclining figure of the rain god Chac-Mol.

Below: The Temple of Kukulcan, popularly known as 'El Castillo' (The Castle), is the most famous building at Chichén Itzá and has been carefully reconstructed.

limestone crust of which the whole peninsula is formed. Into its dark waters, 98 feet (thirty metres) sheer below, women were thrown in times of drought to appease Chac-Mol. They were thrown in at dawn, and at midday a rope was lowered; if they had survived they were hauled up to safety. When an American archaeologist, E.H. Thompson, dredged the well he discovered countless precious objects which had been thrown in to propitiate the rain god, including gold which came from as far as Colombia and Peru. He also found many bones of middle-aged women, disproving the legend that the women sacrificed to Chac-Mol were always young virgins.

The Grand Canyon

Of all the gradual events which have modified and changed the earth's surface, few have had such spectacular results as the cutting of the Grand Canyon by the Colorado River in north-west Arizona. Ranging in width from 655 feet to 18 miles (200 metres to twenty-nine kilometres), and about 5315 feet (1620 metres) deep at its deepest, this mighty gash in the Colorado Plateau winds its way from east to west for about 217 miles (350 kilometres), from Marble Gorge near Arizona's northern border to Grand Wash Cliffs near the Nevada border. The canyon's north rim, at 8202 feet (2500 metres) above sea level, is about 1200 feet (366 metres) higher than the south rim. Apart from the Colorado River itself, the canyon floor is desert country, but forests grow along the rims.

The scenic splendour of the Grand Canyon is not just a matter of sheer, awe-inspiring size; it derives also from the canyon's intricately sculptured and infinitely varied rock formations: the many peaks, buttes and subsidiary canyons lying between the two rims, and the step-terrace effect of the canyon walls. The buttes are towers of rock which nature has carved out in almost architectural blocks, some resembling ancient temples. The overall impression of colour is red, but this shifts with changing sunlight. Each rock layer or group of layers has its own shade: grey, green and pink and, lower down, brown and violet.

The exposed strata of its walls make the Grand Canyon a geologist's paradise. Nowhere else in the world presents such a display of the processes by which the earth's crust has been made and shaped. The canyon strata are mostly sedimentary rocks: limestones, shales and sandstones. The

bottom layer of rock through which the Colorado River flows is composed of unstratified, much contorted granite and schist, and is about 4000 million years old.

The Grand Canyon is not only a geological record but a dramatic record of the slow millenia of the evolutionary process. Its sedimentary strata are rich in fossils of plants and animals, from primitive algae to trees and from sea-shells and trilobites to the remains of dinosaurs, camels, horses and elephants. One of the most exciting finds in the canyon has been the footprints of dinosaurs, embedded in sandstone.

The speed and volume of the Colorado River, and the mud, sand and gravel it carries, gave it the tremendous cutting power that was needed to gouge out the Grand Canyon. Geologists think that the canyon was cut as the Colorado Plateau moved upwards. Since the Grand Canyon was formed, the arid climate of the region has preserved the canyon's features from erosion by rainfall.

Ruined adobe houses and cliff dwellings in the Grand Canyon show that Pueblo Indians lived there, perhaps from the thirteenth century. Today, a handful of about two hundred Havasupai Indians live in an isolated branch of the canyon. Explorers from a Spanish expedition of 1540 were the first Europeans to see the canyon, but it was not revisited until 1776.

The Grand Canyon (below), one of the most breathtaking spectacles on earth, is a tremendous gash in the Arizona landscape carved by the Colorado River. Far below the canyon rim, many smaller streams, such as Upper Deer Creek (far left), offer fascinating side trips for adventurous rafters.

Today, the Grand Canyon forms a national park, which was created in 1919 and nearly doubled in area in 1975. A paved road and a cross-canyon trail link the north and south rims; other routes lead to all the important features of the canyon's landscape. Mule-back trips and exciting rides down the Colorado River in motorboats and rafts are two of the most popular ways of seeing the canyon – one of the world's great natural wonders.

Below: Trips by mule offer visitors the unforgettable experience of entering the maze of towering pinnacles, rock cliffs and mesas inside the Grand Canyon.

Bottom: Before entering the dramatic landscapes of the Grand Canyon, the Colorado River flows through the narrow rock walls of the stretch known as Marble Canyon.

Cuzco and Machu Picchu

The soaring peaks, high mountain valleys and sheer ravines of the Andes, in Peru's southern highlands, hardly seem a favourable environment for one of the world's greatest civilizations to have taken root. Yet it was the Valley of Cuzco, in this region, which became the starting point of the largest, most highly organized state of the ancient Americas: the Empire of the Inca. Settling in this valley in about AD 1250, the Inca people were one small tribal state among many in the neighbourhood until 1438. Then, under the leadership of the Inca (emperor) Pachacuti, they began a tremendous campaign of conquest. In scarcely thirty years they gained a vast empire which covered almost all of Peru, most of Ecuador, a large part of Bolivia and parts of Chile and Argentina.

The skill with which the Incas governed this empire has always astonished historians, for there had been nothing quite like Inca society before or since. People's lives were organized down to the last detail, so that everyone had enough land and enough to eat. Great cities, fortresses, irrigation works and roads were built. All this was achieved in a pre-technological society which used no money and had no writing.

But after 1532, when Francisco Pizarro and a handful of Spanish *conquistadores* seized the Inca Atahuallpa, the empire collapsed like a card house. Such a highly centralized state could not function with its centre, the Inca himself, removed. But for all their easy success, the Spaniards were well aware of the remarkable achievements of the Incas. Few sights impressed them more than the Inca capital of Cuzco.

In the Quechua language of the Incas, the name of their capital meant 'The Navel'. According to legend it was built on the spot where Manco Capac, founder of the Inca dynasty, planted a golden staff. After the beginning of the Inca expansion Cuzco grew greatly, reaching a population of up to 300000. Here, surrounding the court of the Inca, was the administrative and religious centre of his far-flung empire.

The two central points of Cuzco were the Coricancha, or Sun Temple, and the Huacapata, or

The mysterious sacred spring of Tambo Machay, a shrine built by the Incas near Cuzco, has long been popularly known as the 'Baths of the Inca'.

Left: The Calle de Loreto, with its typical sloping Inca walls, was one of the main streets of the old Inca capital of Cuzco and led to the Temple of the Sun.

Right: A series of massive walls mark the site of the fortress of Sacsahuaman, built by the Incas to defend their capital, Cuzco, from the west.

Below: The ruins of the ancient Inca city of Machu Picchu cling to their remote mountain-top site amid the soaring peaks of the Andes in Peru.

great plaza. The Coricancha was a complex of buildings made of great blocks of stone masonry, which fitted together so closely that not even a knife blade could be forced between them. Their perfect fitting, without the use of mortar, was a secret that died with the empire. Inside the temple was the treasure which attracted the Spaniards: huge gold and silver discs representing the Sun God and his wife the Moon.

The great festivals and ceremonies of the Inca people were held in the Huacapata. Here too were the palaces of the Inca nobles – low buildings with rooms grouped around courtyards, something like the atrium houses of ancient Rome in plan.

Apart from Cuzco the Incas built many other cities and forts in the Andes. One of the most striking examples is Machu Picchu in the Valley of Urubamba, famous as the 'Lost City of the Incas'. Really a large, fortified village of two to three hundred buildings, Machu Picchu was never reached by the Spanish and remained unknown to Europeans until 1911, when the long-deserted site was discovered by the American explorer Hiram Bingham.

The fine buildings of Machu Picchu include a Sun Temple with three great windows looking out to the rising sun, and a unique feature – a stone Intihuatana, or hitching post for the sun, the only undamaged one remaining in Peru. Graves at the city showed that most of its last inhabitants had been women – perhaps the Chosen Women of the Inca who had escaped the Spanish.

Lake Titicaca

Imagine an enormous inland sea, cradled by mountains, and so high that visitors from the lowlands suffer from breathlessness and palpitations because of the thinness of the air there. That is Titicaca, highest of the world's great lakes, in the Andes of South America.

At 12500 feet (3810 metres) above sea level, Titicaca lies on the Andean *altiplano*, a wide, bleak tableland so silent and empty that one might be on another planet. In the distance, snowy peaks of more than 19685 feet (6000 metres) are clearly outlined in the pure, cold air.

Partly in Bolivia and partly in Peru, the dark blue expanse of Titicaca stretches across this desolate landscape, an upland sea 120 miles (193 kilometres) long and 62 miles (100 kilometres) across at its widest. With an area of 3205 square miles (8300 square kilometres), the lake is South America's second largest after Lake Maracaibo. Seen from above, the outline of Titicaca resembles a lop-sided dumbell, divided by the narrow Tiquina Strait into a smaller, south-eastern part, the Lago Viñaimarca, and a larger section in the north-west, Lago Chucuito.

More than twenty-five rivers fill Titicaca, draining a basin of 22396 square miles (58000 square kilometres). The largest, the Ramis, enters the lake at its north-west corner. But there is only one small outlet, the Desaguadero, at the southern end. The rest of the water loss is through evaporation by sun and wind. Titicaca's average depth is 328 feet (100 metres), but the lake bottom tilts towards the east, reaching a depth of 590 feet (180 metres) in the north-eastern corner. The limpid, slightly brackish waters vary in level by up to five metres annually, rising in the rainy season from December to March and receding in the winter months. For a long time it was thought that Titicaca was slowly drying up, but it is now known that its level fluctuates over a period of years as well as seasonally.

Titicaca contains more than forty islands, some of them densely populated. The largest, the Isla de Titicaca, lies off the Copacabana Peninsula in Peru. Ruins on the lake shore and islands show that Titicaca was occupied by one of South Amer-

ica's first civilizations. At the main site, Tiahuanaco, at the south end of the lake in Bolivia, there are the remains of temples, stelae and stone figures. Later, Titicaca was part of the Inca Empire. On the Isla de Titicaca the ruins of a temple mark the place where Manco Capac and his wife Mama Ocllo, the legendary founders of the Inca dynasty, were sent to earth by the Sun God.

Aymara Indians have lived on the shores of Lake Titicaca since prehistoric times. There are also groups of Quechua-speaking Indians whose ancestors were probably brought to the *altiplano* by Inca conquest. An ancient lake-dwelling people, the Uru, live on floating mats of dried *totora*, a reedy papyrus that grows in marshy shallows. The Uru and other lake-dwellers still make boats by lashing bundles of dried reeds together.

The Indians are famous for the fiestas which are held on feast-days, particularly at Copacabana, and which blend ancient customs with Roman Catholicism. On one level, the fiestas are a colourful tourist spectacle; on another, a temporary release from the harsh existence of the *altiplano*; and on a third, an affirmation of the age-old culture which grew up in the strange isolation of Titicaca, the world's great rooftop lake.

Opposite page: Lake Titicaca, the world's highest large lake, is surrounded by the high peaks of the Andes on the border between Peru and Bolivia.

Below: A boat made by Uru craftsmen from the reeds that grow around Lake Titicaca has the typical high prow and stern created by lashing the huge bundles together.

Crater Lake, Oregon

Among the most spectacular sights in North America is the brilliant blue, ice-cold Crater Lake, 6177 feet (1883 metres) above sea level in the Cascade Mountains of southern Oregon. Filling a great bowl that was once the site of the volcano Mount Mazama, the lake is about 6 miles (9.6 kilometres) long, and 5 miles (8 kilometres) wide, with a total area of 20 square miles (54 square kilometres). Its great depth of 1932 feet (589 metres) – enough to sink the Great Pyramid nearly four times over – makes Crater Lake the second deepest lake on the continent after Canada's Great Slave Lake. Filled by rainwater and melted snows, Crater Lake's hydrological balance is so perfect that its level hardly changes from season to season or from year to year. The cold, pure water never rises above a temperature of 55°F (13°C) even in the warmest summers, and is claimed to be twenty times cleaner than the purest tap water.

According to Indian legend, Crater Lake was created when the gods of the earth's surface tore a mountain from its base and hurled it after Llao, god of the underworld, as they chased him into his secret passage to the underworld. Landing point down, the mountain blocked Llao's escape route for all time, and created the crater which formed the lake. The geological explanation of Crater Lake is no less impressive. The great volcanic peaks of the Cascade Mountains were formed a mere 10000 years ago: Rainier, Shasta, Adams and, further south, Mazama. Several of these peaks had pockets of natural gas beneath them, and some 6000 years ago one of these pockets exploded, with a force equal to several nuclear bombs, tearing the insides from Mount Mazama. The sides of the mountain then collapsed, forming the great caldera, or volcanic bowl, which gradually filled with water to become Crater Lake.

Towering rock walls between 500 and 2000 feet (152 and 610 metres) high now encircle the lake and offer breathtaking panoramas of the lake from many lookout points. Down below, the deep-blue waters are broken only by two small islands: Wizard Island, a symmetrical volcanic cone some

Above and right: A small volcanic cone known as Wizard Island rises from the deep-blue waters of Crater Lake in the Cascade Mountains of Oregon. The immense circular lake fills the cone of a former volcano that exploded and collapsed thousands of years ago. It and the surrounding country are now protected as a national park.

600 feet (183 metres) high on the western side, and Phantom Ship, an appropriately named pile of lava debris that seems to float on the glassy surface like some ghostly vessel.

The first European to see Crater Lake was a gold prospector, John Wesley Hillman, who stumbled on it in 1853 while searching for a lost goldmine. Its discovery was not publicly announced until 1884, and the few people who knew of its existence called it 'Deep Blue Lake'. Then, in 1885, William G. Steel, an emigré from Kansas, saw the lake and was so enchanted that he spent much of the rest of his life on a campaign to preserve Crater Lake and its surroundings from exploitation by prospectors, lumberjacks and settlers. Steel's efforts were rewarded in 1902 when Crater Lake became Oregon's first and only national park.

With an area of 250 square miles (647 square kilometres), Crater Lake National Park is surrounded on almost every side by forests. A 33-mile (fifty-three kilometre) road runs around the rim of the crater, providing superb vistas of the lake and the surrounding mountainsides. Nearly 100 miles (160 kilometres) of trails, mostly starting from the Rim Road, lead down to the lake's shores or up the nearby mountains. Discovery Point Trail leads to the spot where John Hillman first saw the lake in 1853. This and many other trails and natural viewing points give dramatic views of the Cascade Range in the north and of the vast expanse of the lake below. Serene in its cold, blue purity, Crater Lake seems the very archetype of its kind.

The Panama Canal

A passenger in an aeroplane flying over the republic of Panama sees a memorable sight, if there is a break in the tropical clouds: the Atlantic and Pacific oceans at the same time. And beneath, like links in a silver chain across the dark-green isthmus, a series of lakes and lengths of waterway forms the Panama Canal which joins the two oceans.

The cutting of the Panama Canal, just under 51 miles (82 kilometres) long, between 1904 and 1914, was not only one of the greatest engineering feats of history, it was the fulfilment of a dream which had begun when Columbus sailed westward in the prophetic hope of finding a new passage to India.

When it became obvious that Columbus had not discovered India's outlying islands, as he thought, but a new, and solid, continent, the search was on for a way around it. Until the twentieth century and the Panama Canal the best that could be done was the long detour round Cape Horn. It was tantalizingly obvious that the slender Isthmus of Panama, with its break in the mountain backbone of the Americas, would be the ideal route to the Pacific for a canal. In the nineteenth century Simón Bolívar hoped that the states of the Americas would collaborate in a canal-building project. Then Ferdinand de Lesseps, the builder of Suez, hoped to repeat his triumph at Panama, only to preside over one of history's most monumental fiascos – bringing disease and death to thousands of workers, bankruptcy to his backers and a financial scandal which rocked France.

Finally, President Theodore Roosevelt, seeing the immense advantage of a Panama Canal to the United States, encouraged the Panamanians to break away from Colombia and set up an independent republic in 1903 – which (quite by chance) immediately gave the United States the concession to build the canal, with sovereignty over a canal zone cutting the new republic in two.

Built at a cost of just over $336,500,000, the Panama Canal runs south-east across the isthmus from Colón on the Caribbean Sea to the Pacific inlet of the Bay of Panama. Six pairs of locks are needed to carry the water over the changing levels of the canal, which reaches a height of nearly 85 feet (26 metres) above sea level; the canal's width ranges from 100 feet to 300 feet (30.5 metres to 91.4 metres), and its minimum depth is 41 feet (12.5 metres).

Travelling through the canal from the Atlantic to the Pacific, a ship first passes along a seven-mile (11-kilometre) channel to reach the Gatun Locks – three pairs of concrete locks like giant steps, which raise the ship 85 feet (twenty-six metres) above sea level in three stages. (Ships are pulled through the locks by electric locomotives running on tracks alongside.) The ship then enters the 162-square-mile (420-square-kilometre) Gatun Lake, formed

by damming the Chagres River Valley, and steams some 22 miles (35 kilometres) along the lake to enter the 8-mile (13-kilometre) Gaillard Cut. From the Cut the ship passes into the Pedro Miguel Lock, which lowers it 30 feet (9 metres) to the Miraflores Lake. At the other end of the one-mile (2.4-kilometre) lake, the two sets of the Miraflores Locks lower the ship to the level of the Pacific. It then passes through a final 8-mile (13-kilometre) stretch to the end of the canal. On average, the journey takes eight hours. About 12000 ships use the canal each year, or roughly thirty-three every day.

By shortening the sea voyage between New York and San Francisco to less than 5201 miles (8370 kilometres) compared to the 12987 miles (20900 kilometres) via Cape Horn, the Panama Canal transformed the Western world's shipping routes. Its construction, by United States army engineers, was a technical triumph; at the height of the work, in 1913, more than 43000 labourers were employed on the canal. Just as impressive were the precautions taken to eradicate the yellow fever and malaria which had aborted de Lesseps' project.

One peculiarity of the Panama Canal is that, because of the direction of the land, its Pacific exit is a bit more than 27 miles (43.5 kilometres) *east* of its Atlantic entrance; so the traveller passing through the canal sees the sun rising over the Pacific rather than the Atlantic.

The Panama Canal is a tremendous engineering feat that provides a short route for shipping between the Atlantic and Pacific Oceans, avoiding the long voyage south round Cape Horn. Ships using the canal pass through several locks, including the three steps of the Gatum Locks (below).

Monument Valley

All fans of vintage Western movies have the image of Monument Valley imprinted in their mind's eye, for this extraordinary desert region of Utah and Arizona was the backdrop for a series of classic Westerns by the great director John Ford, beginning with *Stagecoach*.

The vast scenic area of Monument Valley stretches for several thousand square kilometres from the San Juan River in south-east Utah into north-east Arizona. From the flat, sandy desert floor rises a landscape which it is hard to believe was created by nature, a landscape of sculptured rock on an epic, monumental scale.

The starkly isolated 'monuments' are a series of red sandstone formations, some rising to 984 feet (300 metres) or more. They are the remnants of sandstone strata deposited during the Permian period. Aeons of subsequent erosion have eaten away these strata to leave only flat desert – except where the sandstone was capped by layers of Triassic rock, more resistant to erosion. The result is that the forces of nature have carved out massive, detached buttes and mesas of a marvellous grandeur, so sharply etched that they might indeed be monuments made by a race of giants. Here and there, as well, huge natural bridges and arches of sandstone have been formed.

Among the most striking examples of Monument Valley's formations are the Two Mittens, neighbouring buttes which by a geological quirk have been eroded into an almost identical form,

resembling a vast pair of mittens sticking out of the desert as though their owner was buried beneath it. Each mitten consists of a truncated pyramidal base, surmounted by a broad, square-topped block – the finger compartment of the mitten – with a narrow thumb of rock sticking up next to it. Many other prominent landmarks are known by colourful names, such as Brigham's Tomb, the Stagecoach and the Totem Pole.

Depending on the time of day and the angle of

Above: Rugs of great beauty and craftsmanship are woven by Navajo Indians who inhabit the vast reservation that encloses Monument Valley.

Right: A familiar backdrop used in many a Western film, the distinctive rock formations of Monument Valley create a landscape of impressive beauty.

the sun, the valley's sandstone formations constantly change colour. The most striking time, though, is when the sun begins to go down and the buttes cast long, sinister shadows over the flat desert. The famous Totem Pole casts a shadow no less than 35 miles (56 kilometres) long.

The remains of early cave dwellings, rock paintings and artifacts show that Monument Valley, despite its inhospitable appearance, was inhabited from early times by tribes of Indians. The petrified remains of ancient animal life have also been found. Today, the valley is part of the vast expanse of territory set aside as a reservation for the Navajo Indians. The Navajo live in traditional earth or log *hogans* and raise sheep, work as silversmiths, weave beautifully patterned rugs or work in the neighbouring towns. Their occupation of Monument Valley dates from the 1860s, when Chief Hoskinini led his people into the area to avoid their deportation to New Mexico.

Amazonia

The Amazon River and its many tributaries, together with the tropical rain forest that surrounds them, are among the earth's greatest natural wonders. The Amazon itself, as South America's longest and, after the Nile, the world's second longest river, is staggering enough. Rising in the Peruvian Andes less than 99 miles (160 kilometres) from the Pacific Ocean, the river flows nearly 3977 miles (6400 kilometres) across the continent, collecting the waters of more than one thousand known tributaries before emptying into the Atlantic Ocean. Here it dilutes the ocean's salinity for over 99 miles (160 kilometres) out to sea. The area drained by the Amazon is greater than that of any other river; it collects about a fifth of all the water that runs off the earth's surface. The volume of water discharged by the Amazon is about 6568492 cubic feet (186000 cubic metres) each second; four times that of the Zaïre River and ten times that of the Mississippi.

Strictly speaking, the river only becomes the Amazon at its confluence with the Rio Negro in central Brazil. From its source to Iquitos in Peru it is the Marañón; from there to Manaus in Brazil, where it joins the Rio Negro, it is the Solimões. Ocean-going steamers can navigate the Amazon for about 2300 miles (3700 kilometres) to Iquitos; its greatest port is Manaus which is 994 miles (1600 kilometres) from the Atlantic.

The Amazonian forest stretches from mangrove swamps near the Atlantic coast of Brazil to the treeline of the Andes in the west. It occupies an area larger than Europe, totalling about 2.7 million square miles (seven million square kilometres). The forest contains an enormous variety of trees, so many that botanists have counted 60 species in just over one square mile (2.5 square kilometres). Beneath the forest ceiling, formed by giants such as silkcotton, para nut and sucupira trees, grow shade-loving trees often festooned with orchids, ferns, bromeliads, creepers, vines and many other plants. Little sunlight penetrates to the forest floor, making it easy to lose oneself. Even the forest Indians do not venture too far into the forest from their riverbank settlements.

Insect, animal and bird life abounds in the Amazonian forest. Over eight thousand species of insects have been collected and classified, and many are still unclassified. Butterflies provide an extraordinary sight as they gather in thousands on humid sands near river banks, or on islets, often covering several square feet. Among the animals are many monkeys (hunted and eaten by the Indians), armadilloes, deer, giant anteaters and boa constrictors. Brilliantly coloured parrots,

toucans, hangnests, ovenbirds, scarlet ibis and the jabiru (great South American marabou stork) are just a small sample of Amazonia's rich bird life.

The Amazon River and its tributaries are no less rich in life. There are about two thousand species of fish, among them many brightly coloured small fish, such as the neon tetra and discus. Some of the best-known larger species are the piracura, giant catfish, stingray and electric eel. The notorious Amazonian piranha is not nearly as deadly as it is reputed to be: it will finish off victims rather than simply attack them. Besides the fishes there are manatees or sea-cows, caimans, turtles and anacondas or giant water snakes. Cooked anaconda, tasting like tender chicken, is a particular Indian delicacy.

Taken together, the vast expanse of the Amazonian forest acts as a huge, green lung, literally enabling the world to breathe. It has been calculated that during photosynthesis the trees of Amazonia release up to half the oxygen in the atmosphere. At the same time, by absorbing

Opposite page: Manaus, near the junction of the Negro and Solimões rivers, is a major city of Brazil's interior forest region.

Below: The Amazon and its tributaries drain an immense area of South America's tropical forests.

carbon dioxide, the Amazonian forests prevent a build-up in the atmosphere which would otherwise have serious effects on the earth's climate.

The trees, plants and animals of Amazonia make up a finely balanced ecological system of great complexity. One surprising aspect of this is that the forest soil is actually thin and infertile: very little humus builds up because dead organic matter is immediately recycled by the forest. It takes very little interference from man to upset Amazonia's ecological balance. The Amerindians who have lived there for millenia are part of this balance, with a simple life-style based on hunting, gathering and a little agriculture. But modern attempts to exploit the resources of Amazonia are having a disastrous effect, both on the forest and on its Indians – fewer than 100000 of whom are thought to survive. The conservation of Amazonia, and its inhabitants, may be one of the most urgent tasks facing mankind.

The Amazon region is a kaleidoscope of colourful sights that include exotic vegetation, such as the beautiful Angel's Wings, or Caladium (right); rivers swollen with flood water that meander sluggishly through the forest (below); Indians and their dwellings (opposite, top); and simple cabins deep in Colombia's jungle (opposite, bottom).

Antarctica

The midnight sun, Antarctica

Antarctica

Antarctica, the world's most remote continent, is a vast sheet of ice and frozen rock covering an area of more than 5405823 square miles (fourteen million square kilometres) – nearly half the size of Africa. Apart from two great bays of the Ross and Weddell seas, and the Antarctic Peninsula, stretching from West Antarctica towards the tip of South America, Antarctica is more or less round in outline. The Transantarctic Range, from 6562 feet to 13123 feet (2000 to nearly 4000 metres) high, divides Antarctica into two unequal parts, the smaller part known as West Antarctica and the larger part, East Antarctica.

The South Pole itself – the still point of the earth's rotation – lies about 994 miles (1600 kilometres) inland. It is not at all like the North Pole, where there are open seas. Surrounded by an immense, flat tableland of ice of vast thickness, the South Pole is very high – some 9843 feet (3000 metres) above sea level. Nothing can grow or survive there; it is the coldest, most desolate place on the face of the earth. For nine months in every year the South Pole is cloaked in continuous night.

Except for its raging blizzards, the South Pole and the interior of Antarctica is a world of complete silence and stillness. But the coast is very different; here, there is movement and life. The landscape has great splendour, with glaciers reaching down from the mountainsides into the sea. On the sea itself, floating pack ice breaks up and drifts away as tremendous icebergs, some more than 328 feet (100 metres) high.

The Antarctic coast shelters vast rookeries of seabirds. There are about seventy-five species, though only three breed exclusively on the continent: the emperor penguin, antarctic petrel and south polar skua. Most of the birds leave the continent each autumn to follow the pack ice as it builds northwards. Only the emperor penguins stay behind through the long winter night, congregating in closely packed colonies of up to 40000 birds. Standing nearly 4 feet (1.2 metres) high, these huge, flightless birds weigh up to 99 pounds (45 kilograms). Each autumn the female lays a single egg, which the male incubates by holding it over his broad, webbed feet, tucked beneath a fold of abdominal skin to keep it warm.

The Antarctic land is almost completely barren of plant life, the only ones being lichens, mosses, liverworts and some microscopic fungi. But the Antarctic seas are almost as rich in life as the land is barren. Plankton abound, and there are about one hundred species of fish, and many sea mammals: seals, porpoises, dolphins and whales. The baleen or whalebone whales, including the nearly extinct blue whale, the world's largest mammal, feed on the enormous concentrations of shrimp-like krill. With their comb-like baleen plates, they can strain meals of a tonne in a few minutes.

For most of its geological history, Antarctica was actually ice-free, and fossil discoveries show that it once had a luxuriant plant and tree life, and reptiles and amphibians similar to those of other southern continents in the Mesozoic Period. Forty to fifty million years ago, in the early Cenozoic Period, the continent began to freeze over, for reasons which are not completely understood. Today, Antarctica is covered by about nine-tenths

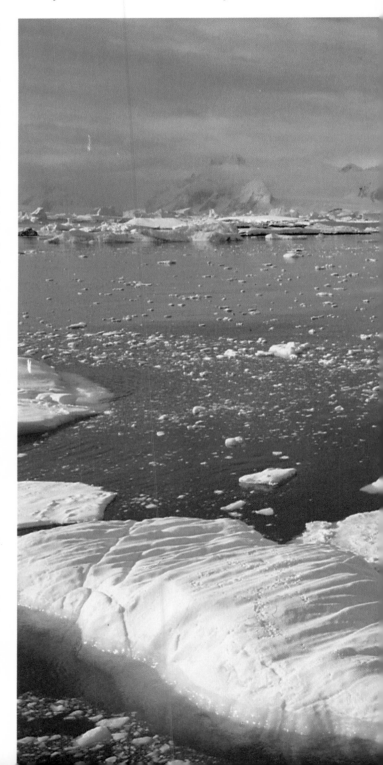

of the world's ice, amounting to roughly seven million cubic miles (29 million cubic kilometres). But in the future, it is quite possible that Antarctica could become ice-free again. If the ice melted, geologists think that it would reveal West Antarctica as an island archipelago the size of Indonesia, and East Antarctica as the size of Australia. The melting ice would raise the sea level by up to 196 feet (60 metres), with world-wide effects on climate and weather patterns (to say nothing of The Netherlands!).

Though its existence was long suspected, Antarctica was the last of the world's continents to be discovered. (On the other hand, it was the first continent to be *literally* discovered, because no people were living there already.) It was possibly approached by Polynesian navigators as early as the seventh century AD. James Cook circumnavigated the Antarctic pack ice in 1772–5, virtually proving there was a southern continent, but he could not penetrate the ice far enough to sight land. The first actual sighting was made in 1820, probably by the Russian expedition led by von Bellingshausen, though there were rival claims in the same year by British and American navigators.

A smooth-topped ice floe provides a relatively comfortable surface for basking seals amid the bleak, inhospitable landscapes of Antarctica.

By the 1900s, Antarctic exploration was in full swing. The South Magnetic Pole was reached in 1909 by British explorers, T. W. E. David and Douglas Mawson, and in December 1911 the Norwegian Roald Amundsen reached the South Pole itself, just ahead of the British team led by Captain Scott. In 1929 Commander Richard Byrd, of the USA, was the first to fly over the South Pole. In International Geophysical Year, 1957–8, twelve nations co-operated in a massive programme of Antarctic research and exploration, setting up many bases and scientific stations. This was followed in 1959 by the Antarctic Treaty to preserve international co-operation in Antarctica.

Many countries have claimed different sections of Antarctica, and as exploration reveals the existence of more mineral wealth, the ideals of the treaty may be threatened by international competition. It is to be hoped that when the treaty is reviewed in 1991, Antarctica will remain a unique example of peaceful international collaboration in research and the most unspoiled place on earth.

Antarctica was once the private domain of such hardy wild creatures as emperor penguins (below). But during the present century human beings have intruded into this remote wilderness to explore and to establish scientific research bases (right). Despite such developments, Antarctica is still an unspoiled region of outstanding natural beauty, nowhere more spectacular than on the Antarctica Peninsula (below right), a long finger of land extending north toward South America.

Asia

A water taxi on a lake in Kashmir

The Taj Mahal

The feelings and responses evoked by the world's great buildings are as diverse as the buildings themselves. The Egyptian pyramids and the Great Wall of China stun the imagination with their sheer scale; one is overawed by the absolute and pitiless power implied in the ability to organize such massive undertakings. A great Gothic cathedral impresses us with the intense faith that motivated its builders. The Parthenon, by contrast, expresses the ancient Greek love of rationality and proportion.

The Taj Mahal, the superb mausoleum built by the seventeenth-century Mogul emperor of India, Shah Jehan, for his queen, Mumtaz Mahal, has something of all these qualities, but over and above them the feeling it conveys is of romance in the purest sense.

India's Mogul rulers, of whom Shah Jehan (reigned 1628–58) was the fifth, had many contradictory characteristics. On the one hand, they were as capriciously cruel and devoted to hunting, war and debauchery as any despots in history. On the other, they were often tolerant and just, devout and great patrons of the arts and learning. Shah Jehan and his father Jahangir shared all these qualities, together with a remarkable devotion to their wives. So it was that when Shah Jehan's queen died in childbirth in 1631, the fourth year of his reign, the heartbroken emperor immediately decreed the building of the Taj Mahal – in response, it is said, to his wife's final wish. The chosen site was on the banks of the sacred Jumna River near Agra, the Mogul capital of northern India.

The Taj Mahal (the name means 'crown of the queen') stands in a large rectangular garden enclosed by a tall wall of red sandstone. At the other end of the garden is the fine gateway, also of sandstone and inlaid with ornaments and Koranic calligraphy in white marble.

The garden, geometrically designed in the style of a Persian formal garden, forms an integral part of the mausoleum complex. (Both here and in many other aspects of the Taj Mahal the influence of Persian art and architecture is strong). Two marble canals meet in the centre of the square garden to divide it into four equal parts; at the centre, midway between the gate and the tomb, is a marble fish tank perfectly positioned to reflect the tomb.

At the far end of the garden vista rises the shimmering white marble structure of the tomb itself. The Taj Mahal, basically a square with the corners cut off, stands on a square red sandstone platform with an elegant minaret at each corner; the platform, in turn, rests on a solid stone terrace. The crowning feature of the building is the magnificent, swelling dome rising from the centre of the building. It is 70 feet (21.3 metres) in diameter and the building overall is 120 feet (36.6 metres) high. At its corners are four smaller domes, and on each side of the building a pointed arch forms a grand entrance to the tomb. The entrance arches are flanked by smaller arches, one placed above the other. The magnificent effect of the building lies in the superb symmetry and proportion of its parts, qualities which, despite the difference of style, the Taj Mahal shares with the finest architecture of ancient Greece or Renaissance Italy.

A uniquely Islamic feature of the building is the calligraphic designs which are inlaid in various colours of marble, and which are said to include every chapter of the Koran. They are not merely decorative but form an integral part of the design of the whole building.

Above: A Mogul painting of about 1630 portrays Shah Jehan, the builder of the Taj Mahal, out riding with his son.

Right: The beautiful Taj Mahal, Shah Jehan's magnificent memorial to his dead wife, Mumtaz Mahal, is one of the world's truly great works of art.

The octagonal main chamber of the Taj Mahal contains the richly decorated marble sarcophagi of Mumtaz Mahal and Shah Jehan. Their bodies, however, are buried in a vault below. (In fact, Shah Jehan did not intend to share his wife's tomb; this decision was made by his son Aurangzeb, to avoid the colossal expense of building another tomb to rival the Taj Mahal.) The false coffins are decorated with floral mosaics, including thirty-five kinds of precious stone, and calligraphic inscriptions glorifying the queen, the emperor and Allah. Surrounding the coffins is an alabaster screen, carved in lace-like filigree, with an octagonal shape echoing that of the main chamber. Four smaller rooms, also octagonal, surround the main chamber. Goethe's celebrated dictum that architecture is frozen music is especially relevant to the chambers of the Taj Mahal, which are renowned for their beautiful acoustics.

On either side of the Taj Mahal is a red sandstone building, the one to the west being a three-domed mosque. Its twin on the other side of the Taj Mahal is known as the *ja-wab* ('answer'). Facing away from Mecca, it was never used for prayer and probably its only purpose was architectural: to balance the mosque.

The architect of the Taj Mahal is unknown but the names of the master craftsmen who carried out various expert tasks were recorded. They came from many parts of Asia, and especially Persia, to make up a team of thirty-seven, including dome builders, mosaicists, calligraphers, sculptors, masons and engineers. In addition, there was a labour force of about 20000. The whole complex probably took about twenty-two years to complete. Together with the architect's work, the most important task was that of the master calligrapher, Amanat Khan of Shiraz. His is the only signature to appear in the Taj Mahal; on the base of the inside of the dome it reads 'written by the insignificant being, Amanat Khan Shirazi'.

The interior of the Taj Mahal is richly decorated with beautiful relief carvings and inlaid stone of the most exquisite craftsmanship.

Everest

Chomo Iungma in Tibetan, *Sagarmatha* in Nepalese, Everest in English, are the names given to the world's highest peak at 29028 feet (8848 metres), straddling the border between Nepal and Tibet. Translated, Everest's Tibetan and Nepalese names mean Goddess of the Wind – a suitably poetic description for the mightiest of mountains. One might suppose its English name to have been inspired by a similarly poetic impulse, but the truth is more prosaic: the mountain was named after Sir George Everest, Surveyor General of India from 1830–43.

In the geological time scale, the formation of Everest and the other colossal peaks of the 1500-mile (2400-kilometre) Himalayan Range is relatively recent. Geologists now believe that the Himalayas were thrown up about fifty million years ago by the collision of two of the vast plates which form the earth's crust. The more southerly of these tectonic plates, carrying India, Australia and the Indian Ocean, crunched its way into the Eurasian plate which carried Europe, Central Asia and China. The ensuing impact thrust part of the Tibetan Plateau high into the air and the Himalayas were born. Over millions of years, the forces of wind, snow and ice sharpened and shaped the peaks and ridges of the Himalayas to their present outline.

Above the 21000-foot (6400-metre) contour line the snow which is driven on to the Himalayas never melts except close to the mountain ridges which are warmed by the sun. Between the ridges the snow is compacted into ice, which fractures and grinds its way down the mountain sides to form glaciers in the cwms or valleys enclosed by the mountains. These glaciers are the eventual source of the mighty rivers of the Indian subcontinent, great rivers like the Indus, Brahmaputra and Sutlej.

The brooding summit of Mount Everest towers above nearby peaks in the mighty Himalayas, the roof of the world.

The trinity of peaks formed by Everest and its massive companions Lhotse at 27870 feet (8495 metres) and Nuptse at 25899 feet (7894 metres) cradle the Western Cwm, into which a constant supply of young ice is forced. From the cwm, a 1969-foot (600-metre) icefall descends to the bend leading to the Khumbu Glacier. At the foot of the Ice Fall is the site of the base camps which are the starting points for the decades of mountaineering expeditions which have responded to the lure of Everest.

Although Everest had been recognized as the world's highest mountain in 1852, Tibet and Nepal were firmly closed to visitors, and it was not until 1920 that the Tibetan government agreed to allow a British expedition to travel to Everest. Between 1921 and 1938 there were seven major British attempts to reach the summit. The most famous of these took place in 1924, when George Mallory and Andrew Irvine disappeared while climbing the North Ridge. Their bodies have never been found, and it will never be known for certain if Mallory and Irvine succeeded in reaching the summit.

After World War II many countries joined in the race. The Chinese invasion of Tibet in 1950–1 closed the former northern approach to the mountain, but Nepal was persuaded to admit Western mountaineers. Now, it seemed that the southern side of Everest offered better chances of success. Though this meant passing the treacherous Ice Fall

to reach the Western Cwm, and then climbing the steep Lhotse Face to reach the South Col, the southern route would give more protection from gales and the final climb to the summit from the South Col would be less steep.

In 1952, Swiss climbers made two strong attempts at reaching the summit from the southern route. But the final victory went to the British expedition of 1953, when on 29 May the New Zealand climber Edmund Hillary and Tenzing Norgay, his Sherpa guide, became the first men to stand on top of the world's highest mountain.

Since then Everest has been scaled by mountaineers from many countries, including the United States of America, China, India, Japan, Italy and South Korea as well as Britain, either repeating the South Col route or trying more difficult ones, such as the South-west Face. Though there are more demanding peaks in the Himalayas, the Goddess of the Wind remains an irresistible challenge.

The vertical rock faces and treacherous ice fields on the upper slopes of Mount Everest (below) are a formidable challenge even to experienced climbers. The first successful ascent was made by Edmund Hillary and Tenzing Norgay during the British expedition of 1953 (opposite page, top). The climb involves negotiating many hazards, including the unpredictable Ice Fall (opposite page, bottom).

The Great Wall of China

The conflict between nomadic raiders and settled communities is a recurring theme in human development. But nowhere has it been symbolized as dramatically and permanently, or on such an epic scale, as by the Great Wall of China, which snakes its way across hills and mountains of northern China as far as central Asia. The building of walled frontiers between Chinese kingdoms dates from at least the fourth century BC, in the 'Warring States' period, and was a development of the idea of the walled city.

In the third century BC the powerful emperor Shih Huang Ti unified China. To protect his empire from the Hsiungnu (Huns) to the north, he ordered the existing walls on the northern frontier to be linked to create the Great Wall. Contemporary texts state that 300000 men laboured for ten years on this gigantic task, which took up nearly all the revenues of the empire. The Wall was built in earth and stone; the eastern sections faced in brick.

After the Han dynasty, a series of short-lived dynasties exhausted themselves in internal power struggles and no rulers kept the Wall in a state of repair. In 1234 the Chin dynasty was overthrown when Genghis Khan led his troops over the Wall and established the Mongol dynasty. In 1368 the Ming dynasty finally drove the Mongols back out of China. The Ming rulers transferred their capital from Nanking to Peking to strengthen the northern frontier, and in 1420 the Emperor Yung Lo ordered the reconstruction of the Great Wall.

The average height of the rebuilt Wall was from 22 feet to nearly 26 feet (6.7 metres to 8 metres). At the base it was 21 feet (6.4 metres) thick, tapering to 18 feet (5.5 metres) wide at the top. The Wall was built of stone with a core of earth and rubble; the top was faced with three to four layers of carefully pointed brickwork, with a crenellated battlement on the north side. Every 590 feet (180 metres) there was a square watch tower with observation terraces, and arched gateways were built through the Wall at intervals. At important passes, especialy north of Peking, the Wall formed two-fold and three-fold branches across the caravan road to form defence areas.

With all its ramifications the Wall is about 2486

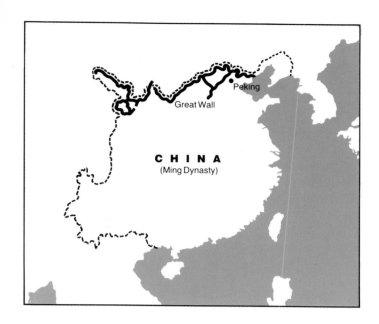

miles (4000 kilometres) long, and contains 47277956 cubic feet (1338750 cubic metres) of earth and another 15759318 cubic feet (446250 cubic metres) of stone and brick. Altogether the Wall is the greatest building enterprise ever undertaken, and is thought to be the only man-made structure which could be seen from Mars.

The Great Wall was mainly defensive but it had other uses, particularly as a way of communication through mountain ranges where movement was otherwise difficult. Virtually a raised roadway, its width on top is enough to take five or six horses abreast.

Basically the Great Wall of China is a stupendous piece of military engineering, with no artistic embellishment. Nevertheless, the way in which it has been fitted into the landscape follows the Chinese belief that every man-made structure must obey the laws of the place where it is built. This meant that the Wall had to follow the crests of the hills in order to form a crest to the 'dragon' of the landscape contour. Apart from its sheer size and length, it is this striking marriage between the Wall and its surroundings which has caught the imagination of the world and ranks it as a work of art.

The Great Wall of China (below left) snakes over the hills of northern China, a stupendous monument to the engineering skills of the builders who began the work more than two thousand years ago. Spaced at regular intervals along this impressive defensive fortification are huge square watch towers (below).

Bali

The small Indonesian island of Bali, just over a narrow strait from the eastern tip of Java, is perhaps a closer approximation to an earthly paradise than any other place in the world. The paradisiacal qualities are both natural and human: Bali's fertile volcanic soil and brilliant green jungle provide the sustenance and setting for one of the world's most richly elaborate traditional cultures, long famous for its art, music and dance.

With an area of 2173 square miles (5628 square kilometres) and a population of about two and a half million, Bali is unique in Indonesia for having preserved its Hindu religion. Brought direct by Indian colonists about two thousand years ago, Hinduism in Bali stood its ground against Islam, which swept through the rest of Indonesia in the sixteenth century. Balinese Hinduism is, however, influenced by Buddhism and also by early Malay ancestor cults.

The art, music and dance of Bali are bound up so closely with religion and everyday life that the Balinese have no separate words for art (or the arts) and artist in the Western sense. Bali is sometimes called the 'island of a thousand temples', but ten thousand is probably closer to the real number. The volcano Mount Agung is, at 10308 feet (3142 metres), the highest point in mountainous Bali; to the Balinese it is the 'navel of the world', and it is the site of the island's most sacred temple, the *Pura Besakhi*. The temple is divided into three sections, each dedicated to one of the main Hindu deities, Vishnu, Siva and Brahma.

At the temples the Balinese celebrate a stream of religious festivals with great feasts, dances and prayer. The high points of the year include the ceremony to drive out evil spirits, prayer days for

Bali probably has the highest proportion of places of worship per head of the population of any country. They range from the great 'mother temples' to domestic 'backyard' shrines. Below: The Menqwi Temple, Taman Ajan.

ancestors, thanksgiving to the goddess of rice and the birthdays of all the important gods.

Each Balinese village is a self-contained community, worshipping a common ancestor and usually divided into co-operative societies which carry out various communal functions such as maintaining temples and organizing festivals and rites. Every village has one or more gamelans – the world-famous percussion orchestras which provide the complex music that accompanies the temple ceremonies, dance dramas and shadow plays of Bali.

Balinese dance is no less intricate and beautiful. One of the most popular dances, the *Legong*, is performed by three girls in bright, jewelled costumes, and features rapid eye and body move-

ments; it often tells the story of a cruel king who woos an unwilling princess.

The Balinese are also famous for their artistic ability as painters, in carving wood, stone, ivory and other materials, and for delicate ornaments in gold, silver and copper.

Despite its sophistication, Balinese culture has a quality of primal innocence which has led the island to be described as 'the morning of the world'. Today, despite the impact of tourism, Bali retains much of the magical charm for which it has long been fabled.

Traditional ceremonial dances are a special feature of Balinese life and a great attraction for the many tourists who flock to this beautiful island.

114

The Temple-palace of Angkor Wat

The main cultural influences on South-East Asia have come from India, in the form of Hinduism and Buddhism. Along with these two religions came two basic types of religious building: the Hindu shrine designed to house the statue of a god, and the solid shrine or stupa of Buddhism. Both types tended to become the centres of temple complexes including monasteries, rest-houses and further shrines.

The Hindu temple, especially in South-East Asia, was seen as a microcosm of Semeru, the mountain at the world's axis. If built as a tower, the central shrine could symbolize the world's axis as well as housing a god. Gradually the tradition developed of a five-fold arrangement of towers consisting of the shrine in the middle of a platform and four more towers on the corners of the platform.

This tradition reached its peak in the great temple of Angkor Wat in Cambodia, probably the world's largest religious structure. The temple is in the Siemreap region, the site of the capitals of the old Khmer Empire, and its building was begun by the Khmer king Suryavarman (reigned AD 1113–50).

The walled complex of Angkor Wat is surrounded by moats, 625 feet (190.5 metres) wide, representing the outer ocean of Hindu mythology.

An immense symmetrical complex of ornamented buildings, enclosures and gateways forms the beautiful temple-palace of Angkor Wat, Cambodia.

The walls, forming a rectangle of 4275 by 4905 feet (1303 by 1495 metres), represent the world's peripheral mountains. From the west side a wide, balustraded causeway crosses the moat and leads to the temple's first inner enclosure, which has entrances in three sides. The main entrance is a ceremonial gateway or *gopura*, with three pavilions crowned by towers. Through this gateway, a ceremonial way leads to a second inner enclosure, forming the temple proper and provided with a covered gallery. Within this enclosure is a third enclosure, also with a gallery, which rises by two terraces to the fircone-shaped central tower which is Angkor Wat's innermost shrine. The tower contained a god statue which has disappeared; it was almost certainly of King Suryavarman as the god Vishnu. Each corner of the central terrace carries a similar but smaller tower.

Besides its impressive layout and architecture Angkor Wat is famous for its ornamental sculpture, ranging from decorative scrollwork adorning the pillars to superb narrative bas-reliefs of Hindu mythology which fill the galleries. All this ornamentation is skilfully integrated with the building

so that the sculptors' virtuosity is shown to full advantage without dominating its surroundings, resulting in an aesthetic balance which distinguishes Angkor Wat from many other great Khmer buildings.

Perhaps the best way to regard Angkor Wat, in Western terms, would be as a combination of Orléans cathedral and the Palace of Versailles, since it was not only a temple but also the royal residence. The temple-palace housed an image, the *deva-raja* (literally, god-king), which was believed to contain the essence of kingship and with which the king became identified after his death. During his reign, however, the form of the temple-palace, as a microcosm of the world, made the king a true world ruler or *chakravartin*.

Among the special features of Angkor Wat's design are its magnificent profile, dominated by its elaborate towers (below); its central enclosures and ceremonial gateways (opposite page, top); and its finely carved relief sculptures portraying themes from Hindu mythology (opposite page, bottom).

The Dead Sea

Despite its name, the Dead Sea is a landlocked lake, the end of the line for the River Jordan, with no outlet for its waters except by evaporation. Forming part of the border between Israel and Jordan, this saltiest of lakes is about 50 miles (80 kilometres) long and ten miles (16 kilometres) wide; it covers an area of 405 square miles (1049 square kilometres). With its surface 1299 feet (396 metres) below the level of the Mediterranean, and its greatest depth 1296 feet (395 metres) below that, the Dead Sea is the lowest body of water on earth – so low that visitors' ears pop as they descend to its shores from Jerusalem.

Right: The Qumran Caves, near the Dead Sea, hid the biblical manuscripts now known as the Dead Sea Scrolls until their discovery by a shepherd in 1947.

Below: The intense heat of the sun creates a haze of moisture in the still air as it evaporates huge quantities of water from the surface of the Dead Sea.

In the Middle Ages, travellers reported that no birds flew over the Dead Sea because the air was poisonous. In fact the Dead Sea climate is healthy and bracing, especially in winter. There are no birds about simply because there is nothing for them to eat: no fish (those that are carried into the lake by the Jordan die immediately), and very little plant life. The lake is much too salty. Nearly a quarter of its volume consists of dissolved solids, mostly common salt, but also chlorides of magnesium, potassium and calcium, and magnesium bromide.

This chemical saturation accounts for the well-known fact that the Dead Sea is the ideal place to learn to swim – its density is so great that it is impossible to sink.

It seems surprising that the Dead Sea should be nine times as salty as the ocean when the Jordan and several smaller streams pour over four million tons (four million tonnes) of fresh water into it every day. But this fresh water simply has no chance to dilute the Dead Sea, or even mix with it very much, before it is sucked up by the intense heat of the sun, which can rise above 125°F (52°C).

The lake shores are covered with lava, sulphur and rock salt, reminding us that the Dead Sea is in a zone of volcanic activity. In fact, the 350-mile (563-kilometre) trench occupied by the Jordan and the Dead Sea is the northern extension of the Great Rift Valley stretching through East Africa. Like the Dead Sea, most of the lakes along the Rift are thick with chemicals which have bubbled up along this line of weakness in the earth's crust.

To the east of the Dead Sea, the white limestone walls of the Plain of Moab rise to 4396 feet (1340 metres), while on the west the Plateau of Judea rises to 2986 feet (910 metres). To the Arabs the Dead Sea is *Bahr Lut*, the Sea of Lot, and on the lake's south-western corner stands the pillar of salt – actually a low mountain – into which Lot's wife was supposed to have been turned. The sites of biblican Sodom and Gomorrah are thought to be submerged in the southern part of the Dead Sea, possibly as the result of an earthquake or volcanic eruption. On the south-western shore is Masada, where the Jews made their last stand against the Romans in AD 72. Few places as barren as the Dead Sea can be richer in historical association than this dramatic mountain-top site.

It was near the north-west shore of the Dead Sea, in a cave in the Qumran Valley, that a Bedouin shepherd boy discovered the first group of Dead Sea Scrolls in 1947. These, the earliest known manuscripts of the Bible, are thought to have been part of a library belonging to the Essenes, a Jewish sect who may have lived near the Dead Sea from about 100 BC to AD 70.

Hong Kong

The British colony of Hong Kong, a handkerchief-sized territory precariously poised on the southern edge of the Chinese mainland, is one of the world's most unlikely places. About four and a half million people live there, nearly all of them Chinese, jammed into an area of just over 386 square miles (1000 square kilometres). If Hong Kong were part of China, it would be the third largest Chinese city, and easily the richest.

Hong Kong is located on the coast of China's Kwantung province (China's 'southern gateway') at the mouth of the Hsi Chiang River. It consists of two parts: Hong Kong proper, including Hong Kong Island, Stonecutters Island and the mainland peninsula of Kowloon; and the New Territories, comprising some mainland and more than 230 tiny surrounding islands.

Most of Hong Kong is steep and hilly and there is little farmland. The highest peak is Tai Mo Shan at 3140 feet (957 metres) on the mainland. Hong Kong's longest river, the Sham Chun, forms the border with China. The most heavily urbanized parts of Hong Kong are Victoria, the capital, on Hong Kong Island, and the Kowloon peninsula opposite. Overlooking one of the world's most superb natural harbours, Victoria is a crowded, bustling city of skyscrapers.

Hong Kong's purpose has always been simple – to make money: first, as a great entrepôt for trade between China and the West, and, more recently, as a major centre of industry as well. Its port handles more than 7000 ships a year and Hong Kong is a great producer of textiles, toys, plastics and electronics. It is also one of Asia's main centres of banking and finance.

Since World War II Hong Kong's population has tripled, so that today it is one of the world's most densely populated regions, with an average 11700 people to every square mile (2.6 square kilometres). There is a chronic housing crisis, and Hong Kong has a large floating population of permanent boat dwellers. This great population increase made it harder for Hong Kong to survive only on trade, as before, and it has been one of the main reasons for the development of Hong Kong's industry.

The founding of Hong Kong in 1842 was a piece of classic British colonialism. Although the Manchu government in China had made opium trading illegal, the East India Company had joined in the profitable business of importing opium into Canton in 1834. In 1839, the Chinese surrounded all the foreign warehouses in Canton and refused to allow anyone to leave until the European traders had surrendered all their opium stocks and signed agreements to stop its import. After a six-week siege the British surrendered more than 20,000 chests of opium. Then, however, the British government sent an expeditionary force to compel China to accept a commercial treaty and to cede an island to Britain so that it could carry on its trade without interruptions. This, the First Opium War, ended with the Treaty of Nanking in 1842, by which Britain gained Hong Kong Island. Kowloon was added in 1860, and in 1898 Britain obtained a ninety-nine year lease on the New Territories.

Hong Kong today is a vigorous remnant of nineteenth century imperialism, but it will revert to China in 1997. Meanwhile Hong Kong continues as before because it serves a balance of interests. For China also it is economically useful in providing a point of contact with the West; for the West, Hong Kong is a window on China.

The prosperity of Hong Kong (below), place of 'sweet waters', was originally based on shipping. It has one of the finest natural harbours in the world. There is chronic overcrowding in Kowloon and many parts of Victoria. This has led to numerous land reclamation schemes and the development of towns in the New Territories. Many families still prefer to live in 'sampans' like these seen (right) at North Point.
Left: A crowded street on Hong Kong Island.

The Shwe Dagon

It was in 1755 that the city of Dagon became the capital of Burma, in south-eastern Asia, and changed its name to Rangoon. Burma is perhaps the most devoutly Buddhist of all countries, and the entire way of life of the Burmese has been deeply imbued with the piety of Buddha's teachings. This can be seen in the veneration accorded to the Shwe Dagon, the remarkable Buddhist stupa which dominates Rangoon, and commemorates the capital's former name.

It its history of more than 1000 years, the Shwe Dagon has been repeatedly enlarged and reno-vated. Its most recent rebuilding took place between 1768 and 1773 and was undertaken not simply to honour Buddha but also to create a monument which would be worthy of the new capital and command the attention of the whole of Burma.

To achieve these aims, a huge mound was raised, 299 feet by 226 feet (91 by 69 metres) at the base and 164 feet (50 metres) high, and on this was erected a great brick-cased stupa soaring to a height of 351 feet (107 metres). The entire surface of the stupa and mound was then covered with exceptionally hard plaster which was polished to a glassy smoothness and finally coated with layer after layer of gold leaf. Around the base of the

Shwe Dagon cluster a medley of little shrines and chapels, each topped with its own miniature gilded stupa.

At the top of the main, bell-shaped stupa is a reliquary decorated with lotus blossom wreaths, surmounted by a richly carved baldachin with ornamental umbrellas encrusted with rubies and diamonds. The stupa is traditionally believed to contain relics of the Gautama Buddha and three Buddhas who were born in ages before him.

Whereas the great stupa-temple of Borobudur, in Indonesia, is a completely Javanese realization of Buddhist concepts, the Shwe Dagon borrows both its design and concept from India and Sri Lanka. The reliquary and umbrellas of the Shwe Dagon conform to the design of those of the Buddhist stupas at Sanchi in India, while the idea of the bell-shaped stupa originated in Sri Lanka. On the one hand, the Shwe Dagon recognizes the idea of the stupa as Buddha's tomb; on the other, it incorporates the old idea, expressed also by Angkor Wat in Cambodia and Borobudur, of the world mountain Meru, the central belief in Indian cosmology.

Burma's greatest religious shrine is a vision of shimmering gold towers, domes and steeples, dominated by the massive gilded pile of the Shwe Dagon, which can be seen from anywhere in the capital. The modern name Rangoon means 'the end of conflict'.

Ellura and Ajanta

If you want to make an edifice out of stone, there are two ways of going about it. The most usual way is to quarry the stone and cut it into masonry blocks, which are then assembled at the desired site. The other way, which is really an extension of sculpture, is to carve an edifice out of rock *in situ*, as at the ancient city of Petra in Jordan. Apart from Petra, probably the world's most famous examples of this approach are to be found at Ellura and Ajanta in Maharashtra state, western India.

At Ellura, the most outstanding monument is the huge Kailasa Temple, hewn from a solid rock outcrop in the eighth century AD. This vast undertaking was intended to symbolize and to picture the mountain home of the Hindu god Siva. The method of construction was to cut three trenches into the cliff face and carve the temple from the block of stone remaining. The disadvantage of this approach could have been that it left the temple

The Kailasa Temple (below) is not really a building but a piece of sculpture, perhaps the single most impressive work of art in India. It is an example of a very rare phenomenon – a freestanding building that was started at the top!

Opposite: Some of the rock caves of Ellura.

at the bottom of a deep pit. This was overcome by placing the temple on a very high base, with a deeply carved frieze of elephants and lions appearing to hold the temple on their backs. The rest of the temple is carved with monumental reliefs of Hindu myth and legend.

Near the Kailasa Temple are the fascinating rock caves of Ellura, whose carvings again typify the Indian passion for sculpture. The oldest of the caves, dating from the fourth and fifth centuries AD, were built by the Buddhists as monasteries and prayer halls. Later, the Hindus created very similar cave sites. Finally, in the ninth or tenth centuries the Jains added the last few structures, so that the Ellura caves represent a virtual symposium of Indian religion.

The walls, pillars and particularly the entrances of all the caves provide an excuse for lavish sculpture, and every available space is covered with richly detailed ornamentation.

The Ajanta Caves are Buddhist sanctuaries and monasteries hollowed out of granite cliffs on the side of a 72-foot (22-metre) high ravine in the Wagurna River valley. There are about thirty caves, which were excavated between the first century BC and seventh century AD. Like the Ellura Caves, the Ajanta Caves are noteworthy for their fine sculpture, but their chief glory is the fresco-style paintings which adorn their walls and ceilings.

The most famous paintings at Ajanta are in Cave I, dating from the fifth to early seventh century. The cave is a square hall with its roof supported by rows of pillars. At the back of the sanctuary a deep niche contains a rock-cut image of a seated Buddha, flanked by two colossal painted figures of Bodhisattvas (beings who, though capable of reaching Buddhahood, renounce this goal in favour of ministering to humanity). The left-hand Bodhisattva is one of the most beautiful paintings in Buddhist art.

On the ceiling the paintings are in a flatter, more decorative style. The space is divided into panels filled with figures and ornamental motifs. One composition, repeated four times with slight variations, shows a bearded man attended by musicians and cup-bearers, probably representing Kuvera, the god of riches.

The technique of the Ajanta paintings was similar to fresco. The rough wall surface was covered with a layer of clay mixed with chopped straw or animal hair. This was smoothed and levelled and covered with a layer of gesso (fine white clay or gypsum), on which the painting was done. Finally the paintings were burnished to give a lustrous finish.

The Ajanta caves (below) lie in the horseshoe bend of a river, a wild and desolate spot which offered refuge as well as peace. To enable the painters to see what they were doing in the dark caves, metal mirrors were set up outside to reflect sunlight.

Opposite: The interior of one of the caves.

The Vale of Kashmir

If there is a perfect mountain valley in the world, it is almost certainly the magical Vale of Kashmir, in the southern centre of the Himalayan state of Jammu and Kashmir. Hidden between the snow-ranges of the main Himalayas to the north-east and the Pir Panjals to the south-west, the valley is an ancient lake basin 87 miles (140 kilometres) long, 20 miles (32 kilometres) wide and 5315 feet (1620 metres) above sea level. Well-watered and fertile, it is drained by the great Jhelum River and ornamented by a string of lakes. Woodlands and groves of Indian cedar, plane, walnut, willow and poplar abound. Higher on the valley sides are evergreen forests of fir, pine and spruce, followed by birch, and, above 11800 feet (3600 metres), alpine meadows of rhododendrons, dwarf willows and honeysuckle.

Since partition in 1947, the possession of Jammu and Kashmir has been bitterly disputed between India and Pakistan, and today an uneasy line of demarcation places the vale under Indian rule. But for more than four hundred years, the Vale of Kashmir has held visitors spellbound as a mountain refuge of ultimate peacefulness. The Mogul emperors, who conquered it in the sixteenth century, found it the perfect escape from the heat of their North Indian dominions. When the vale

eventually came under the suzerainty of the British, the new rulers were equally enchanted, and its fame inspired Thomas Moore's long, romantic poem, *Lallah Rook*.

Srinagar, the fifteenth-century capital of the vale, and now the summer capital of Indian Kashmir, stands between four lakes; it is intersected by the Jhelum River and criss-crossed by ancient canals, almost like an Asiatic Venice. Around Dal Lake are the great Mogul pleasure gardens of Shalimar, Nishat, Cashma Shahi and Nazim Bagh – superbly blending the formal and the natural, with rose-covered terraces, fountains, waterside pavilions and tall, spreading trees.

Downstream from its Westernized sector, Old Srinagar, with its dwellings of blackened cedar wood, mosques, bazaars and narrow, labyrinthine alleys, has all the classic ingredients of the orient. To a great extent, though, life is lived on the water, in barges, punts, canoes, skiffs, motorboat taxis and, above all, houseboats. The traditional Kashmiri houseboat is a thatched affair like an ark,

The idyllic situation of the Vale of Kashmir (far left) is partly the result of geographical accident. Most of the 'happy valley' is sheltered from the monsoon by the high Pir Panjal, while the 'dry' season is comparatively damp. Below: 'Shikaras' (water taxis) cross Dal Lake at sunset beneath the fort on Hari Parbat hill built by the Emperor Akbar.

bristling with cooking pots, chicken coops and washing lines. The British (who were not permitted to own land in Kashmir) evolved another standard type of houseboat, almost a water villa, with its own cookboat tied astern, many of which are still to be seen moored along the banks and canals of Srinagar.

The countryside of the vale is dotted with villages with tall, thatched farms, grain stores, wood piles and flocks of chickens, geese and ducks and by the graceful ruins of ancient Hindu temples. During the early summer, the purple crocus-like flowers of the saffron crop bloom in great swathes across the valley. From the moun-

tainsides descend lively, trout-filled streams, fed by the snows above.

But it is from its high rim that the otherworldly character of the Vale of Kashmir is best appreciated. Here, it literally seems to float among the clouds, as a disembodied mountain Eden.

Srinagar, summer capital of the state of Kashmir, stands on the banks of the Jhelum River. The buildings are a quaint mixture (no two are alike), and with its numerous gardens and waterways and its backdrop of mountains, Srinagar is one of the world's most picturesque cities. Below: The gardens of the Nishat Bagh run down in terraces to Dal Lake. Opposite page, top: Boats used for transport. Bottom: Srinagar houseboats.

Borobudur

The great Buddhist temple-mountain of Borobudur in central Java, Indonesia, is one of the most impressive monuments created by mankind. Both a temple and a complete exposition of Buddhist belief, it was designed as a whole, and completed as designed, with only one major change. Built in about AD 800, Borobudur seems to have fallen into neglect by about 1000 and became overgrown. Early in the twentieth century it was carefully excavated and restored by the Dutch colonial government.

The building appears as a huge square plinth on which stand five gradually diminishing terraces – like a ziggurat in principle, but with a more complex outline because the corners of each terrace are doubly recessed. On the fifth terrace stand three circular diminishing terraces, crowned by a large circular stupa (solid shrine). A long staircase runs up the centre of each side to the highest terrace through lavishly carved archways, none of which takes precedence as a main entrance.

Each of Borobudur's square terraces is enclosed by a high wall which prevents visitors on one terrace from seeing into any of the other levels. The exterior façades of each wall are carved with garlands and other motifs, and contain ornamental niches which enshrine life-size Buddha figures. Each side of the monument has a total of 108 Buddhas – a number of great importance in Indian numerology. The Buddhas on each side are distinguished by a different hand position, and each group represents one of the so-called dhyani-Buddhas which are associated with the four cardinal points of east, south, west and north.

The top three circular terraces are unwalled. They support seventy-two smaller stupas built with half-open walls. Inside each of these is a large stone Buddha.

Only the bottom plinth seems to have been added as an afterthought to the original design. It consists of a mass of stone masonry pressed up against the original lowest storey, and actually obscures an entire set of reliefs (some of which have been uncovered today). Probably the plinth was added to buttress the bottom storey and to prevent the whole structure from shifting under its massive weight.

The whole of Borobudur symbolizes a Buddhist transition from the lowest levels of reality at the base to the final enlightenment at the summit. Also, since the monument is a unity, it proclaims the unity of creation and does not banish the world of ordinary life. The message is that the difference between ordinary life and enlightenment is in the individual mind. The forms of the Buddha figures at different levels symbolize the stages leading to enlightenment: at the lower levels they appear as human, at the higher levels as transcendent.

A pilgrim usually pays reverence to a Buddhist stupa by walking round it, keeping the monument to his right. The terraces of Borobudur have on their walls a great series of narrative relief sculp-

tures, which the visitors read from right to left as they walked around each terrace. There are nearly 1500 of these reliefs, which if placed end to end would stretch nearly 5 miles (eight kilometres).

The reliefs on the original lowest level, which were hidden by the added plinth, show the workings of good and bad deeds, especially bad ones, in successive reincarnations: for example, how people who kill and cook living creatures are themselves cooked in hell, and how inferior people waste their time. The reliefs on the first terrace show the life of Buddha up to his first sermon at Banares, and stories of his earlier incarnations. On the terraces above, the self-discovery and education of the Bodhisattva are illustrated. The second gallery shows some specially noteworthy scenes of paradise – which came relatively low in the Buddhist scheme – in which superbly jewelled figures sit beneath ornate pavilions among trees with gem-like strings of fruit. Even without their religious significance, the art of the carved reliefs, with their wonderfully naturalistic and expressive treatment, would ensure Borobudur a high place among the world's great buildings. They are a rich source of information on many aspects of medieval Javanese life, from styles of houses to dress, weapons and jewellery, and the plants and animals, especially monkeys and elephants, the Javanese countryside are beautifully portrayed.

As a beautiful monumental expression of Buddhism, Borobudur is unrivalled. Unlike Angkor Wat, for which it may have been a prototype, Borobudur does not seem to have been the centre of a royal cult, but a monument for the whole people, a permanent reminder of their religious beliefs.

In January 1985 terrorists exploded nine bombs in the temple of Borobudur. Damage was limited and repairs put in hand. One of the world's greatest architectural masterpieces survived.

Borobudur is the largest Javanese monument devoted to Mahayana ('Great Vehicle') Buddhism, the liberal form of Buddhism founded about the 1st century BC. It is essentially a great stupa, situated on a stone-dressed, terraced and galleried mound. It seems to have been soon abandoned: the Buddha image in the main stupa was never finished.

Mount Fuji

Great volcanic peaks have always had a special fascination for mankind; on one hand, for their awesome destructiveness when they erupt, and on the other, because they are undeniably among the most elegant of natural creations. This beauty is somewhat paradoxical. A volcanic eruption, like a tidal wave, tornado or avalanche, is nature at its most irrational and violent. Yet the end result, the towering cone of ash and debris which forms around the crater, can have a placid symmetry which inspires quite different emotions. To contemplate the peaceful majesty of an extinct volcano is a uniquely calming experience.

From this point of view, Japan's Mount Fuji is surely the world's most beautiful volcanic peak. Rising to 12388 feet (3776 metres), Fuji is high enough to dominate its mountainous surroundings in central Honshu for great distances in every direction. But it is not so much by its sheer height as by its proportions that Fuji impresses. At its base, the mountain is about three times as wide as it is high, so that its concave sides rise gently rather than precipitately from the landscape below. For eight to nine months every year, Fuji's purity of outline is enhanced by a cap of snow.

At the foot of Fuji is Lake Hakone, or the Lake of the Reeds, in which the peak is reflected upside down, forming the famous 'double Fuji'. The surrounding countryside gives many unexpected views of Fuji, rather like a tall landmark in a city which pops unexpectedly into view as you turn a corner. The counterpoint between Fuji and its surroundings was beautifully captured by the Japanese artist Hokusai (1760–1849) in his famous series of colour prints, 'Thirty-six views of Mount Fuji'. In one of the most imaginative of these, the mountain is seen framed by a curving wave.

Not surprisingly, the Japanese used to regard Fuji as a sacred mountain. Every summer in July and August, thousands of people climb to the top to see the famous *Goraiko* (sunrise) and a long view of the Japanese Alps and the Pacific Ocean.

As a volcano Fuji has been dormant for a long time. In its last eruption, in 1717, volcanic ash was carried as far as Tokyo, where it clogged the streets. In an earlier eruption, in the ninth century, lava flowed from the volcano between the neighbouring lakes. On this lava flow a primeval forest of Aokigahara trees took root, forming the so-called 'Sea of Trees'. Since 1707 there have not been any signs that Fuji is likely to erupt again.

For eight to nine months every year, Mount Fuji's purity of outline is enhanced by a covering of snow.

Persepolis

It was in the reign of Darius I, the Great (522–486 BC), that the ancient Persian empire of the Achaemenid dynasty reached its peak. The successor to Babylon, Egypt and Assyria, the Persian empire outdid them all in size and population, stretching from the Mediterranean to Central Asia. Its most outstanding memorial is the ceremonial city-fortress of Persepolis, near Shiraz, where each New Year the representatives of all the varied peoples of the empire gathered to bring tribute and pay homage to the King of Kings.

When Darius became king he decided to build Persepolis as a new spring capital, perhaps to commemorate his reign as a fresh start, since he had not been in the direct line of succession. The site, overlooking the plain of Marv Dasht 50 miles (80 kilometres) south of the old capital, Pasargadae, was a natural rock terrace backed by a sheer cliff face. The building began in 520 BC and continued in the reigns of Darius' successors Xerxes I (486–466) and Ataxerxes I (466–426). Unlike similar projects in other nations at the time, Persepolis was built by free, paid labour rather than by slaves.

The terrace of Persepolis, a colossal platform of 1476 feet by 984 feet (450 by 300 metres), is formed partly from natural rock and partly from enormous fitted limestone blocks, and rises to a height of 66 feet (20 metres). A complex network of drainage and water channels cut into the terrace suggests that the layout of the city was planned carefully before building began.

The main entrance to Persepolis is on the west, where a wide ceremonial stairway leads up to the terrace. At the top of this stairway is the Gateway of All Nations, built by Xerxes I. Opposite its southern exit is the largest and most fascinating of the buildings of Persepolis, the Audience Hall or *Apadana* built by Darius and Xerxes. Constructed on a stone platform, the *Apadana* was reached by impressive double staircases on the north and east walls. These staircases are famous for their superb bas reliefs of the tribute-bearing processions of delegates from all parts of the Persian empire, and lines of guards, dignitaries, horses and chariots, all sculpted in almost photographic detail.

Persepolis was an awe-inspiring piece of imperial architecture which, even in its ruined state (it was first sacked by the followers of Alexander the Great), retains an imposing grandeur. The remains of the palaces (below: Palace of Darius I) on their huge platforms, the many-columned halls and the great carved gateway of Xerxes I (opposite) convey the power of the Achaemenid monarchy.

The *Apadana* was more than 66 feet (20 metres) high, with a square main hall enclosed by thick mud-brick walls with a side length of 198 feet (60.5 metres). The ceiling beams of teak, ebony and cedar were gold-plated and inlaid with precious metals and ivory.

The doorways of the Palace of Darius, immediately south of the *Apadana*, have huge bas reliefs of the king and his attendants. Their splendour was originally embellished with jewellery, gold and other precious metals. In the small rooms, where the king bathed and changed, are reliefs of his personal servants carrying items such as towels, fly whisks, a scent box and royal parasol.

To the south of this palace is the Palace of Xerxes, on the highest part of the terrace. Approached by a northern porch with twelve columns, its central hall with thirty-six columns has five doorways with reliefs showing Xerxes and his attendants entering or leaving the palace. North of Xerxes' palace is the small Central Palace with three entrances. On the portal of the eastern doorway Darius is shown on his throne, carried by people of twenty-eight countries with Xerxes, as crown prince, standing behind. On the east of the terrace, at the foot of the mountain, is the Royal Treasury, which covered more than 107643 square feet (10000 square metres). Clay and stone tablets discovered here reveal the exact wages paid to the labourers who built Persepolis. Immediately

to the north of the Treasury is the Hall of One Hundred Columns, the largest of the palaces, measuring 230 by 230 feet (70 by 70 metres). This was the throne room.

Impressive as they are, their remains give little idea of the sheer splendour of these buildings, which combined architectural grandeur with a wealth of colourful decoration. Delicately patterned gold covered the great wooden doors; heavy gold lace curtains kept out draughts; and the upper walls were decorated with glazed and terracotta tiles in pink, yellow and blue, portraying animals and plants.

Ironically it was Xerxes, whose contribution to Persepolis was second only to that of Darius, who sowed the seeds of the city's eventual destruction when he sacked the Acropolis of Athens in 480 BC. This act was never forgotten by the Greeks, and when Alexander the Great captured Persepolis in 330 BC he burnt it down in revenge.

However, enough was left, in its great staircases, majestic doorways and myriad columns, and above all its matchless reliefs, to show that Persepolis was the grand finale to the mastery of Babylon, Assyria and Egypt, a summary and synthesis of the ancient world's achievement.

The artistic imagery at Persepolis is of course Persian, with many Assyrian influences, but much of the actual carving was done by Greek craftsmen.

Jerusalem

Jerusalem – the word itself evokes the spiritual appeal of this ancient Middle Eastern city, the centre of three great world religions: Judaism, Christianity and Islam. Founded some four thousand years ago, Jerusalem was an obscure hill town until about 1000 BC when King David made it the capital of the newly united Israelite tribes. King Solomon, his son, built the first Temple of the Jews there, and ever since, Jerusalem has been the emotional focus of Judaism. For Christians the city has an equal significance through its association with many events of Christ's life and as the scene of his crucifixion. For Muslims Jerusalem is the third holy city of Islam, after Mecca and Medina; from Jerusalem, they believe, Muhammad rose to heaven and returned with the message of Islam.

Jerusalem's long history is one of many conquests: by the Babylonians, Persians, Greeks, Romans, Arabs, Crusaders and Turks. As the capital of Palestine the British controlled the city from 1917 to 1948; after the Arab–Israeli war of 1948 it was divided between Israel and Jordan. In the 1967 war the Israelis captured the whole city, and have since held it as their capital. Spiritually, though, Jerusalem remains the common property of its three religions.

At an altitude of 2500 feet (762 metres), Jerusalem lies on two rocky hills in the heart of the biblical Holy Land, about 13 miles (21 kilometres) west of the north end of the Dead Sea. The city, with more than 300000 inhabitants, is divided into West Jerusalem, with a mainly Jewish population and modern buildings and industry, and East Jerusalem, which is mainly Arab. East Jerusalem includes the walled Old City, a maze of narrow, cobbled streets divided into Armenian, Christian, Jewish and Muslim quarters. In the Old City are the holiest places of Jerusalem's three religions – the Wailing Wall, the Church of the Holy Sepulchre and the Dome of the Rock.

The Wailing Wall, in the south-east of the Old City, is the holiest of holy places for Jews throughout the world. Built of huge limestone

The Dome of the Rock was built by Abd al-Malik in 691 and probaly intended as a substitute for the Kaaba – the Muslim shrine in Mecca.

blocks, it forms a sheer cliff 69 feet (21.14 metres) high and 160 feet (49 metres) long. It was a section of the retaining wall built by King Herod when he enlarged the site of Solomon's Temple. After the Romans destroyed Herod's Temple in AD 70 and drove the Jews into exile, the Wall was all that was left. For the exiled Jews it became the symbolic focus for the lost Jerusalem and the object of intense longing and veneration. In the fourth century AD the emperor Constantine allowed the Jews a yearly pilgrimage to the Wall, at which they would weep and tear their robes. From these sorrowful prayers, the Wailing Wall received its name.

In the north-west of the Old City, surrounded by the Christian quarter, is the Church of the Holy Sepulchre. Built over the traditional sites of Christ's crucifixion and entombment, it is the holiest shrine of Christianity. Rather than a single church it is a cluster of chapels, holy places and historic buildings maintained by six Christian sects: Abyssinians, Greek Orthodox, Franciscans (for the Roman Catholic Church), Syrians, Copts and Armenians.

The church began as a basilica built by Constantine the Great in the fourth century AD. The Persians destroyed it in 614 and its replacement was destroyed in turn by the caliph of Egypt in the eleventh century. Then the Crusaders, during their brief rule of Jerusalem, built the Romanesque church which, heavily restored by the Greek Orthodox sect in the early nineteenth century, is the centre of the complex today.

Leading from the Muslim quarter into the Christian quarter and to the Church of the Holy Sepulchre is the Via Dolorosa (Way of Sorrows), since Crusader times the traditional route that Christ followed to Calvary. The fourteen Stations of the Cross are marked by shrines along the route. Each Friday, processions of pilgrims led by Franciscan monks retrace Christ's steps to Calvary.

The Dome of the Rock, Jerusalem's holiest Islamic place, stands near the Wailing Wall, and, in fact, has a close spiritual connection with it. The Dome shelters the Rock of Jerusalem, the outcrop on which the altar of Solomon's Temple stood. Muslims believe that Muhammad flew to the Rock on his sacred horse, *El-Burak*; from the Rock the angel Gabriel lifted Muhammad to heaven, where he spoke with God, and returned to earth with the message of Islam. (Islam, of course, accepts Abraham and Christ as earlier prophets of Allah.) Therefore, the Arabs already regarded Jerusalem as a Holy City when they captured it in 638. The Dome was built in 691 by the caliph Abd-al-Malik. Covered in brass gilt, it collapsed in an earthquake in 1016 and was rebuilt in dull lead. Today, the Dome has been restored to its original hue with modern gold-plated aluminium.

The Dome rests on a richly decorated octagonal building, with four entrances exactly aligned to the points of the compass; the south entrance faces towards Mecca. The style of the building shows how the Arabs were influenced by other cultures: the Dome is held up by ancient Roman columns and its diameter exactly matches that of the dome of the Church of the Holy Sepulchre. The inside of the Dome is decorated with rich arabesques in plaster, a masterpiece by fourteenth-century Indian craftsmen.

Perhaps the most fascinating aspect of Jerusalem is the way in which the physical proximity of its three great faiths emphasizes what is, for all their historical rivalry, their underlying similarity. The city is the living memorial to a revolutionary development in human ideas: the worship of one god, rather than many.

Jerusalem contains sacred relics and shrines of three major religions. *Right:* Orthodox Jews pray at the Wailing Wall, containing (according to tradition) stones from Solomon's temple. *Below:* The Mount of Olives rises up behind the Dome of the Rock, outside the walls of the Old City. Such was the importance of Jerusalem in the early days of Islam that the 'mihrabs', which now traditionally indicate the direction of Mecca, indicated the direction of Jerusalem in many early mosques.

Isfahan

Of all the cities of Iran, Isfahan is the most typically Persian in the sense in which westerners visualize that country. The saying *Isfahan–nisf-i jahân* (Isfahan is half the world) is justifiable hyperbole, for within a relatively small space the city has some of the finest examples of Islamic architecture: the pavilioned bridges, the long central *maidan* where the shah's court once played polo, and the palace, mosques and market which surround it.

Isfahan probably existed in the Achaemenian period (550–330 BC), and became a provincial capital under the Parthians. Under Arab rule from about AD 640 to 931, Isfahan became famous for its silks and cottons, which it still produces. In the Seljuq period (*c* 1000–*c* 1218) the rulers Tughril Beg, Alp Arslan and Malik Shah contributed much to Isfahan's beauty. Malik Shah, however, was murdered by the Assassins, who also destroyed the city's famous library at the Masjid-i Jami mosque. In 1235 the Mongols captured Isfahan. In 1397 Tamurlane the Great slaughtered 70000 Isfahanis and heaped up their skulls to make minarets.

Isfahan's golden age began in 1598, when the Safavid ruler Shah Abbas I, the Great (1586–1629), made it his capital. Shah Abbas, the contemporary of Queen Elizabeth I and Akbar the Great, decided to make Isfahan the first city in the world; he laid out its great squares and avenues and built many of its finest buildings. During his reign Isfahan reached a splendour which astonished contemporary western visitors and which was to last until the eighteenth century.

Historically, Isfahan's richest building is the great Masjid-i Jami (Mosque of Congregation), which embraces eight hundred years of Persian Islamic architecture from the eleventh to the eighteenth centuries. On the mosque's median line (from north-east to south-west) there are two tall baked brick domes. The larger one, on the south-west, stands over the main sanctuary with its *mihrab*, the prayer-niche giving the direction of Mecca. This, the oldest complete part, was built in about 1080 by Nizam al-Mulk, prime minister to the Seljuq ruler Malik Shah. The smaller north-eastern dome was built by Nizam al-Mulk's political rival Taj al-Mulk in 1088. It is thought to

In Seljuq Iran, refined techniques of bricklaying and plasterwork were employed on a huge scale to decorate the surfaces of buildings. A unique development was the use, for the same purpose, of glazed bricks or tiles, and this is largely responsible for the glittering effect of Shah Abbas's capital city. Brilliant examples can be seen in the Masjid-i Shah (below) and Masjid-i Jami (right).

have been designed by the great poet and mathematician Omar Khayyam, who lived at Isfahan at the time. Of mathematically perfect proportions, this beautiful dome has survived without a crack for nearly nine hundred years. Both domes have their original patterned brickwork.

Built around a central courtyard, the mosque has a great variety of brick vaulting, especially over the corridors and arcades by the southern entrance, with decorated columns and ornamented brick-plugs which are typical of Seljuq architecture. Many additions and extensions were made over the centuries.

Shah Abbas's greatest buildings in Isfahan surrounded the oblong Royal Quadrangle or Maidan-i Shah, to the south of the Masjid-i Jami.

At the west end of the quadrangle is the royal palace of Ala Qapi; at the north the Qaysariyya Gateway leading to the Royal Bazaar; at the east is the mosque of Shaikh Lutfullah; and at the south end is the Masjid-i Shah (Royal Mosque). On the bazaar gateway were frescoes of Abbas's conquests which have now faded, but its exquisite mosaic tiling still remains. The bazaar itself, a great arcaded market which is possibly the finest in all Asia if not the world, is still active.

The impressive Masjid-i Shah was set at an angle to its gateway so that its *mihrab* could be aligned to Mecca. The great portal was so richly decorated in mosaic tiling that it took four years to complete (1612–6), and Shah Abbas ordered the decoration of the interior to be done with simpler, square painted tiles.

In contrast, the mosque of Shaikh Lutfullah is entirely decorated with mosaic, both inside and out, except for the marble floor. The dome, with its *café-au-lait* background colour, is perhaps the most perfect of all Isfahan's domes [below].

The Ala Qapi, also commenced by Shah Abbas but completed by his successors, appears to consist of two large storeys, the lower one of tile-decorated brick, the upper one a large, flat-roofed balcony. In fact, there are seven interior storeys, approached by a spiral staircase. From the balcony the Shah and his guests watched the spectacles which took place on the *maidan*.

Apart from the Royal Quadrangle, Shah Abbas's other great projects included the spacious avenue called the Chahar Bagh (Four Gardens), leading down to the river.

The smaller buildings of Isfahan include countless minarets, some no longer attached to mosques but free-standing, many fine tombs, and a number of smaller mosques (Isfahan has more than two hundred) which, though dominated by the city's great mosques, are masterpieces in their own right. Isfahan is also famous for its bridges over the Zayanda-rud river; the finest is the Khaju bridge, built by Abbas II on the old Shiraz road.

Since its heyday as the Safavid capital, Isfahan has survived invasions by Turks, Russians and Afghans to become a thriving modern city. But thanks to careful restoration, its original beauty is almost intact.

The mosques of Isfahan are splendid monuments, political and artistic as well as religious. The builders of the mosques used three basic structural elements, the pointed arch, the dome and the squinch, but all was covered with abstract and calligraphic ornament – in plaster, brick and mosaic. Vaults were patterned with ever more complex honeycomb designs, and everywhere mass disappeared under decoration and alternating patches of light and dark, so that the buildings themselves appear insubstantial, ethereal, not earthly edifices but heavenly dreams.

145

Göreme

In the Göreme Valley, gateway to the mountainous region of central Turkey known since ancient times as Cappadocia, nature and man have combined to create one of the world's strangest and most interesting landscapes. Walled in by soaring cliffs, the valley is a shady desert, broken here and there by unexpectedly luxuriant vegetation and by fields and vineyards fertilized by pigeon droppings. At the bottom of the valley, the soft tuff-stone has been cut by streams (many of them long since vanished) and worn by wind and rain into a bizarre medley of shapes: columns, irregular pyramids, chimneys, needles and twisted cones, some

supporting great flat slabs of stone balanced like hats.

According to local legend, this weird landscape was created when a neighbouring king came to make war on the defenceless people of the valley. The people gave prayer to Allah, who took pity on their plight and turned the king's warriors to stone. Whatever the explanation, the result resembles an eerie moonscape.

But this is just a start. The entire valley, from the cliff sides to the innumerable pinnacles, seems to be a giant rabbit warren. In fact, it is riddled with caves which have been dug out over thousands of years of human habitation.

A large number of the Göreme caves are ancient Christian churches, chapels and sanctuaries. Soon

after Christianity gained a foothold in Asia Minor, anchorite hermits, in search of solitude, began to settle in Cappadocia. Many of them came to Göreme. Between the end of the fifth century AD and the ninth century there was a new influx of Christian refugees, escaping from the iconoclastic conflicts and the expansion of Islam. These pressures caused the originally solitary anchorites to unite with the newcomers and built religious communities for their mutual protection. But rather than build houses, the Christians simply hollowed out shelters in the soft rock of Göreme.

In the cave churches is an amazing series of frescoes, some dating back to the fifth century. Tokali Kilise, the largest of the Göreme churches, is hollowed out of a rock pillar. Its frescoes, in ochres, yellows, reds and occasional greens, depict the life of Jesus, the Apostles, the Annunciation and the seizure of Jesus by Judas and the Roman soldiers.

The extraordinary interiors of the chapels and churches in the Göreme valley are carved out of rock with all the architectural elements typical of normal Byzantine churches – domes, apses, naves and aisles. Monasteries complete with refectories, monks' cells and workshops were created entirely inside the rock formations. The walls are covered with cycles of paintings made over several centuries.

Nara

Nara, Japan's most historic city, lies about 26 miles (42 kilometres) west of Osaka on Honshu Island, at the foot of the nine wooded hills called the Kasugayama. Founded in AD 709, Nara became the first permanent capital of the Japanese empire, and early Japan's chief centre of Buddhist religion and art. Its surviving temples make Nara a place of pilgrimage for the Japanese and for all devotees of Japanese culture.

The old city of Nara was laid out on the plan of Ch'ang-an, the famous capital of the Chinese T'ang dynasty: a rectangle of 2 by 1½ miles (3.2 by 2.4 kilometres), with nine wide, intersecting streets. A succession of rulers built palaces, temples and public buildings until 784, when the emperor Tenno moved the capital to Kyoto, where it was to remain until 1868. Some of Nara's buildings were dismantled and transported to the new capital (all were of wood), but others were left.

Today, only Nara's temples remain, most of them in a huge and beautiful park, the largest in Japan, which lies outside the modern city. Mingling with the temples are sacred deer, ancient maple trees, pines and Japanese cedars, shapely and with delicate leaves.

On one of the Kasugayama hills enclosed by the park is the beautiful Kasuga-jinsha. This Shinto temple was founded in AD 768 by the Fujiwara family as a tutelary shrine. While Nara was the capital, Buddhism became firmly established in Japan. Shōmu, the most devout of the Buddhist

emperors, built the Todai-ji, the most famous of the 'seven temples of Nara', and entrusted to its monks the task of propagating Buddhism and supervising temples throughout Japan.

The Todai-ji was set in a 1¼-square-mile (3.2-square-kilometre) enclosure in the eastern sector of Nara. The monastery's great hall, originally 284 feet (86.5 metres) long and 427 feet (130 metres) high, is the largest wooden building ever built with one roof.

The central hall of the Todai-ji was intended to house the great bronze Buddha, more than 53 feet (16 metres) high and weighing over 541 tons (550 tonnes). It is sheathed with gilt from a vein of gold discovered nearby. Both the Todai-ji and its Buddha were so large that their construction

The Todai-ji (below) became the centre of Buddhist learning, and an illustrious Chinese monk, Ganjin, was invited by the Emperor to train Japanese priests. After encounters with pirates, storms, shipwreck and other disasters, he arrived at the sixth attempt in 754, old, blind and feeble. Nevertheless, he presided over a magnificent opening ceremony, and is commemorated by a superb portrait in carved lacquer in the Todai-ji. Left: The bronze Buddha. Opposite: Kasaga shrine.

almost emptied the imperial treasury. Apart from its size, which made it one of the wonders of the ancient east, the Buddha figure has played an important part in Japanese history because its construction brought about a reconciliation between the rival religions of Buddhism and Shintoism.

Although the bronze Buddha was conceived by the emperor Shōmu in 735, the project was not started for ten years because of a shortage of contributions from the people. Finally, Shōmu turned to an unorthodox monk, Gyōgi, who started a successful fund-raising campaign by making a pilgrimage to Japan's most sacred Shinto shrine, at Ise, where he presented a Buddhist relic as an offering. After this, donations for the Todai-ji Buddha came pouring in from Shintoists and Buddhists alike, and the figure was finally inaugurated by Shōmu's daughter Kōken in AD 756. A Shinto emblem was enshrined at the Todai-ji, and after that every important Buddhist temple in Japan was built under the guardianship of a nearby Shinto shrine.

Behind the hall of the Great Buddha of Todai-ji is the famous Shōsōin treasure house. Windowless and made of timber, it is raised ten feet (three metres) from the ground by many rows of pillars. Inside are the finest of Emperor Shōmu's personal belongings, including cabinets, swords, textiles, musical instruments, screens, horse trappings, gaming boards, pottery and wooden masks. In their quality and decoration all these and many other items are superb examples of the arts and crafts of eighth-century Japan.

On 22 July 756, the forty-ninth day after Shōmu's death, the treasure was dedicated to the Vairocana Buddha by the dowager empress Kōmyo and the Shōsōin was closed with the imperial seal. From then on it was opened only at the emperor's command. After 1884, the doors of the Shōsōin were opened once a year, in October, by the emperor's messenger but since the Second World War it has been easier to see the treasures.

For many visitors to Nara the most unforgettable experience is the seated wooden image of the Buddhist goddess of mercy at the Chūgū-ji convent – the Nyorin Kwannon, or Omnipotent Kwannon, the Japanese version of the goddess's Chinese name, Kuan-Yin. The statue, dating from the late sixth or early seventh centuries, is behind a curtain. Visitors may look at it for two or three minutes before the nuns cover it again.

The atmosphere of Nara is one of great peace, partly because of its religious associations but equally because its timber architecture of temples and low, curving roofs blends with nature rather than asserting itself like Western architecture.

The Jordan River

No river evokes so many religious associations as the Jordan; like the holy city of Jerusalem, it is equally revered by Jews, Christians and Muslims. For such a famous river, the Jordan is neither long nor large: from its sources in Syria and Lebanon it flows southwards for 224 miles (360 kilometres) through Israel and the Kingdom of Jordan before disappearing into the Dead Sea. Because of its meandering habits during the last part of its course, the distance from source to finish is even less, as the crow flies, a mere 124 miles (200 kilometres). But the Jordan is the world's lowest river, and the one with the steepest gradient. Its Arabic name means 'that which goes down', and so it does: from 259 feet (79 metres) above sea level to 1286 feet (392 metres) below, an average drop of 4 feet (1.3 metres) to every mile.

Traditionally, the Jordan springs from a limestone cave below snow-capped Mount Hermon (Jebel esh Sheikh), on the border between Lebanon and Syria. In fact, there are at least three main sources, all rising at the foot of Hermon: the Hasbani, Dan and Nahr Baniyas. The three

streams unite in the Ard el Hula, or Hula Basin. This plain was formerly malarial swampland with papyrus, waterlilies and yellow pond lilies, and a rich wild life. Most of it has been drained to provide fertile farmland; a small section has been left as a nature reserve, with otters, wild boar and herons.

After the young Jordan has left this basin it passes through Lake Hula (the biblical Waters of Merom) and dives below sea level into the black basalt gorge of the Jordan Valley (the beginning of the great, volcanic Rift Valley system which stretches through the Red Sea into East Africa). By the time the Jordan reaches harp-shaped Lake Tiberias, or the Sea of Galilee, it has fallen 902 feet (275 metres) in seven miles (eleven kilometres).

After Galilee, the river valley narrows again, and the Jordan receives its largest tributary, the Yarmuk, which almost doubles the Jordan's flow. It is then joined by two more tributaries, the Harod on the right bank and the Yabis on the left. Now, the river plain spreads out into the huge, 15-mile (24-kilometre) wide depression of the Plain of Ghor. Here, far below sea level, the Jordan seems to do all it can to delay its demise in the Dead Sea; it slows down and adopts a meandering, snakelike path, spinning out the 65 miles (105 kilometres) between the Sea of Galilee and the Dead Sea to a course of 135 miles (217 kilometres).

The Plain of Ghor descends 656 feet (200 metres) by a series of flat, arid terraces to the wide river valley below. They are cut by wadis and rivers into rocky pinnacles and towers that resemble a lunar landscape. The valley itself, known as the Zor, was covered by thickets of reeds, willows, tamarisk and poplars, and was often flooded. Today, since dams have been built to control the river, this land has been turned into cultivated fields.

Just before it reaches its destination, the Jordan passes within a few miles of Jericho – a region which has been settled by man for at least ten thousand years. Finally, passing the Plains of Moab on the left, the Jordan reluctantly drains into the Dead Sea over a large, gently sloping delta. Here is the end of the line; there is no escape for the waters of the holy river except to be sucked into the atmosphere by the merciless heat of the sun.

Lake Tiberias (the Sea of Galilee) was probably formed by volcanic action. Its surface lies about 700 feet (213 metres) below the level of the Mediterranean.

Petra

In 1812 a young Swiss explorer, John Burckhardt, in the disguise of an Arab merchant, was making his way across the Biblical lands of Jordan. As he came to the mountainous hills of ancient Edom, he became fascinated by Bedouin stories of a mysterious ancient city buried in the heart of a mountain. Burckhardt could not openly declare a desire to visit this place, since this would have blown his cover, so he announced that he wished to make a sacrifice at the tomb of Aaron, which he had heard overlooked the ruined city. Following his guide along a dry water course which led through a long narrow gorge in the mountainside, Burckhardt was amazed to come upon a wealth of temples and tombs cut into the living rock. He had rediscovered the ancient city of Petra, the location of which had passed from Western memory for nearly a thousand years.

Apart from its scientific interest, the rediscovery of Petra, like the earlier unearthing of Pompeii, made a deep impression on the Romantic sensibility of the times. This is summed up by the famous – but inaccurate – poem by the English clergyman Dean Burgon, in which he described Petra, without having seen it, as a 'rose-red city'. In fact the sandstone bands from which Petra is cut range almost through the spectrum, from white to blue, salmon pink, grey and brown as well as (very occasionally) deep red.

Its visual impact, situation and mixture of architectural influences (Mesopotamian, Egyptian, Hellenistic and Roman) make Petra quite unlike any other ancient city. But like most other splendid cities, Petra's rise depended on trade. Today, Petra's location, tucked away in a cliff-surrounded mountain basin, seems eccentric. In fact, the city lay at the crossroads of some of the most important overland trade routes of the ancient Middle East. Only at Petra was there a convenient route through the high mountain ridges over which the trans-Arabian caravans had to pass to reach the Red Sea and Mediterranean. Added to this, Petra had the advantage of an abundant water supply.

The ancient Nabateans saw the possibilities of the Petra site, and, by about 300 BC they started to carve out a city there. Soon, Petra became a great trading emporium and the capital of a powerful

Little remains of the original city of Petra except the building known as the Treasury (right), which is late, and the tombs of the Nabateans. They were Arabs who controlled an important entrepôt of trade, and their influence reached deep into Arabia. Petra was defensively formidable, impervious to the marauding hordes of the desert.

Nabatean kingdom, which lasted until AD 106 when Petra was conquered by the Romans. As a Roman province, Petra's importance continued for some time, and its architecture was strongly influenced by Roman styles. But its commerce gradually dwindled as the Romans developed alternative trade routes. By the middle of the sixth century the city seems to have been deserted. In a final disaster, Petra was hit by an earthquake, probably in the middle of the eighth century. A millennium of total obscurity faced the once proud city before its rediscovery.

Almost nothing remains of the free-standing buildings which once occupied the centre of Petra. But the many tombs and temples which were cut into the surrounding cliff faces survive almost intact.

The most famous and most beautiful of these is the Khasneh, which stands opposite the inner end of the Siq, the narrow gorge leading to Petra. The façade of the Khasneh appears in a narrow strip of brilliant daylight framed by the walls of the gorge.

Probably built in the first century BC, the Khasneh has a two-storied façade. The lower storey is like a Greek temple entrance, with columns crowned by a triangular pediment. This alone would have been dwarfed by the tall cliffface, so the architect built a second colonnade above, skilfully designed to complement the lower façade, but without duplicating it or distracting from it. The central part is recessed, leaving 'broken' pediments on either side; in the recess is a round pavilion or kiosk. Sculptured decoration completed the monument. Inside the Khasneh is a central sanctuary 40 feet square (12.2 metres square), flanked by two smaller rooms, presumably for priests.

The Khasneh was certainly a temple and may also have been a tomb. Its Arabic name, meaning Treasury, came from the Bedouin belief that the sculpted urn on top of the central pavilion contained the treasure of an Egyptian pharoah. The local Bedouin used to fire at the urn with their rifles in the hope of breaking it open and being showered with treasure. The treasure of Petra is, however, the remains of the city itself.

El Deir, the monastery, Petra. Christianity came early to Petra but was swept away by the Muslim conquest in the 630s. In Crusading times, however, Petra was part of the Latin kingdom of the Franks.

Samarkand

Samarkand, on the edge of the Central Asian Desert in the Soviet Union, was already an old city by the fourth century BC, when Alexander the Great knew it as Marakanda. Beautifully located in the fertile valley of the Zeravshan River, 180 miles (290 kilometres) south-west of Tashkent, Samarkand lies between the western spurs of the Alai Mountains. To the east, the still higher Tien Shan Mountains tower in the distance, half in China – a reminder that Samarkand was one of the great staging-posts on the old overland silk route between China and Europe. Today, though, for travellers from the west, the 'golden road to Samarkand' is a train journey of many days across the Kirghiz steppe, with little to see except the two-humped Bactrian camels of the Kazakh, carrying heavy loads in summer or pulling sledges over the snow-covered desert in winter.

The old and new cities of Samarkand are separated by a citadel and a depression in the ground. The modern city, an important industrial centre built since the Russian Revolution, could be nearly

Interior of a tomb at Samarkand, built in the time of Tamerlane.

anywhere in the Soviet Union, except for the tell-tale sprinkling of Mongoloid people wearing national Uzbek costume of long, brightly striped gowns and embroidered caps.

Crossing into the old city, the contrast is total, almost as if the modern world had ceased to exist. Here everyone wears the national costume, and many buildings survive from the great days of Samarkand, which the Mongol conqueror Tamerlane made his capital in 1370. Tamerlane's repu-

tation as a destroyer is only half the story. Like many Asian potentates he was a patron of arts and poetry, and from the cities ransacked by his Mongol hordes he collected artists and craftsmen to beautify Samarkand.

The buildings raised by Tamerlane and his successors are decorated with strongly patterned tiles in deep, varied colours. A fine example is Tamerlane's own tomb, built early in the fifteenth century. Tamerlane lies buried under the world's

largest slab of jade. Other fine buildings are the Koranic schools which line three sides of the superb square, El Registan. The starred design on the tilework of one of these announces that it was built by Tamerlane's grandson, the astronomer Ulugh Bek, who made Samarkand into a centre of art and science. On the outskirts of Samarkand, Ulugh Bek had an observatory dug into the ground to keep out all extraneous light, from which he recalculated, for the first time since Ptolemy, the positions of 992 stars. The observatory's ruins can still be seen.

After Tamerlane and his successors, Samarkand gradually declined until, by 1700, it was almost uninhabited. But during the eighteenth century the city revived as it passed first under Chinese rule and then under the emir of Bukhara. After a bitter struggle it was finally taken by the Russians in 1868. Today, the Soviet city of Samarkand still evokes its vivid Asian past.

Shah-i Zindeh (left) is a necropolis outside the old city of Samarkand where a variety of small mausoleums, or tomb buildings, are preserved. They are of simple design but exquisite decoration, whole surfaces being covered with glazed tiles, often moulded in relief and glazed deep blue or turquoise, among other colours. Their rich decoration gives some idea of the lost palaces and mosques of Tamerlane. The buildings on this page are of later date. Below: The façade of the 17th century Shir-Dar Madrasah in the El Registan square.

The Terracotta Warriors of Xi'an

For many centuries in ancient times, the Chinese city of Chang'an (now Xi'an), in the province of Shaanxi, served as the capital for eleven ruling dynasties. It was here that many of the emperors had their impressive mausoleums constructed, among them the First Emperor of the Qin Dynasty. In accordance with custom, he ordered work to begin on his tomb soon after he came to the throne as King Zheng at the age of thirteen in 246 BC. Through a series of ruthless military conquests the young king unified China under his rule and brought to an end two and a half centuries of constant warfare known in Chinese history as the Period of the Warring States (475–221 BC). In 221 Zheng proclaimed himself the First Emperor of the new dynasty of Qin, a period of harsh rule that survived for only three years after his death in 210.

The First Emperor's tomb was built by over 700000 labourers and craftsmen some 15 miles (24 kilometres) east of present-day Xi'an. The place chosen was in beautiful countryside on the north bank of the Wei River near Mount Lishan. Deep below ground the workmen constructed what was in effect a lavish palace, packed with treasure and fitted with ingenious mechanisms to make rivers and pools of quicksilver flow and to trigger crossbows to shoot at intruders. Around it two concentric walls were built, the square inner one about 2.5 miles (4 kilometres) in length, the rectangular outer one 3.5 miles (6 kilometres). On completion, thousands of the workers were buried alive in the tomb, as were the emperor's concubines at his burial.

Today, a great mound of earth some 154 feet (47 metres) high, shaped like a pyramid and covered with trees, marks the site. But unknown until recently, the First Emperor of Qin had left other wonders below the ground for later generations to discover and marvel at.

In March 1974, farm labourers sinking a well one mile (1.5 kilometres) east of the tomb were astonished to dig up a group of lifesize terracotta figures. When experts arrived to investigate and dig further, they unearthed one of the most amazing and important archaeological treasures in Chinese history: a whole army of thousands of pottery soldiers, complete with cavalry horses, chariots and metal weapons, arranged in immaculate formation and frozen in time since their burial 2200 years ago.

In the years since the discovery, several huge pits have been excavated at the site. Pit 1, the first and largest, has revealed that the terracotta figures stood on a brick floor inside a wood and masonry structure that was burned down soon after completion and collapsed on to the figures. Many of these have since been dug out, repaired and replaced in the pit, which is now enclosed in a large on-site exhibition hall 755 feet (230 metres) long and 246 feet (75 metres) wide and covered by an immense arched roof. This now forms the Museum of the Terracotta Warriors of the First Emperor of Qin, opened in 1979. Similar excavations have been made in the other pits nearby, which are less extensive in area but equally rich in terracotta figures.

The finds reveal the high degree of technical skill attained by the sculptors working in clay at the time of the Qin Dynasty. The figures, once painted in bright colours now faded with time, represent infantrymen, archers, cavalry soldiers, and officers of the imperial army of the time, and show the current styles of military uniform, hair styles and other personal details. Many of them display individualized facial expressions. Towering above them all is the majestic figure of the 6.5-foot (two-metre) tall commander of the army, his armour-plated tunic covered with knotted decorations.

Each of the figures was individually modelled, not shaped in moulds. The hollow heads and torsos and solid legs were made separately as

Opposite: Inside the museum the reaction of a visitor on first seeing the amazing terracotta army of the Emperor Zheng is one of bewilderment, almost disbelief. China is a country full of historical paradoxes, but this array of warriors is a perfect freak of artistic enterprise. The sheer size of the project comes near to reducing it to absurdity. What on earth was it all for? Never have the expedients arising from the disinclination of man to accept his own mortality risen to a greater pitch of megalomania. Above: The Emperor's tomb.

rough shapes and then assembled with strips of clay. A layer of finer clay was then added, into which were carved details of facial expressions and items of dress. The figures of horses were made in a similar way.

Thousands of metal weapons – swords, spears, arrowheads, bows and crossbows – have also been uncovered alongside the terracotta figures, the bronze swords and arrowheads still as sharp as when they were made over 2000 years ago.

The significance of this vast terracotta army is still unresolved, and many ideas have been put forward. It has been suggested that the First Emperor's mausoleum, just to the west, symbolizes an ideal imperial city, the tomb inside the inner wall representing the emperor's palace protected inside the private 'forbidden city'. In accordance with this notion, the soldiers uncovered in the pit excavations may represent the military garrison which is stationed just outside the city.

More finds continue to be made as excavations are extended to other areas around the central mausoleum. Yet even now, before the First Emperor of Qin has yielded up all his secret treasures, the terracotta army at the Xi'an tomb must rank as one of the most amazing archaeological discoveries in China's long history.

Baalbek

Modern Lebanon, between Israel and Syria on the eastern Mediterranean coast, was the home of the ancient Phoenicians, history's first great trading peoples. Their god, and the god of their predecessors the Canaanites, was the sun-god Baal. His centre of worship was Baalbek, on the lower western slope of the Anti-Lebanon Mountains overlooking the fertile Bekaa plain. To the Greeks, who conquered Phoenicia in 332 BC, Baalbek became known as Heliopolis, 'City of the Sun', and it kept this name when it became a Roman colony in the time of Julius Caesar.

During the Graeco–Roman period, Baalbek-Heliopolis was a city of great size and importance, and many fine buildings were erected, especially in the reign of the Roman emperor Antoninus Pius (AD 138–161). The temple ruins for which Baalbek is famous are all Graeco–Roman; nothing is left of the older temple sites over which they were built.

The temples are grouped on a great acropolis high above the surrounding countryside, which is reached by a magnificent flight of stairs. These lead to a hexagonal forecourt, followed by the main courtyard of the acropolis. The courtyard, which measures 449 feet (137 metres) long by 371 feet (113 metres) wide, was originally surrounded on three sides by a covered portico supported by eighty-four giant pillars. These pillars, like the rest of the pillars in Baalbek's temples, were cut from granite quarried at Aswan in Upper Egypt. (It has been calculated that it took at least three years to carry them to Baalbek).

In the centre of the main courtyard is a great altar, which has been reconstructed. Here, bulls were sacrificed to the gods. On either side of the altar are two pools, surrounded by walls carved with nymphs, cupids and tritons. The pools were used for ritual ablutions.

The most beautiful part of the acropolis is the temple of Jupiter, beyond the main courtyard. Of the temple's fifty-four original columns, six are still standing; they are considered to be some of the finest ever built. Each one consists of three blocks and together with its base and capital is nearly 66 feet (20 metres) high and has a diameter of 7 feet (2.28 metres). Above the capitals is an entablature about 16 feet (five metres) high. Between the architrave and cornice is a frieze of bulls' and lions' heads strung together with garlands. The cornice is richly sculpted with modillions, rosettes, dentils, eggs (symbolizing life), darts (symbolizing death), acanthus leaves and lion's-head waterspouts.

To the south of the Jupiter temple, at a lower level, stands Baalbek's best-preserved temple, the temple of Bacchus. Measuring 225 feet (68.5

metres) long by 110 feet (33.5 metres) wide, it is raised on a platform on a southern projection of the acropolis. In the temple are carvings of Bacchus, his head encircled with grapes.

Below the acropolis, to the south-east, is the small, circular temple of Venus, with eight Corinthian columns supporting a projecting entablature. Constantine the Great turned this into a church dedicated to St Barbara; the inside walls have carved crosses, painted in vermilion, with Constantine's monogram above them.

In the seventh century AD the Arabs turned Baalbek into a fortress, concealing many of its features. But from the eighteenth century archaeologists began to restore the acropolis and clear it of additions. Today, in their magnificent setting, the temples of Baalbek create an impression which has been described as second only to the Athenian Acropolis.

Baalbek (below) is the finest classical archaeological site in the Middle East. The buildings have nothing to do with Baal, the god of the Canaanites (whose priests received such a comeuppance from the Prophet Elijah), but are later Roman works. The interiors of the temples are sumptuously ornate and in detail highly unorthodox – according to classical rules. Like the Treasury at Petra (page 153), they represent a daring, eastern version. Opposite: Temple of Bacchus. Left: Temple of Jupiter with a sculpted lion's head in the foreground.

Australasia
and Oceania

The tropical Pacific island of Maui, Hawaii

Easter Island

The mysterious stone statues of Easter Island, surrounded by the empty vastness of the East Pacific, are one of the great puzzles of archaeology. More than six hundred of these figures, ranging from life-size to giant-size, are scattered around this small volcanic island in the middle of nowhere. Not only the statues, but also superbly built masonry walls and temple platforms, show that Easter Island was once occupied by people highly skilled in stone-working.

These people were not Polynesians, for nothing like their art exists anywhere else in Polynesia. Today, however, almost all the people of Easter Island are of Polynesian descent. But their culture has many non-Polynesian traits, suggesting that they were strongly influenced by their statue-building predecessors. Who these people were, where they came from and why they should have turned a place as remote as Easter Island into something like the world's biggest open-air sculpture exhibition have puzzled many researchers.

With an area of just 45 square miles (117 square kilometres), Easter Island is 1180 miles (1900 kilometres) east of the equally remote Pitcairn Island and 2299 miles (3700 kilometres) west of Chile. The first European to arrive there was a Dutch Admiral, Jacob Roggeveen, in 1722, who named it Easter Island for the day of its discovery.

Today there are just over 1000 Easter Islanders. Their oral history relates that there was once a time when Easter Island was inhabited by two distinct groups, Polynesians or 'short-ears' and non-Polynesians or 'long-ears', who lengthened their ears as a sign of status. The great majority of present-day Easter Islanders claim descent from the short-ears, but a few families claim descent from the long-ears – who were the statue-builders. After a long period in which the short-ears helped the long-ears build statues, they became tired of their labour and turned on the long-ears, exterminating most of them.

This tradition is borne out by the most numerous of the Easter Island statue: the long-eared, legless figures which were mounted on stepped stone temple platforms called *ahu*. These statues were a single, stylized type made from yellow-grey tuff, a volcanic rock quarried from the crater of Rano Raraku, one of the island's three extinct volcanoes. Inside and outside the crater walls where the statues were quarried are many unfinished figures and thousands of simple stone axes, suggesting that the sculptors' work was suddenly interrupted.

In the 1950s archaeologists made some experiments to see how these massive statues might have been handled. They showed that 180 islanders could pull a medium-sized statue over the ground. Twelve people took eighteen days to lift a 25-ton (25-tonne) statue ten feet (three metres) from the ground and tilt it on to an *ahu*, using only two logs as levers. This was done by wedging stones under the statue to make a slowly rising cairn.

Archaeologists believe that the long-eared statues that stood on the *ahus* were the product of a middle period of Easter Island culture beginning in about AD 1100. But before that, an earlier culture was responsible for a series of smaller statues of four different types, one of which became the prototype of the *ahu* figures. This early culture, dating from about AD 380 or before, also built a solar observatory aligned to the sun's annual movements, with megalithic walls of beautifully-fitted masonry. Nothing like the statues and constructions of this early Easter Island culture is known in the Pacific. But they do resemble monuments built in the first millennium AD by the pre-Inca peoples of the South American Andes. The great *ahu* figures of the middle period have no parallel anywhere. Yet another feature of this period was circular stone buildings with roof entrances, associated with a bird cult. Similar buildings are common in the adjacent parts of South America.

For these reasons it is possible that the stone-builders of Easter Island's early and middle periods may have come from the west coast of South America, in two widely separated migrations. If so, they were possibly sun worshippers who, perhaps because they were defeated in war, decided to take to the sea and follow the sun-god westwards.

At some later stage, possibly in the fifteenth century, there was also a Polynesian migration to Easter Island. The Polynesians adopted the stone-builders' culture and religion and at first were subservient to them, but finally revolted and brought the era of *ahu* figures to an end.

This began a third or late period of Easter Island culture, in which wood carving and small stone figures replaced statues and Polynesians became the majority of the population. Amidst general war and destruction the upright *ahu* figures were overthrown. Only the temporarily raised statues at the foot of the quarry were impossible to topple because silt from the quarry had buried them up to the chest. It is these great heads, sightless because they had not yet been given their eyes, which have remained standing to the present day, and given Easter Island its fame.

A seductive hypothesis concerning the Easter Island statues suggests the builders came from South America.

Tahiti

No Pacific island has made a greater impression on the Western imagination than Tahiti, the largest of the Society Islands of French Polynesia in the South Pacific. To the European navigators who reached it in the eighteenth century, after many months of hardship at sea, this lush and fertile speck of volcanic land, and its welcoming people, seemed like an earthly paradise. Their reports of Tahiti began one of the great myths of modern times – the idea of the 'Noble Savage', living in primeval innocence untroubled by the neuroses of civilization. Though this was a superficial view of a way of life which was to disappear through the very contacts which made the myth possible, Tahiti still retains a unique, and justified, appeal.

About 33 miles (53 kilometres) long and covering an area of 400 square miles (1036 square kilometres), Tahiti is shaped like a lop-sided hourglass. The main part, Big Tahiti or Tahiti-nui, is nearly circular and very mountainous. In the centre is the highest peak, Orohena, which rises to 7333 feet (2235 metres) and can be seen from nearly 62 miles (100 kilometres) out to sea. A narrow isthmus in the south-east joins Big Tahiti to the broad, oval peninsula of Little Tahiti or Tahiti-iti. Most of the island is circled by coral reefs, providing safe lagoon anchorage. Beyond the lagoons, the Pacific swell breaks on the reefs, with a light, ceaseless thunder.

Thickly covered with tropical forest, the mountain slopes of Tahiti descend to flat, fertile shores fringed with groves of extraordinarily tall coconut palms, which bend out over the lagoons. Behind the palms are groves of breadfruit trees, with round, green fruit. Though hot and humid, the tropical climate is not oppressive. Mountain cataracts and waterfalls provide fresh water in abundance, and flowers and fruit grow everywhere: red hibiscus, frangi-pani, white *tiare Tahiti*, yellow jasmine; wild bananas, yams and sugarcane.

The first European navigator to visit Tahiti was the Portuguese, de Queirós, in 1606. After that, it was forgotten for over 150 years until it was rediscovered and claimed for Britain by Samuel Wallis in 1767. Next year Louis de Bougainville claimed Tahiti for France, but did not press his claim. The first Europeans to visit the island for a lengthy period were Captain James Cook and the crew of the *Endeavour*, who stayed on Tahiti for three months in 1769.

To Cook and his men, Tahitian society seemed idyllic. The men were tall and well-proportioned; the women were not only beautiful beyond dreams, but happy to bestow their favours on their visitors. The Tahitians hardly needed to work, as there was food all around them: fish in the lagoons, fruit for the taking, and small wild pigs and fowls which they baked in underground ovens. Their main entertainments were surfing in the Pacific, dancing and singing to the music of drums and flutes, play-acting and wrestling.

This apparently perfect life had its complications, however. Tahitian society was divided into tribal groups, each with its upper class and ruling family. Below them was a middle class and a class of serfs. Despite their friendliness and good nature the Tahitians engaged in vicious tribal wars, and in human sacrifice to assure and celebrate victories. There were many strictly observed

taboos. European contact was limited, its idyllic side persisted.

Captain William Bligh and the crew of the *Bounty* arrived in Tahiti in 1788 and stayed for five months, collecting and transplanting breadfruit seedlings to transport to the West Indies. The famous mutiny after their departure was caused, not so much by Bligh's sternness as by the undermining of the crew's discipline during their long stay on Tahiti. Each man had had his Tahitian girl, and had found it unbearable to leave. Having put Bligh overboard in an open boat, the mutineers sailed back to Tahiti, where some settled, and others went with Tahitian women to Pitcairn Island.

As the fame of Tahiti spread, so it attracted more visitors. Missionaries came, anxious to reform the easy-going Tahitian morals, and so did whaling crews, equally anxious to debauch them. Venereal disease and alcohol took their toll of the population. The missionaries did their best to counter these evils but at the same time did much to stifle the Tahitian spirit. By 1843, when France annexed the Society Islands, the romantic dream of Tahiti was past. Today, its old customs survive only as tourist spectacles. But Tahiti is still one of the world's most beautiful islands.

Cook's Bay. To grubby, hard-worked, 18th-century mariners, Tahiti was a paradise.

Sydney

In 1788 a British fleet arrived on the coast of New South Wales to establish a convict settlement at Botany Bay, which had been discovered eight years before by Captain Cook. But the British commander, Captain Phillip, sent a reconnaissance party up the coast to search for fresh water and soon discovered a superb natural harbour, Port Jackson. He considered this to be a much more suitable site for the new colony and thus ignored his instructions to settle at Botany Bay.

The new settlement, at first called Albion, soon became known as Sydney, after the British Home Secretary, Lord Sydney. Today, after less than two hundred years, it has become Australia's largest city and one of the greatest cities in the southern hemisphere, with a population of 3143800.

Perhaps only San Francisco, Cape Town and Rio de Janeiro have a setting which compares with Sydney. The harbour opens with a narrow passage from the Pacific, less than 1 mile (two kilometres) wide between a rocky gateway. Once inside, a broad fairway reaches nearly 12 miles (20 kilometres) between shores which are so indented with bays, coves and branches that the total coastline of Port Jackson is about 139 miles (224 kilometres) long.

The harbour runs south from the Pacific Ocean, parallel with the coast and protected from the thundering Pacific surf by a narrow peninsula, before turning west towards the estuaries of the Lane Cove and Parramatta rivers. The bays of the peninsula are fringed with old mansions and modern houses and apartments with long terraces and high lawns and, underneath, swimming pools and yacht anchorages. Farther up the fairway are the grassy shores of the Botanic Gardens, the city's main park, and Sydney Cove, where the first

settlement was established. Here, the narrow streets of the waterfront climb to the city's lofty modern skyline.

Overlooking the harbour on Bennelong Point, the eastern prong of Sydney Cove, is Sydney's newest landmark, the famous Opera House. Built of steel, glass and silvery white concrete and tiles, it is surmounted by two sets of three overlapping shells, opening towards the harbour. Seen from different points around the harbour, the dramatic structure seems to rise unexpectedly from the sea like an enormous butterfly or a beautiful yacht with spinnaker racing before the wind.

Walking inside the Opera House is rather like being inside a sculpture, or even an intricately structured, semi-translucent seashell. Forming an entire cultural complex, the building contains restaurants, cafés, a concert hall, a drama theatre and a music room as well as an opera hall, and can accommodate more than 6000 people.

A little way to the west of Sydney Cove, the steel arch of Sydney Harbour Bridge spans the harbour to link the southern and northern sections of the city. Designed by J. C. C. Bradfield, the rail and road bridge was built between 1923 and 1932. Its total length is 3766 feet (1148 metres); its main span is exactly the width of the harbour between Dawes and Milson's Points, 1650 feet (503 metres). The highest part of the span is 437 feet (133.3 metres) above sea level.

Since its completion, the Harbour Bridge has become world-famous as the symbol of Sydney, only perhaps now to be challenged by Joern Utzon's magnificent opera house.

Perhaps only in Australia would the Sydney Opera House (below, left) have been built. Its construction was beggared by problems which suggested the plan was unworkable, but the final result is a triumph. Below: Gracious ironwork balconies in Hurstville.

Ayers Rock

In the south-west of Australia's Northern Territory, not far from the very centre of the continent, lies the extraordinary natural monolith known as Ayers Rock. Roughly oval in shape, and a startling reddish colour, the Rock is about two miles (2.5 kilometres) long and one mile (1.6 kilometres) wide, with a circumference of about five miles (eight kilometres). It rises 2851 feet (869 metres) above sea level and 1099 feet (335 metres) above the surrounding plains.

Possibly the world's largest single piece of stone, Ayers Rock is, technically speaking, an inselberg or 'island mountain'. It consists of a hard, pebbly felspar sandstone called arkose, arranged in vertical strata which have been boldly etched out through weathering and erosion. The top of the Rock is scored by gullies, some 19½ feet (six metres) deep, lightning-scarred ridges and rockholes which act as rain traps.

The Rock stands on an open plain of sandy ridges which are swept by local storms created by the Rock itself. Its sides rise so abruptly that someone standing on the level ground can rest

their hands on the vertical sides of sheer precipices rising to over 984 feet (300 metres). At the bottom of the Rock are water soaks and shallow caves. The caves are decorated with aboriginal paintings and carvings.

To the Aborigines, who called it Uluhru, the Rock was a sacred landmark for many centuries before the arrival of Europeans in Australia. The first European to notice the Rock was Ernest Giles, who saw it from the northern side of the salt depression of Lake Amadeus, 23 miles (37 kilometres) to the north, in 1872. When he reached it in 1873, William Gosse, another explorer, had already examined the Rock and named it after Sir Henry Ayers, the Premier of South Australia.

Lying in the South-Western Aboriginal Reserve, the Ayers Rock area is now a national park. Tourists visit the Rock from Alice Springs, the centre of Australia, some 249 miles (400 kilometres) away to the north-east.

Ayers Rock, said to be the largest monolith in the world, is an overwhelming sight close-to. It changes colour as the Sun moves over it, appearing sometimes red, sometimes brown, sometimes almost black. From 150 miles away it appears as a great purple mound.

North Island, New Zealand

Together with Iceland, New Zealand is perhaps the world's outstanding example of a land shaped by volcanic forces. In the North Island of New Zealand, volcanic activity which began in the Pleistocene Epoch (two and a half million to ten thousand years ago) and is still continuing, has created a richly fascinating landscape of rugged volcanic peaks, myriad lakes and boiling, bubbling thermal regions, all amid the lushness of a gentle, temperate climate.

Lake Taupo, in the centre of the North Island, is New Zealand's largest lake, with an area of 238 square miles (616 square kilometres). Formed by an ancient volcanic subsidence, it is in the middle of a region of intense thermal activity. To the

north-east, the thermal area of Waiotapu includes strange silica terraces, like a river frozen in full spate, and the famous Lady Knox Geyser which ejects, punctually at 10.30 every morning, a 69-foot (21-metre) jet of boiling water. Also at Waiotapu is the small, bright blue Champagne Lake, with steaming waters that fizz like champagne when a handful of sand is thrown in.

To the south of Lake Taupo, the Tongariro National Park has three of New Zealand's best-known volcanic peaks, Tongariro (6456 feet/1968 metres), Ngauruhoe (7513 feet/2290 metres) and Ruapehu (9173 feet/2796 metres). All three are peacably active.

Flanking Mount Tongariro is the most bizarre of New Zealand's thermal regions, the Ketetahi Springs. Here are hissing and burbling gas vents, small geysers hurling boiling water into the air and

breathing sulphurous steam clouds, boiling mud pools, hot springs gushing from rock fissures, roaring blowholes and everywhere a smell of sulphur hanging in the air.

Ruapehu, the southernmost of the three volcanoes, is famous for its ski slopes, and its warm Crater Lake. Although surrounded by snow and ice, the lake is hot, because Ruapehu is still active; occasionally it erupts and the lake is replaced by smoking lava. In contrast to the rugged, eroded outlines of Tongariro and Ruapehu, Mount Ngauruhoe has a symmetrical cone.

To the north of Lake Taupo is the Wairakei Valley, one of the country's most famous thermal regions. A vast reservoir of hot water beneath the thin crust of the valley is tapped by the Wairakei Geothermal Power Project, which generates 175000 kilowatts of electric power. The valley is a place of great scenic beauty, with examples of nearly every kind of thermal activity: mud pools, hot springs, geysers and gas vents. The most dramatic feature is the Karapiti Blowhole, at the top of a 400-foot (122-metre) hill. Often called 'The Safety Valve of the North Island', this blowhole is thought to be a pressure outlet for a far greater area than the Wairakei Valley. Karapiti emits a continuous, high pressure steam blast from a single vent at 50000

Warfare was endemic among the Maori and fortifications vital. Opposite: The ornamental gateway in a stockade surrounding a village. Below: The snow-capped peak of Mount Ngauruhoe in a fizzing volcanic landscape. An early explorer wrote, 'I have been wandering about . . . New Zealand for over 5 and 30 years, always finding something in Nature new to me.'

pounds (22680 kilograms) per hour. Its steam is so dry that the jet will carry sparks from a smouldering sack thrust into it to a height of more than 197 feet (60 metres), producing a brilliant display at night. Local Maoris used this idea as a warning beacon. If an enemy tribe approached, smouldering flax was held into the jet to send up a rocket-like signal which could be seen from a distance.

Just south of Lake Rotorua in north-central North Island is New Zealand's most famous thermal region, the valley of Whakarewarewa – 'The Place of the Rising Steam'. In the western side of the valley are steaming mud pools, hissing and roaring gas vents, silica terraces and several great geysers. The Pohutu Geyser, on the peak of a frozen wave of alum, plays several times daily for up to forty minutes at a time, sending its jet to a height of 59 to 98 feet (18 to 30 metres) depending on its mood. Nearby is the Prince of Wales' Feathers, a triple geyser which usually plays before Pohutu. Another famous geyser, Papakura, sprays a continual jet of boiling water over the cold Puarenga Stream running through the valley.

South-east of Lake Rotorua is the volcanic peak of Mount Tarawera (3642 feet/1110 metres). In 1886, Tarawera erupted, showering the surrounding countryside with red hot rocks and ash. The land tilted violently, swallowing up much of nearby Lake Rotomahana and destroying its famous Pink and White Terraces of silica, and the thriving Maori village of Te Wairoa was buried in a matter of hours. The site has been excavated and is a fascinating glimpse of Maori life in the last century. Near Rotomahana is Waimangu Valley, another notable thermal area. As well as the world's largest boiling lake, the valley contains many geysers and boiling pools, including the Waimangu Geyser, which once played to a height of 1499 feet (457 metres) and was reputed to be the world's largest, but is now much diminished.

The original 'Geysir' is a hot spring in Iceland (see page 211). Geysers are fairly uncommon and usually occur in areas of recent volcanic activity, such as New Zealand, Iceland and Yellowstone National Park in the United States. Opposite: Rotorua geysers. Below: 'The Cathedrals' – rocky spires in the Waimangu region.

Maui

In the middle of the Pacific Ocean an archipelago of volcanic peaks reaches up from the sea bed forming the Hawaiian Islands. The island of Maui, the second largest island of the group, lies between the largest, Hawaii itself, and Oahu, the group's third largest island. Maui's popular nickname, the Valley Isle, comes from the valley isthmus which links the island's two volcanic masses. Maui is about 48 miles (77 kilometres) long and 26 miles (42 kilometres) wide, with a coastline of 120 miles (193 kilometres); its area is about 728 square miles (1885 square kilometres). The population of Hawaiians, Japanese, Filipinos and Europeans is about 71000.

Maui is named after the Polynesian god who pulled the Hawaiian Islands out of the sea. To gain more time for fishing, his favourite pursuit, he captured the sun and forced it to allow more daylight. It was also Maui who brought the Polynesians the gift of fire.

The island's most famous feature is the dormant 10023-foot (3055-metre) volcano Haleakala – the House of the Sun – now a national park. With an area of about 25 square miles (65 square kilo-metres), Haleakala's crater is the largest in the world. All of Manhattan Island could fit inside it, and the tallest of skyscrapers would not rise above its 3000-foot (914-metres) rim.

The western slopes of Haleakala fringe one of the most beautiful and fertile sections of Maui. The road to the summit winds upwards through sugar plantations and aromatic groves of eucalyptus, spruce and pine. Also growing on Haleakala's slopes is the famous silversword plant, with spiky, upthrusting silver leaves. After years of growth, the plants send up long stalks which burst into yellow and purple flowers, which last for a week before they fade and the plant dies.

From the crater rim the view resembles the surface of the moon with nine lesser cinder cones rising from the crater's floor. They appear small, but even the smallest is taller than a good-sized

Below: Clouds linger above the crater of Haleakala, 'House of the Sun', which is part of Hawaii National Park. The northern slopes of the big volcanic dome receive more than 300 inches (662 cm) of rain a year; water is carried by irrigation ditches to the sugarcane plantations (right) in the central lowlands.

skyscraper. Their colours range through subtle gradations of brown, grey, black and yellow with a faint purple tinge.

Haleakala is famed for its cloud effects, especially at sunset and sunrise. Sometimes, atmospheric conditions produce the fascinating phenomenon known as the Spectre of Brocken (so-called because it appears on Mount Brocken in Germany's Harz Mountains). The spectre is one's own shadow projected in a rainbow halo on mist and cloud formations inside the crater.

When the weather is clear, the view from the summit stretches more than 99.5 miles (160 kilometres) out to sea. The unpolluted air and high altitude of Haleakala make it a superb location for scientific observations; there are several observatories and a satellite tracking station on the rim.

As a contrast to twentieth-century science, the valley of Hana on the eastern slope of Haleakala, with its cliffs, waterfalls and rich profusion of tropical trees and flowers, is a quintessential piece of Polynesia.

The Great Barrier Reef

The Great Barrier Reef stretches more than 1243 miles (2000 kilometres) along the eastern coast of Australia, from Torres Strait at the continent's northern tip to just south of the Tropic of Capricorn. Its name suggests a continuous barrier, but this amazing natural formation is much more complicated: it is a maze of coral reefs, channels, cays, lagoons, rocky islands and shallow pools, teaming with every kind of underwater life, altogether covering 100004 square miles (258990 square kilometres). Lying on the shallow continental shelf off Queensland, the Great Barrier Reef reaches out to sea for up to 200 miles (320 kilometres), to the line where the shelf plummets into the depths of the Pacific Ocean. The eastern edge is formed by a nearly continuous chain of reefs which gives the Barrier its name; this is separated from the

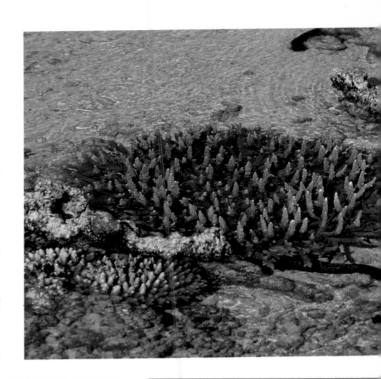

mainland by a long lagoon channel, sprinkled with rocky islands formed by the peaks of a sunken coastal mountain range.

About one third of the region is taken up by the numberless separate reefs. Some are small patch reefs the size of a table, while others may reach more than 19 square miles (50 square kilometres) in area. They may be so close to the surface that waves break over them, or many feet deep. The coral islands, called cays, rise above the reefs. Built

The coral caves and recesses of the Great Barrier Reef harbour every kind of marine creature, from hammerhead sharks to the exquisite array of tropical fish (opposite below); from giant turtles to unappealingly squashy creatures such as the sea cucumber (left). In terms of productivity, the Reef is probably the greatest structure in Nature. The chief threat is a starfish which eats the living polyps. Below: Masthead Island.

up by accumulating sand and coral debris, they are eventually colonized by plants from seeds carried by birds, wind and sea.

Along the outer line of reefs, Pacific breakers pound away to form a continuous line of surf. During the summer, between November and February, heavy rains beat down on the Reef. Occasionally, the Reef is struck by cyclones sweeping in from the Coral Sea. They whip up immense waves which may wash away some of the smaller coral islands and uproot reefs from the sea bed.

The Great Barrier Reef withstands these elemental batterings because it is an organic, self-renewing entity – the work of countless millions of coral polyps. The tiny, sea anemone-like animals form external limestone skeletons which divide and branch into elaborate colonies in many shapes and forms. The reefs are formed by the skeletal remains of generation after generation of polyps as they continually build towards the surface.

The constantly growing and changing coral of the Great Barrier Reef provides an environment for an astonishingly rich and diverse marine life: anemones, sponges, marine worms, sea urchins and starfish, crabs, lobsters and shrimps, mussels, oysters and clams, cowries and spider shells, flagtails, snappers and a multitude of other fishes of every shape and colour. All these and thousands of other organisms make up an ecological network so complex that it boggles the minds of marine biologists.

The Great Barrier Reef has long been famous as a natural wonder. Until recently its position as an unspoilt wilderness was protected by its inaccessibility and the dangers of navigation. But the pressures of modern development may threaten the future of the Reef. Some of the coral islands have been mined for limestone fertilizer. Oil and minerals are thought to lie beneath the Reef and exploration has begun. Farming, industry and urban development on the mainland coast discharge pollutants into the sea. Tourists hack away at the corals and collect rare shells.

It is thought that the pressure of human activities may have altered the Reef's ecological balance in some way which has contributed to a major threat to the Reef: the appearance of hordes of voracious crown-of-thorns starfish, which have devastated large stretches of coral.

It would seem that these hungry starfish are now on the decline and that the explosion of their numbers was a cyclical occurrence. However, strict conservation measures are still necessary to preserve the Great Barrier Reef as an extraordinary and unique treasure-house of marine life.

Waitomo Caves

Waitomo Caves, a national reserve in New Zealand lying 120 miles (193 kilometres) south of Aukland in the North Island, would be little different from many other limestone cave systems in the world were it not for one remarkable feature – their famous Glow-Worm Grotto.

The caves are reached through a countryside of green meadows, luxuriant trees and gentle hills: a typical limestone landscape. There is nothing to suggest that under the visitor's feet lies a magical cave world lit up by a million points of eerie glow-worm light.

In the Maori language Waitomo means 'water-in-going', and the caves were known to the Maoris for the underground river that links the system. The caves came to wider attention in the nineteenth century after a New Zealander navigated the river on a raft he had put together from the tough stems and leaves of New Zealand flax.

Today, tourists enter the caves through a small door in the hillside about 59 feet (18 metres) above the point where the waters flow into the caves. To begin with there are many galleries, chambers, grottoes and glistening stalactite and stalagmite formations, all interesting enough but differing little from scores of other caves. Finally, the path slopes downwards to a large subterranean lake, overarched by limestone vaulting.

The visitors push out in a boat, and the electric lights are switched off. Ordering silence, the guide pulls the boat along by a cable stretched over the water.

At this point, in the darkness and silence, a gradual transformation takes place, rather like sitting in a cinema as the lights are dimmed – but in reverse. Looking upwards, visitors see a faint dawn creep into the velvet darkness as myriad points of green-blue light appear on the cave roof nearly 50 feet (15 metres) above.

Soon there is enough light to tell the time by a wrist-watch. The cave has become a natural planetarium, with a galaxy of stars twinkling in the roof. Hanging down from the roof, a network of beaded, cobwebby filaments catches the light from the green-blue stars which are Waitomo's glow-worms. The effect is unearthly.

Unlike the European glow-worm, which is a beetle, the New Zealand glow-worm which lights up the Waitomo Caves is the larva of a kind of gnat, *Arachnocampa luminosa*. It not only lives in deep caves but is quite common in dark, damp habitats elsewhere in New Zealand. The larva's rear end is luminescent. Sitting inside a thread hammock attached to the cave roof, the glow-worm extrudes as many as twenty filaments, glittering with sticky droplets. Like moths to a light, the midges which breed on the water below are attracted by the glow-worms' glimmering posteriors and become ensnared by the dangling filaments. The glow-worms then haul in the lines and feast on their catches, sucking the life out of them. Despite their behaviour towards their prey, these glow-worms are sensitive creatures. They dislike light or noise, either of which causes them to extinguish their own glow.

The luminescent inhabitants of Waitomo Caves switch on to attract midges and – less agreeably – tourists.

Europe

Peaks of the Dolomites, northern Italy

The Acropolis

The Acropolis of Athens, overlooking the city from a steep, rocky outcrop, is the centre of myth, art, archaeology and history which epitomizes the golden age of Greece. Most of the ancient Greek city-states had an acropolis built on high ground, serving as a fortress, palace and place of worship, but the Acropolis of Athens is without doubt the most famous of these 'upper cities'.

Since their construction more than 2400 years ago the great public buildings of the Acropolis have endured many vicissitudes. They were converted into Christian churches and then Turkish mosques, and were even used as gunpowder stores, with ruinous results for the Parthenon. But since the eighteenth century their battered remnants have been recognized as architectural masterpieces of the ancient world. The Acropolis is also famous for the sculptures and friezes which adorned its buildings. (In the early nineteenth century many of these were rescued or looted, depending on your point of view, by Lord Elgin, and can now be seen in the British Museum, as the Elgin Marbles.)

An inhabited site since Neolithic times, the Acropolis became the stronghold-palace of the early Athenian kings and later, by the classical period, the centre for the worship of Athena, patron goddess of Athens. In 480–79 BC Athens and the Acropolis were sacked and destroyed by the Persians. But by mid-century the resurgent Athenians, now led by Pericles and at the head of the Delian League (an alliance formed by the Greek states to fight the Persians), decided to use the League's funds to replace the temples destroyed by the Persians. It is to this decision to mis-appropriate the funds of Athens' allies that we owe the architectural masterpieces of the classical Acropolis.

Of the three major buildings on the Acropolis – the Parthenon, Erechtheum and Propylaia – the temple of the Parthenon is the most famous, and probably the world's best-known single building. By the time the Parthenon came to be completely appreciated, however, it had already been partly destroyed; in 1687, gunpowder stored in the Parthenon by the occupying Turks exploded while the Acropolis was under siege by the Venetians, causing extensive damage.

The Parthenon was built between 447 and 432 BC by the architects Kallikrates and Iktinos, super-vised by Pericles's friend the sculptor Pheidias. Nearly a double square in plan 228 feet (69.5 metres) long and nearly 102 feet (31 metres) wide, the temple faced east and west. Except for a wooden inner ceiling it was built entirely of marble. The interior building was divided into two rooms: one, more or less square and entered from the west, was called the *parthenon*; the other, entered from the east, was oblong and called the *hekatompedos neos*. Two rows of ten Doric columns divided the latter into a nave and two aisles and towards the end of the nave stood the great gold and ivory statue of Athena.

The walled interior of the Parthenon was surrounded by a peristyle or colonnade of Doric columns, with seventeen columns on each side

and six at the front and back. Each column was built of nine fluted marble blocks, with no base. To compensate for the illusion of concavity caused by perfectly straight columns, the columns were given a slight swelling or entasis. At each end of

In this view of the Acropolis from the south-west the buildings visible are, from the left, the Propylaia, with the temple of Nike Athena; the Erectheum; and the Parthenon. Left: Detail from the west frieze of the Parthenon, illustrating the quadrennial procession in honour of Athena.

the building was a porch crowned with a triangular pediment and containing a second row of six columns.

The colonnade supported an architrave or stone beam, on which rested a series of blocks called triglyphs. The spaces or metopes between these were filled with blocks decorated with sculptures representing gods, giants and episodes from Greek mythology. The pediments at either end of the roof were also filled with sculptures, but unfortunately these have mostly been destroyed.

The finest decoration of the Parthenon – and fortunately the best preserved – was the sculpted frieze above the inner colonnades of the porches and above the wall of the interior chamber. One of the world's greatest works of art, the frieze represented the procession of the Panathenaic Festival; this was celebrated every four years and passed by the Parthenon to the summit of the Acropolis.

The temple of the Erechtheum, to the north of the Parthenon, was completed after the Parthenon, probably by about 404 BC. It was a smaller and more complex building, and its overall form was less perfect; however its Ionian style had great elegance. The building had a walled room or *cella* divided into three parts, and had three porches. On the south-west corner was the famous Caryatid Porch – a balustrade on which six sculptures of young women supported a flat roof. One of the Caryatids was removed by Lord Elgin and is now in the British Museum; it has been replaced in the Erechtheum by a cast.

Overlooking the hill's steep western slope is the

Propylaia, the grandiose entrance gate to the Acropolis. Designed by the architect Mnesikles and built in 437–432 BC, it was intended to consist of a central gate flanked by a wing and a hall on either side, but the halls were not completed. The entrance was covered by a roofed porch faced with six Doric columns crowned with a pediment. The space between the two centre columns was a chariot gate and the other four spaces provided foot gates.

Two bastions built out of the hill protected the approach to the Propylaia. On the south-western bastion stands the beautiful little Ionian temple of Athena Nike (the warrior Athena), probably completed between 427 and 424 BC. The architect may have been Kallikrates, who was also involved with the Parthenon. Like the Erechtheum and Parthenon it consisted of a walled room or *cella*, and at either end were four Ionic columns, with an architrave and frieze above them.

Despite its decay, the Acropolis is still an awe-inspiring sight, rising magnificently on its rocky plateau above modern Athens. How splendid it must once have looked, when it was first built centuries ago.

The Parthenon (opposite) is the grandest of Doric temples and once contained some of the finest sculptures ever made. Its purpose was to house the gold and ivory image of Athena, by Pheidias. Below: The Caryatid porch of the Erectheum. The replica is the rear figure on the left.

Matterhorn

At 14770 feet (4502 metres), the Matterhorn is not Europe's tallest peak – Mont Blanc tops it by 1000 feet (305 metres) – but it has always been considered one of the most impressive, inspiring painters, writers and mountaineers alike. Standing half in Italy and half in Switzerland in the Pennine Alps, the mountain tapers like a rough amethyst out of quartz, showing dark, snow-streaked striated faces which look as if they had been carved out by a gigantic axe.

The Matterhorn's personality was unremarked until 1789, when the Swiss savant H. B. de Saussure camped nearby and studied the mountain. Then, in 1800, a party of English travellers passed by and admired the Cervino (as the mountain is called in Italy). To the locals, the Cervino was a lump of rock in an area infested by wolves, bears and bandits; they could not imagine what attracted foreign visitors. Yet the mountain proved to have a particular appeal to the taste of the romantic era (a taste which had been resensitized to the wilder aspects of landscape). The Cervino gathered a rich harvest of adjectives and epithets; it was compared to giants, animals, archangels and Gothic towers. John Ruskin lavished prose on the mountain in his *Modern Painters*: it was an alpine tower hewn 'by the axe of God'; it was thrust up into 'the great war of the firmament'. Above all, it was inviolable; Ruskin admiringly gloried 'in those firm grey bastions of the Cervin – overhanging, smooth, flawless, unconquerable'.

Up to the 1860s, the Matterhorn, in the words of Edward Whymper, was 'the great Alpine peak which remained unscaled – less on account of the difficulty of doing so, than from the terror inspired by its invincible appearance'. This reputation for being unclimbable was successfully challenged by Whymper when he at last reached the summit with three Englishmen and guides on 14 July 1865, after a race against Italians climbing from the other side. But on the descent, disaster struck. One of Whymper's party slipped and the rope joining the climbers gave way. 'For a few seconds we saw our unfortunate companions sliding downwards on their backs and spreading out their hands, endeavouring to save themselves. They passed from our sight uninjured, disappeared one by one, and fell from precipice to precipice on to the Matterhorn glacier below, a distance of nearly 4000 feet (1,218 metres) in height.' The body of one of the four climbers, Lord Francis Douglas, was never found.

Since Whymper's tragic conquest the Matterhorn has been climbed countless times. A. F. Mummery, another British mountaineer, who climbed it no less than seven times, wrote: 'I have sat on the summit with my wife when a lighted match would not flicker in the windless air, and I have been chased from its shattered crest and down the Italian ridge by the mad fury of thunder, lightning and whirling snow'. Each of the Matterhorn's four faces has been scaled by every combi-

nation of routes and gradation of difficulty. Nowadays, with ropes, cables and ladders fixed at tricky points, Ruskin's 'smooth, flawless, unconquerable' peak has perhaps become too easy for mountaineering purists. But, despite this, the visual grandeur of this archetypal mountain remains unimpaired.

The Matterhorn rises into the sky, resembling the axe-head of some Stone-Age giant. Although from the Swiss side it appears to be an isolated peak, it is actually the butt end of a ridge, and the ascent is not as steep as it looks. From the Italian side, with its imposing terraced walls, it is a considerably greater challenge.

Versailles

During the long reign of the Sun King, Louis XIV (1638–1715), the French monarchy reached the peak of its power and glory. France was then the strongest state in Europe and its king personified the absolute monarch, ruling by Divine Right. To Louis XIV the glory of France meant just one thing, his own glory, and his entire reign was dedicated to furthering it. The Palace of Versailles, which he built, was the greatest monument to this glory, and made such an impact that it became the model for royal palaces in nearly every European country.

As a young man Louis was in the habit of entertaining his friends at the hunting lodge which his father had built at the village of Versailles, 12 miles (twenty kilometres) south-west of Paris. The idea of transforming the lodge came to him in 1661, when he was invited to the house-warming of the magnificent château of Vaux-le-Vicomte, built by his finance minister Nicolas Fouquet. Louis decided that such grandeur was not to be tolerated in a subject, especially as he suspected Fouquet of embezzlement, and promptly clapped him into jail. The king then appointed the three men who had created Vaux, the architect Louis Le Vau (1612–70), the artist Charles Le Brun (1619–90) and the garden designer André Le Nôtre (1613–1700), to help him in his own project at Versailles.

None of Louis' courtiers or ministers could understand his determination to build his palace at Versailles. His courtiers did not want to live in the country and his new finance minister, Colbert, considered the project a colossal waste of money. All this was to no avail and Louis pressed ahead.

The gardens and parkland, with their terraces, sculptured cascades, fountains and lake were laid out by Le Nôtre from 1665. In 1668 Le Vau began the work of 'enveloping' the hunting lodge in the new palace. Leaving the entrance front of the lodge as it was, he extended it in a long rectangular block by adding wings to either side. For the west front, facing the gardens, Le Vau designed a more

The Baroque style of Louis XIV could be somewhat ponderous, but Versailles is saved from too heavy and severe an appearance by a rich array of statuary; see the Garden Façade (left). The sheer scale of the palace is its most impressive feature; however, it does have some frivolities. The Petit Trianon was the favourite residence of Marie Antoinette. Above: In its 'English' garden is this superb little 'Temple of Love', with a statue of Cupid by Bouchardon. There was also a little farm where the Queen could pretend to be a milkmaid.

191

majestic stone façade, with a terrace joining the two wings. From 1678, after Le Vau's death, the architect Jules Mansart (1646–1708) extended the palace yet again by filling in the terrace to provide another impressive room and by adding further wings to the building, giving an immense façade of 1969 feet (600 metres) to the garden front. The fittings for Versailles were designed by Le Brun, who also decorated its finest rooms, the Galerie des Glaces, the Salon de la Guerre and the Salon de la Paix, as well as the magnificent staircase known as the Escalier des Ambassadeurs.

Generations of workmen were employed at Versailles, for Louis was forever making additions and alterations. The cost of building Versailles was 400 million francs – a colossal sum in the seventeenth century.

As Louis intended, the splendour of Versailles became famous throughout Europe, and other European rulers wanted their own Versailles, down to the last detail. Colbert, who had been opposed to building Versailles, recognized its value for French exports. He organized factories to make luxury goods which could be seen at the palace by the foreign visitors who flocked there.

Equally, Versailles became the hub of French culture. The great playwright Molière performed his brilliant comedies there, and Racine lodged at Versailles as the king's official historian. Jean-Baptiste Lully, the pioneer of French opera,

provided the music for the elaborate fêtes and ballets at the palace.

But for all its glory there was something soulless about Versailles. In spite of their earlier reluctance, the nobility flocked there. But there was little to do except involve themselves in palace intrigues and the minute etiquette of court life. The king's mistress Mme de Maintenon wrote to her brother: 'I know of no one more unfortunate than the highest in the land, except for the people who envy them.' And Versailles was uncomfortable: an always inadequate water supply meant that sanitation was nearly non-existent, and in the winter only the royal family's rooms were kept warm.

By cooping up the nobility around him at Versailles, Louis kept them under his eye and prevented them from plotting against him in the provinces. But in depriving them of a role in government, while preserving their privileges, Louis widened the gap between the nobility and people which was to lead to the French Revolution. As well as symbolizing *la gloire* of the Sun King, Versailles symbolized this gap.

Opposite: The Hall of Mirrors (Galerie des Glaces), by Mansart, 240 feet (73 metres) long, 43 feet (13 metres) high. The ceiling paintings show scenes from the life of Louis XIV, and the whole ensemble provides an unsurpassable setting for lavish regal ceremonial. Below: The Salon de la Guerre, *with a relief portrait of the King in warlike array.*

Stonehenge

Standing alone on Salisbury Plain in Wiltshire, the mysterious massive stone circle known as Stonehenge is Britain's most famous and impressive prehistoric site. Long before the beginning of modern archaeology Stonehenge appealed to popular imagination, though its origin and purpose had passed out of memory before the Romans arrived. In the Middle Ages it was said that the Wizard Merlin had transported Stonehenge from Ireland to England. Later, in the eighteenth century, it was romanticized as a Druid temple where human sacrifices were made. There was no evidence for this belief, however, and we now know that Stonehenge was built in the late Neolithic and early Bronze Age periods, long before the Druids arrived in Britain. It may have been a centre of sun or sky worship, and may have continued in use beyond the Bronze Age.

Like a medieval cathedral but much more so, Stonehenge was the product of several stages of building over a long period, from about 2800 BC to 1600 BC. The earliest construction, in the late Neolithic Period, was an outer circle 322 feet (98 metres) in diameter, consisting of a bank surrounded by a ditch. Just inside the bank a ring of fifty-six pits was dug, but these were filled in again soon afterwards. They are called Aubrey Holes after John Aubrey, the diarist and antiquarian who discovered them in 1666 (and who first suggested that Stonehenge had been a Druid temple). In the north-east a gap in the bank forms an entrance to the circle. A large stone, popularly known as the Slaughter Stone, lies flat at one side of this entrance. When the idea of a Druidic Stonehenge was popular, this stone was thought to be a sacrificial altar. Flanked by two earth banks, a pathway called the Avenue leads from the entrance. About 98 feet (30 metres) along it is another large stone, called the Heelstone.

The second building stage, about 2400 BC, was probably carried out by newly arrived early Bronze Age people known as Beaker Folk. They began to put up two circles of bluestones in the centre of the site. The stones were probably quarried in Wales and brought to Stonehenge by river.

However, the bluestone circles were never finished. In the third and most important stage, about 2100 BC, the bluestones were taken out and replaced by the massive sarsen sandstone blocks which form the main structure of Stonehenge as it

Stonehenge is set in the middle of Salisbury Plain, an appropriately deserted spot although, unfortunately, the site's popularity with tourists has inevitably led to a loss of 'atmosphere' in recent years.

is today. These stones, some more than 30 feet (9 metres) long and weighing up to 49 tons (50 tonnes), were brought from the nearby Marlborough Downs. They were set up in a perfect circle of 102 feet (31 metres) diameter, consisting of thirty uprights capped with a ring of lintels or cross pieces. Inside the circle a horseshoe arrangement was made of five 'trilithons', each consisting of a pair of sarsen uprights supporting a lintel. The open end of the horseshoe points at the entrance and Heelstone.

Over the centuries some of these mighty stones have fallen and others have been broken up and dragged away. But more than half of them are still standing, and make up Europe's most impressive megalithic monument. The construction was very skilful. The lintel stones do not just sit on the uprights. They are carefully held in position by mortice and tenon joints, each lintel having two holes underneath so that it locks on to knobs on top of the uprights. Also, the lintels are dovetailed into each other, and to make a smooth circle they are curved on their outer and inner faces.

In the last building stage, the bluestones which had been dismantled were put up again to form a smaller circle inside the sarsen circle and a second horseshoe inside the sarsen trilithons. Nearly in the centre of the monument, inside the bluestone horseshoe, is a flat stone known as the Altar Stone. Like the bluestones, it comes from Wales, but is sandstone.

The purpose of Stonehenge has fascinated many researchers. The main clue is the fact that the monument's line of symmetry, north-east from the centre through the Heelstone, lines up with the midsummer sunrise. From this, it is at least likely that Stonehenge was a centre of sun worship, as apparently reported to the ancient Greeks. But it may be that Stonehenge was not simply a temple but also functioned as a kind of observatory for studying and predicting the movements of the moon as well as the sun. This possibility is strengthened by recent measurements which suggest that Stonehenge (together with many other megalithic sites) was laid out with an advanced knowledge of geometry. For these reasons, some experts now think that the early Bronze Age people of north-west Europe had a much more sophisticated understanding of astronomy and geometry than was previously realized.

However, it is likely to be a long time before there is complete agreement on the meaning of Stonehenge. In the meantime, a sense of unsolved mystery continues to be part of the attraction of this strange, solitary collection of stones, with a silhouette like some megalithic Parthenon.

Venice

Built in a lagoon of the Adriatic, two miles (four kilometres) from the mainland of north-east Italy, the city of Venice seems almost to rise from the sea which surrounds and criss-crosses it. No other western city has been so uniquely placed to make its fortune from the sea, and none has put its wealth to better use in creating a treasure house of art and architecture.

The story of Venice begins in the fifth and sixth centuries AD, when the mud flat islands of the lagoon were settled by mainland Italians fleeing from barbarian invaders. There the settlers were able to build houses on wooden piles which they

drove down through the marshy ground to rest on the hard clay below.

At first Venice was a province of Byzantium, the eastern half of the old Roman Empire. But by their sea-borne trade with the eastern Mediterranean, the Venetians soon became rich and strong enough to declare themselves an independent republic, with their own elected government.

Until the sixteenth century, Europe's supply of tropical luxuries, such as cloves and spices, came overland from Asia to the eastern Mediterranean. Venice's sea power gave her a monopoly of this trade, and by the fourteenth and fifteenth centuries she was Europe's wealthiest city. The Portuguese discovery of the Indian Ocean finally broke Venice's commercial power and from the sixteenth century Venice entered a long decline. But the centuries of wealth had done their work in making Venice the most beautiful of cities, whose magnetic attraction for poets, writers, artists and tourists is still unrivalled.

The focus of Venice is the Piazza San Marco, the city's only large square. At its east end is Venice's chief glory, the Cathedral of St Mark. This magical building was beautifully described by John Ruskin: 'a multitude of pillars and white domes, clustered into a long low pyramid of coloured light; a treasure heap, it seems, partly of gold, and partly

A view of the Grand Canal looking east from the Academy Bridge. Venice is slowly sinking, but attracts international conservationist effort.

198

of opal and mother of pearl, hollowed beneath into five great vaulted porches, ceiled with fair mosaic, and beset with sculpture of alabaster, clear as amber and delicate as ivory.'

More than any other building, St Mark's is the symbol of Venice's past independence, wealth and power. In the ninth century, the Venetians wanted to show their independence of Byzantium by getting rid of their Greek patron saint, St Theo-

dore, and adopting St Mark instead. So they hijacked St Mark's relics from Alexandria and built a church for them. This first church was burnt down and the present St Mark's was built to a Greek design between 1063 and 1094. From then until the sixteenth century, the inside and outside were constantly enriched with sculptures, mosaics and precious marbles, including spoils taken from Venice's successful wars, until St Mark's came to resemble an Aladdin's Cave.

St Mark's Campanile (tower) stands separately from the church. It was from the top of the Campanile that Galileo demonstrated his telescope to the Venetian merchants – who were thus able to obtain advance warning of the return of their ships from trading voyages.

Opposite: The church of Santa Maria della Salute, a cluster of domes and bell towers dominating the Grand Canal. The scroll-like forms help to spread the weight of the dome. The Doge's Palace (below) is a truly remarkable building in a unique amalgam of architectural styles known as Venetian Gothic. There is nothing like it.

Next to St Mark's is the scarcely less famous Doge's Palace. The Venetian Republic was controlled by the Great Council of the city's richest families; the Doges, who were the elected heads of state, had little power but important ceremonial duties. Each year, for instance, the Doge boarded the State Barge to re-enact the ritual marriage between Venice and the sea on which the city's wealth depended.

The first Doge's Palace was built in AD 814 and was burnt down at the same time as the first St Mark's. Rebuilt, it took its present form in the fourteenth century. At ground level is an arcade of Gothic arches, supporting a second row of narrower, decorated arches, above which rise the beautifully patterned and multicoloured palace walls. Besides the Doge's apartments, the Palace includes council chambers and law courts. Its three floors are linked by the famous Scala d'Oro (Golden Staircase), decorated with gilt reliefs and painted panels from the sixteenth century.

The wealth of Venetian architecture was matched by the paintings of the many great artists of the Venetian school, including Giovanni Bellini

(*c.* 1430–1516), Carpaccio (1465–1525), Giorgione (*c.* 1478–1510), Titian (1488–1576), Tintoretto (1518–1594), Veronese (*c.* 1528–1588) and Tiepolo (1696–1770). All their work shows a love of the light and colour which surrounded them in Venice.

Today, Venice is probably less spoiled than any other historic city. One reason, of course, is that there are no cars; to get anywhere people must walk or go by gondola or motorboat. But the sea which for so long protected and enriched Venice is now threatening her. Venice is slowly sinking, at two inches (five centimetres) every decade; as she does so, floods which were once occasional are becoming more frequent and serious. To make matters worse, atmospheric pollution from nearby factories is damaging the stone and marble of Venice. An international rescue operation, backed by the United Nations, has been organized to save Venice. The city deserves no less.

To get about the city by boat rather than by bus may seem a quaint procedure nowadays, but in the days when Venice was a rising mercantile republic it was much less unorthodox to take to the water. In most large cities, the river was the main highway. Left: a gondola, the distinctive Venetian alternative to car or taxi, negotiates a narrow 'side street', past buildings that show the effects of age and dampness. Left below: The Doge's Palace and St Mark's, with the campanile of San Giorgio in the background. Below: The interior of St Mark's, looking east.

Spitsbergen

Spitsbergen, the 'pointed mountains', is the largest archipelago of the Svalbard islands in the Arctic Ocean, 360 miles (580 kilometres) north of Norway. Apart from Franz Josef Land and Severnaya Zemlya to the east, and northern Greenland and the Arctic Archipelago to the west, Spitsbergen and Svalbard are the world's most northerly land. Yet, because the tail end of the Gulf Stream, the North Atlantic Drift, bathes their shores in comparatively warm waters, the islands are one of the most accessible parts of the Arctic. In summer, and even in some winters, their coasts and fjords are free of ice.

The Vikings possibly reached Spitsbergen by the twelfth century, but their discovery was forgotten. The first person to see and land on the archipelago in modern times was the Dutch navigator William Barents, in June 1596.

In 1607 Henry Hudson, discoverer of Hudson Bay, found that the right whale (the bowhead whale, called 'right' because it took the trouble to float when dead and thus could easily be fished out by the early whalers) was abundant in the waters of Spitsbergen, and a whaling boom followed. The Dutch built a blubber works at Smeerenburg on Amsterdam Island which, in 1633, was attended by no less than a thousand ships. But from 1640 onwards, overfishing forced the whales away from the fjords and by 1800 the hunting had ceased. From 1715 onwards, Russian hunters established themselves in Spitsbergen hunting bears, walrus, moose, reindeer, arctic foxes and seals.

With an area of 23642 square miles (61229 square kilometres), Spitsbergen is nearly as large as Scotland. The largest island, West Spitsbergen, is nearly cut in half by the great 55-mile (88-kilometre) Icefjord in the west and by the Wijdefjord, which cuts down 50 miles (80 kilometres) from the north. The island is unevenly covered with icecaps from which many glaciers flow into the fjords. Some of the glaciers reach the sea, where they break up to form icebergs.

Spitsbergen's bays and fjords are remarkably beautiful. All of them lie between dissected mountains averaging about 3280 feet (1000 metres) but rising in places to higher than 4921 feet (1500 metres). The highest point is Mount Newton 5672 feet (1729 metres), in the east of New Friesland Island. Spitsbergen is rich in minerals, particularly coal, which today is mined by Norway and the USSR.

Between the central plateaux and the sea is a raised coastal plain averaging about one mile (1.6 kilometres) wide. Here, in the Arctic summer, the melting snow releases a wide belt of alpine flowers and grasses. Otherwise the vegetation consists mainly of lichens and mosses; the only trees are the tiny arctic willow and dwarf birch.

Spitsbergen has a rich and varied bird life, and seals and arctic foxes still abound. There are small native reindeer, and musk-ox, which were introduced by the Norwegians from Greenland.

With the decline of whaling, Spitsbergen's importance centred on its minerals, particularly its coal deposits, and on its use as a base for Arctic exploration. One of the most famous attempts was by the Swedish explorer Andrée, who set off by balloon towards the North Pole in 1897. He and his companions came down on the ice and perished.

An international treaty gave Norway sovereignty over Spitsbergen and Svalbard in 1920 but divided mineral rights between several countries. Apart from a temporary population of miners, scientists and a few trappers, Spitsbergen is uninhabited. But the 'pointed mountains' of the Arctic continue to have a strange fascination of their own.

The name Spitsbergen was formerly given to the Svalbard Islands as a whole. Barents was surprised in 1596 to find leaves, grass and reindeer.

The Colosseum and the Roman Forum

South-east of the Roman Forum, between the Esquiline and Caelian Hills, stand the colossal ruins of one of ancient Rome's most impressive buildings: the immense Flavian Amphitheatre, better known since the Middle Ages as the Colosseum. Yet this tremendous arena is not merely a monument to the architectural genius of Roman civilization but also a symbol of its (by modern standards) degrading cruelty. For this was the setting for great spectacles in which human beings and animals were mercilessly killed for the entertainment of the baying crowds, although there were also less bloodthirsty events such as displays by performing animals, comic mock fights and marvellously staged sea battles for which the central arena was specially flooded.

Devised to replace an earlier amphitheatre in the Campus Martius, which was destroyed in the great fire of AD 64, in the time of the the Emperor Nero, the Colosseum was built on the site of a lake in the landscaped gardens of Nero's famous Golden House, the Domus Aurea. Work began in AD 70 during the reign of Vespasian; the building was dedicated by his successor, Titus, ten years later with a hundred days of spectacles in which thousands of people and animals were slaughtered; and final decorations were completed by Domitian in AD 82. Wandering round the remains of this immense structure today, it is impossible not to be impressed by its sheer size and the technical genius of its design and construction. Oval in plan, the building is 617 feet (188 metres) long, 512 feet (156 metres) wide and 1729 feet (527 metres) in circumference.

The exterior wall, only part of which remains, is 187 feet (57 metres) high and is faced with white travertine stone. The design and decoration on the outside indicate four storeys, each of the lower three consisting of a row of eighty arches separated by piers bearing decorative columns representing Roman versions of the Greek orders, or designs.

On the ground floor, four of the arches, one on each side, served as principal entrances to the arena for the emperor and other dignitaries. The other seventy-six provided access for the general public to the maze of promenades and staircases leading to the seating inside. On the second and third storeys, each of the eighty arches once contained a statue of a divinity or important person.

The top storey consists of a solid wall pierced only by small windows and divided by ornamental pilasters continuing the vertical lines of the columns on the floors below. Corbels around the top of the wall once supported great masts to which was attached a huge canvas awning operated by sailors to shade the interior of the arena from the hot summer sun. On one particularly sweltering day the Emperor Caligula, in one of his more devilish moods, is reported to have had the awning drawn back and to have forbidden anyone to leave.

The central arena itself, an oval measuring 289 by 180 feet (88 by 55 metres) and covered in sand to soak up the blood, was built over a now-exposed maze of underground passages, animal pens, changing rooms for the fight contestants and store-rooms. An ingenious system of hand-operated lifts raised wild animals used in the various spectacles from the pens to the arena above.

Around the arena the seating arrangements were built on a structure of concentric and radial walls pierced with vaults to permit access to the promenades round the building and the staircases leading to the ground-level exits. The design allowed the entire amphitheatre to be cleared of spectators within minutes. This is remarkable, considering that when full to capacity, the Colosseum held over 50000 people, 45000 seated and 5000 standing.

Surrounding the central arena was a raised platform, or podium, 13 feet (4 metres) high, on which the emperor's box occupied the best position in the middle of the long curve on the north side. On the platform, too, were separate marble seats for senators, other high officials, foreign delegates and the Vestal Virgins, all dressed in their resplendent white togas and jewellery.

Above the podium, the seats were divided into sections or tiers for the different social classes. The first tier, with fourteen rows, was for knights; the second, with about twenty rows, for tribunes and citizens; and above a separating wall, the third tier had covered wooden seats reserved for women only. Standing room for the poorest people, dressed in their rough, dark-coloured clothing, was available on the gallery above the women's seats at the highest part of the amphitheatre. Attendance at a spectacle in the Colosseum was free, tickets in the form of tokens or counters bearing the tier and seat number being handed out under a system of patronage.

During the Empire most of the games at the Colosseum were mounted by the emperor himself and consisted of various events that took place throughout the day from sunrise. Many of the

The classical orders of architecture were employed to decorate the exterior of the Colosseum.

unfortunate participants were people condemned to almost certain death in the arena, either in bloody confrontations with starving, vicious animals or in gladiatorial combats for which they may or may not have been trained.

There were various kinds of spectacles involving animals. In some events condemned criminals or slaves armed with knives or spears would be pitted against leopards, bulls, lions, bears or other dangerous animals. In others, unarmed men and women were simply tied to a stake on a platform and then wheeled into the arena, where they would be quickly torn to pieces as the crowd screamed approval. Many of the early Christian martyrs died in this way. There were also contests between different kinds of animals – a bull against an elephant, a lion against a tiger, and so on – and more elaborate spectacles in which deer, wild asses, ostriches and other wild creatures were viciously attacked by hunters armed with javelins and bows and arrows and aided by hounds.

The gladiatorial contests were a blatant method of getting rid of prisoners of war or deserters or of punishing criminals, many of whom were put in the arena with no defensive weapons simply to be killed. Some criminals were, however, sent to the gladiatorial schools where, together with slaves who had been sold and freemen who had volunteered either for glory or money, they were put through a tough training. Once in the arena their guiding principle was simply 'kill or be killed', and those who excelled could expect to be spared by the emperor's thumbs-up signal and eventually to win their freedom.

The day-long events in the arena began with the ceremonial arrival of the emperor, followed by the procession of the gladiators, during which they would pause before the imperial box and shout their famous greeting, 'Hail emperor; those who are about to die salute you.' After the drawing of opponents by lots, inspection of arms and warm-up exercises, a shrill trumpet blast announced the start of combat in earnest, and the bloody spectacle began. During the mid-day break there were often light entertainments with mock fights and then the events featuring animals.

Despite the mass popularity of these spectacles in the Colosseum, there were many prominent citizens who, like the philosopher-playwright Seneca, condemned them, and with the growth of Christianity throughout the Roman Empire they eventually ceased. Gladiatorial combats were officially abolished by Honorius in the Western Empire in AD 404.

During the following centuries, the Colosseum was used as a fortress, a theatre for medieval mystery plays, housing lots for the poor, and a source of building stone for such Renaissance

buildings as the Farnese Palace. Enough of it remains, however, for us to step back in time in our imagination and recreate the horrifying scenes of long ago. Undoubtedly the Colosseum is a masterpiece of architectural ingenuity and construction, but it will always bear the stigma of serving as a torture chamber and slaughterhouse. Perhaps the most moving sight in the whole vast structure is of the simple wooden cross placed in the centre of the arena by Pope Pius IX to consecrate the arena and to honour the memory of the thousands of early Christians exterminated there.

The funeral of the most famous Roman – Julius Caesar – took place in the most fitting part of Rome, the Forum, which is near the Colosseum. This was the public place, which was the centre of every aspect of life in ancient Rome: its politics, law, commerce and religion. For the Romans a city could not exist without a forum where all citizens could meet to deliberate, see justice done, worship and do business – and simply walk around. Wherever they founded cities a forum on the pattern of

The Colosseum (left) is the finest example of the Romans' skill in supporting a massive auditorium on arches and vaults. Below: Statues in the garden of the House of the Vestal Virgins in the Forum, with the columns of the temple of Antoninus and Faustina in the background.

the Roman Forum was an essential ingredient.

Originally the Forum was part of a marshy valley between three of Rome's seven hills, the Capitol, Palatine and Esquiline. It was probably the Etruscans in the seventh century BC who first used it as a public place, immediately after the swamps were drained by the Cloaca Maxima. In the following centuries, as Rome passed from monarchy to republic and finally empire, the Forum gradually acquired its final shape of an oblong stretching eastwards from the Capitol, surrounded on all sides by many of the city's most important monuments, temples and public buildings.

The oldest and most sacred of these was the Temple of Vesta, a small round building on the east of the Forum. It housed the sacred fire of Rome, which was never supposed to go out – though it sometimes did. (If one of the Vestal Virgins, whose job it was to tend the fire, was unlucky enough to let it go out, she was stripped and flogged by the Chief Priest of the temple.) The other problem was that the sacred fire burnt down the temple several times. Each time, however, it was rebuilt in its old shape. Today, some of the façade and columns of the last version of the temple (about AD 200) have been rebuilt. Just east of the temple was the large House of the Vestal Virgins.

The Temple of Saturn stood at the other end of the Forum. All that remains is the base and eight granite columns that formed the porch, topped by their lintel, frieze and cornice, and a fragment of the triangular pediment above. Except for the Temple of Vesta this was the oldest shrine in the Forum. The present remains date from a restoration of the fourth century AD. The temple was the centre of the Saturnalia or Festival of Saturn held every December, when all rules were relaxed and the roles of masters and servants were reversed. It was also the storage place for the bronze tablets on which the laws of Rome were inscribed, and it housed the Treasury, the entrance to which can still be seen in the temple base.

Opposite the Temple of Saturn at the other side of the Forum was the Temple of Castor and Pollux, the Divine Twins who were said to have appeared with their horses in the Forum after helping the Romans win the battle of Lake Regillus in 496 BC. The three elegant columns that survive from the colonnade around the shrine are the most famous sight of the Forum. They date from a rebuilding in the reign of Augustus.

Apart from temples to gods, the Forum had famous temples to Roman rulers who were deified. The Temple of Caesar, built by Octavian (Augustus), stood next to the Regia. Only the base still exists and in a semicircular recess at the front stand the remains of the altar built on the spot where Caesar's body was cremated by the crowd.

The Temple of Antoninus Pius (AD 138–161) and his wife Faustina stands next to the Temple of Caesar. Since it was combined with a baroque church, San Lorenzo in Miranda, in 1602, it is the best preserved structure in the whole Forum. The temple porch in front of the church is made of ten marble columns topped by a finely carved frieze.

Almost certainly Antony gave Caesar's funeral oration from the Rostra, Rome's main public platform, which closed the north-west end of the Forum. The severed head and hand of Cicero, the greatest Roman orator, were displayed on the Rostra, after his proscription and execution for opposing the triumvirate of Anthony, Octavian and Lepidus.

Near to the Rostra was the Comitium, the open space of about 131 feet by 98 feet (40 by 30 metres) which was the meeting place of the Comitia – the assembly of the Roman plebeians, the sovereign body of the state. Standing on the north of the Forum and next to the Comitium is the Curia or

The Forum: the Arch of Septimius Severus and the three columns of the temple of Castor and Pollux.

Senate House, the assembly of patricians. Last rebuilt by Diocletian (AD 284–305) and restored in the 1930s, it can be seen today in something like its original state. For its importance the Senate is modest in size and style: 85 feet (26 metres) long by 59 feet (18 metres) wide, it has a plain façade without columns. But the interior, with the original paving and three rows of senators' seats on either side, is one of the finest surviving interiors of ancient Rome.

On either side of the Forum was a basilica – a great roofed portico imitated from the cities of Syria and Asia Minor. The Basilica Aemilia on the north-east of the Forum was built in 179 BC; in 159 BC it was provided with a water clock, Rome's first reliable public timepiece. On the other side was the Basilica Julia, planned by Caesar on the site of the earlier Basilica Sempronia. While the Aemilia was a business centre, the Julia was important for its law courts.

The last great building in the Forum was the vast Basilica of Constantine completed by Constantine the Great (AD 312–37). This was not a basilica of the same kind as the Aemilia or Julia; its roof was vaulted rather than flat and the design looks forward to future Christian cathedrals. The three great coffered vaults of the north-east end are still standing.

Two out of Rome's three surviving triumphal arches are in the Forum. The Arch of Titus, the simplest and finest, stands over the highest part of the Sacred Way overlooking the Forum from the east. Made of Attic marble, it celebrates the sack of Jerusalem by Titus in AD 70. At the opposite end of the Forum, between the Rostra and Senate, is the more elaborate Arch of Severus (AD 193–211), with three openings.

After the fall of Rome the buildings of the Forum were considerably damaged; their stones were taken for other buildings or burned for lime. By the Middle Ages the Forum came to be known as the *Campo Vaccio* or Field of Cows, as cattle grazed among the confused ruins, but Renaissance architects rediscovered the principles of classical architecture by studying the remains of the Forum's buildings and other ancient buildings of Rome. Beginning with Claude Lorrain in the seventeenth century, many artists and poets were moved by the atmospheric solitude of the Forum. In 1764, Edward Gibbon's walk across the Forum led him to begin his massive *Decline and Fall of the Roman Empire*. Inspired by the great German scholar Winckelmann, the first scientific excavations of the Forum began towards the end of the eighteenth century and have continued until today – enabling us to understand the grandeur of history's most famous meeting place.

Iceland

Surtur was the Nordic god of fire, who was at the same time the creator and destroyer of the world. If he had not existed in the minds of the Vikings who colonized Iceland a thousand years ago, it would have been necessary to invent him, for there could be no apter symbol for the processes of volcanic creation and destruction which have shaped Iceland.

Almost in the middle of the North Atlantic, with its northernmost tip grazing the Arctic Circle, Iceland, with an area of 39712 square miles (102846 square kilometres), is somewhat larger than Portugal. Much of it looks as desolate as the moon.

Because it is warmed by the Gulf Stream, Iceland is not as cold as it sounds. But it is a country of violent contrasts and extremes. Volcanoes by the hundred have pitted, scarred and twisted its barren landscape with craters, jagged crags of lava and great sheets of grey basalt. The windswept countryside is almost treeless, with only a few stunted thickets surviving the northern gales. About one-eighth of the country is covered by one immense glacier, the Vatnajökull, surrounding Iceland's tallest volcano, Mount Hekla 4744 feet (1446 metres). Since people started counting in 1104, Hekla has erupted fifteen times, often horrendously.

Along with its volcanoes, Iceland abounds with more geysers, hot springs and gas and vapour vents than any other country. The largest geyser, Deildartunguhver, ejects 53 US gallons (200 litres) of boiling water each second. The Icelanders use the hot water and steam from the geysers and springs to heat their homes, to provide year-round open-air swimming pools and even to grow tropical fruits under glass. Even so, only a fraction of the country's geothermal energy is harnessed.

In the short summer Iceland's severity is temporarily softened with fragile greenery and dotted with wild flowers. The tumbling glacial streams are brimming with salmon and the air is filled with the song of an astonishingly varied bird population. But in the long winter, snow holds the island in a vice-like grip, blocking off the interior and filling the craters of extinct volcanoes. Throughout the year the weather is freakishly changeable – from blue sky and bright sun to howling blizzard, driving snow-storm and freezing rain, and back again.

Iceland is not the easiest place in the world to live. Yet it has been continuously inhabited for more than a thousand years, and in the present century has become one of the most prosperous of the world's small nations. The first settlers were

Geysir, the Icelandic hot springs which gave their name (meaning 'gusher') to geysers generally in 1847, at the suggestion of the German chemist, Bunsen. Geysir became well known because of early scientific studies of its water temperature. Above: 'Strokkur' (boy), the smaller of the two main geysers, in full spate.

Although we may realise that land forms were created by volcanic activity, we tend to think of that as something long past. The creation of the island of Surtsey was a reminder that it is still happening. Bottom: A fertile spot in the midst of the barren landscape near Mount Hekla, in southern Iceland.

Irish monks, who reached Iceland in the eighth century AD. They were followed, in the ninth and tenth centuries, by Vikings, many of whom brought with them Irish and Scottish wives and slaves. Based on old Norse, the Icelandic language developed, and with it one of the world's richest literatures, the elaborate and often terrifying sagas commemorating the heroes of Viking Iceland. Ruled by Norway from 1262, and by Denmark from 1380, the Icelanders did not regain their original independence until 1944.

Inland, Iceland is almost uninhabited; nearly all the people live along the coast, by the fjords and river estuaries. About a third of the population live in the capital, Reykjavík, on the south-west coast. What little arable land can be found is farmed, but Iceland's income depends almost totally on fishing.

Historically, Iceland is an old nation; geologically, it is a young land. The *Althing*, Iceland's parliament, was founded in AD 930, making it the modern world's oldest continuous parliament. Its original site was Thingvellir, a wide rift valley bordered by mountains, to the east of Reykjavík. It is right on top of the central split in the earth's crust down the Mid-Atlantic Ridge, which is widening as the North American and Eurasian plates move apart. With it, geologists have calculated that Thingvellir is widening by just over a half inch (one centimetre) a year, so that when the first *Althing* met the sides of the valley were more than 33 feet (ten metres) closer.

Associated with this movement in the earth's crust is the volcanic activity which has thrown Iceland up from the seabed over the last fifty million years. Striking evidence that this process is still continuing was recently provided by the appearence of a brand-new volcanic island, Surtsey, off Iceland's southern coast. Poking its tip above the sea in November 1963, Surtsey raged night and day for three and a half years, until its cone had built up an island of nearly 1 square mile (2.8 square kilometres), rising 948 feet (289 metres) from the seabed and 561 feet (171 metres) above sea level. It was the last of a chain of islands, the Westmanns, stretching south into the sea.

In 1973, Iceland's wealthiest fishing port, on Heimaey, the only inhabited island of the Westmanns, was buried by a disastrous eruption of Helgafell, the island's long dormant volcano. Within a year, the Icelanders had cleared 885800 tons (900000 tonnes) of debris and most of Heimaey's inhabitants had returned. However, if Surtsey had shown the fire god's creativity, the disaster of Heimaey, almost as foretold in *The Poetic Edda*, represented his destructive side. Both are part of the continuing drama of Iceland.

The Tower of London

The murder of the Little Princes, thirteen-year-old Prince Edward and his younger brother, the Duke of York, in 1483 is one of the most notorious deeds quoted in the doleful litany of executions and murders woven into the long history of the Tower of London. But there is more than violence to the story of the Tower, which began with the fortress built by William the Conqueror to secure his hold over the capital of his new kingdom. In the Middle Ages, as a richly decorated royal palace, it was the centre of an often gay and carefree court life. Its concomitant role as a state prison dates from 1100, when the agile Bishop Rannulf Flambard, the Tower's first detainee, managed to escape from his top-floor cell. It was not until the Tudor period, however, that the Tower became the pre-eminent venue for the imprisonment, torture and execution of the monarch's enemies (real and imagined). Before that, the Tower served to keep people out as often as in; more than one medieval monarch took refuge there from rebellious subjects.

Coercion, then, was only one of the Tower's functions. From the Norman Conquest until the early nineteenth century it was the site of the Royal Mint, employing such brilliant engravers and medal makers as Nicholas Briot and John Rotier. From the thirteenth century until its removal in 1834 the royal menagerie was housed at the Tower. The Royal Armouries, Britain's oldest museum, is still there, and so, of course, are the Crown Jewels and royal regalia, one of the world's most sumptuous collections of precious objects.

The 18-acre (7.3-hectare) site covered by the Tower complex lies on the north bank of the River Thames in what is now east London, just above Tower Bridge; here, it occupied a commanding position over the old walled City of London. In the centre of the site is the White Tower, the massive fortress which is the oldest structure of the complex. William the Conqueror ordered the construction of this fortress in 1078, as the strongest link of a chain of castles built around London by the Normans; the building was probably supervised by Gundulf, the pious Norman who was bishop of Rochester. Housing a garrison as well as the royal court, the building was 90 feet (27.5 metres) high and measured 118 by 107 feet (36 by 32.5 metres) with massive buttresses supporting the walls. The White Tower acquired its name in the thirteenth century, when Henry III ordered the building to be whitewashed. Since the seventeenth century the White Tower has housed the Royal Armouries, which contain superb collections of armour, hand weapons and cannon. Henry VIII collected many of the items and his own armour is still on show.

Within the White Tower, the austerely beautiful Chapel of St John, spanned by a perfect barrel vault, is one of England's most perfect Romanesque chapels. Dating from about 1080, it is built of Caen stone. Beneath the chapel, juxtaposing sublimity with horror, is the Dungeon of the Little Ease, the smallest of the White Tower's three dungeons. Four feet square (just over a metre), it was too small for a prisoner either to stand or lie in it. Guy Fawkes, leader of the Gunpowder Plot against James I, was one of many prisoners to discover the aptness of this dungeon's name.

The Tower complex attained its present form as the result of much improvement to its defences, especially by Henry III (1216–72) and Edward I (1272–1307). The outermost of the Tower's three lines of defence is a broad moat, water-filled until 1843, when it was drained and filled in with oyster-shells. Next is the wall of the outer ward, with six towers and two bastions built into it; and finally there is the wall of the inner ward, just over 40 feet (12 metres) high and with thirteen towers, which surrounds the large area including the White Tower.

From the west a stone causeway built by Edward I still provides the modern entrance to the Tower, leading to the Middle Tower on the moat's outer bank. From this, a stone bridge leads over the moat to the outer wall's gatehouse, the Byward Tower. Built into the inner wall opposite this tower is the Bell Tower, where Sir Thomas More and the future Queen Elizabeth I were imprisoned. Built into the inner ward just east of the Bell Tower is the Queen's House, where Elizabeth dined as a prisoner and Ann Boleyn, her mother, was held before her execution.

Between the White Tower and the west wall of the inner ward is the Tower Green, scene of many famous executions including those of Ann Boleyn, Catherine Howard and Lady Jane Grey. With many others who died in the Tower, they were buried nearby at the Chapel of St Peter ad Vincula, which was consecrated by Henry I.

Next to this chapel is the vast Waterloo Barracks, built in 1845 to replace the Great Storehouse destroyed by fire in 1841. Since 1967 the barracks has housed the Crown Jewels, which were previously held in the Wakefield Tower built into the southern inner wall. The jewels have been kept in the Tower of London since the Royal Treasury

The Tower of London has been traditionally a multi-purpose building: palace, prison, fortress, armoury, even a zoo. Today it contains one of the finest museums of arms and armour in the world.

was transferred there in the early fourteenth century – following a spectacular robbery in 1303, when thieves broke into the Royal Treasury in Westminster Abbey and made off with £100,000 worth of treasure. Since then only one attempt on the Crown Jewels has come near to success, that made in 1671 by the Irish desperado Colonel Blood whom, surprisingly, King Charles II saw fit to pardon and employ as a spy.

The Wakefield Tower lies next to the notorious Bloody Tower, so named because the Little Princes were almost certainly murdered there. Once the gateway to the inner ward, it has a massive portcullis, the only one in England in working order. Prisoners of the Bloody Tower included Archbishop Cranmer, burned at the stake by Queen Mary, and Sir Walter Raleigh, executed by King James I.

The southern wall of the Tower's outer ward abuts straight on to the Tower Wharf and the Thames. Beneath St Thomas's Tower in this wall is the heavy wood and iron Traitors' Gate, built probably by Henry III. Many famous and countless lesser known prisoners charged with treason were brought here by barge and passed into the Tower, never to return.

Today the Tower of London stages no executions, but is one of Britain's most popular tourist attractions and rightly so, for it stands as a vivid symbol of the splendour and cruelty of England's royal history: a dramatic reminder that sumptuous palaces and torture chambers were two sides of one coin.

Tradition has it that if the ravens which live in the Tower's grounds ever leave, the Tower will collapse and with it, England.

Opposite: The White Tower. Below: The Ceremony of the Keys. The Chief Warder, plus escort, locks the gates every evening at 10 p.m. By the Bloody Tower a sentry challenges him. 'Halt! Who goes there?' He replies, 'The keys.' 'Whose keys?' 'Queen Elizabeth's keys. God preserve Queen Elizabeth.' The sentry says, 'Amen.'

Pompeii

The date: 24 August, AD 79. The place: Pompeii, southern Italy, a prosperous little Roman city on the southern slope of Mount Vesuvius, overlooking the Bay of Naples. As they go about their business the citizens and slaves of Pompeii give little thought to the volcano Vesuvius. It has been inactive for many centuries and the Pompeiians are only vaguely aware of its volcanic nature, for with its thick woods and fertile vineyards it is a pleasantly sylvan background to the city.

Suddenly, without warning, the mountain explodes, raining burning ashes and grit over the city and the surrounding countryside. Panic-stricken, the people try to flee but there is no escape, especially from the deadly volcanic fumes which are everywhere. Within two days the whole of Pompeii is buried under a blanket of debris more than 20 feet (six metres) deep. Only the tops of a few buildings are visible. The city, so recently bustling with life is dead.

What was a tragedy for Pompeii, however, has been a blessing for modern archaeologists. First unearthed between 1594 and 1600, when a canal was being dug, the buried city has been excavated almost continuously since 1748; today, more than

half of it has been uncovered. Precisely because the eruption buried Pompeii almost instantly, the excavated city is wonderfully intact, perhaps better preserved than any other archaeological site. Almost as if time had stopped, Pompeii gives us the best and most detailed picture of life in an ancient city.

Pompeii was built in the form of an oval about two miles (three kilometres) around, and was

The inundation of Pompeii (below left) was so swift, so total, that much of the city was virtually frozen in time. The marks of the traffic are still visible on paved streets (next page), and the wealthier citizens clearly lived in some style, surrounded by works of art. The frescoes of the Villa of Mysteries (below) are of special interest, partly because nothing compares with them in antique painting and partly because the activities of the cult were apparently a shade disreputable. Many statues and artefacts remain to give a clear idea of life in the Roman province. Left: A bronze 'putto' in the House of the Vettii.

surrounded by a wall with eight gates. Its streets, which were paved with lava blocks, crossed each other at right angles. Wheel ruts are still plainly visible, showing how busy the streets then were. At the time of the disaster, Pompeii's population was about 20000.

Pompeii's public buildings are mainly grouped around the city's two open spaces, the Civic Forum in the south-west and the Triangular Forum at the edge of the southern wall. The Civic Forum, with its surrounding porticoes, has the Capitol to the north, a temple dedicated to Jupiter, Juno and Minerva. On the west is the ancient basilica (an early example of the buildings from which the first Christian churches evolved) and various government buildings. To the east is the huge Building of Eumachia, the centre of the *fullones* (fullers) who carried on Pompeii's main trade, the weaving and dyeing of wool cloth. It has a beautiful marble doorway carved with floral patterns. Then there is

a small temple dedicated to the emperor Vespasian; the Sanctuary of the Lares (the city's guardian spirits); and the *macellum* or provision market. The Triangular Forum has a monumental entrance with Ionian columns and is surrounded with a Doric colonnade. It is the site of the Doric Temple, the oldest in the city. At the south-east corner of Pompeii is the amphitheatre, the oldest one known; it was built in about 80 BC.

Public baths were an important feature of Pompeii. The Stabian Baths, one of the best surviving examples, had separate buildings for men and women, each with a hall and *frigidarium*, *tepidarium* and *calidarium* (cold, tepid and hot rooms).

The private houses of Pompeii are particularly interesting because they cover a period of about four centuries. An example of an early *atrium* house, the House of the Surgeon, has rooms grouped around a central *atrium* or entrance hall. The House of the Faun, dating from the second century BC, shows the development of this scheme under Greek influences. At the front of this truly palatial residence are two *atria* (really open countyards) surrounded by various rooms. In the centre of the first *atrium* is a square rainwater basin decorated with the little bronze faun from which the house takes its name. At the back of the house are two splendid gardens surrounded by colonnades. This house is famous for its fine wall decorations and its beautiful floor mosaics.

Pompeii is rich in wall paintings which are remarkable for their realism and freshness of colour. Some of the most interesting are in the Villa of Mysteries on the outskirts of the city. Dating from about AD 50, these frescoes are a complete cycle, possibly showing the initiation of a young woman into the cult of Dionysus.

Cart ruts and stepping stones in a street of Pompeii. The eruption of Vesuvius in AD 79 also buried the nearby town of Herculaneum.

St Paul's Cathedral

The Gothic cathedrals of medieval Europe were masterpieces of architecture – but they were achieved without architects in the modern sense. Often taking hundreds of years to build, it would have been impossible for them to have been designed and carried through by one man. The idea of the individual architect, which had existed in ancient Greece and Rome, did not reappear until the Italian Renaissance, with men like Alberti, Palladio and Bramante. Even then, a vast project like a cathedral was always the work of more than one architect.

The revolutionary influence of Italian architecture did not reach England until the seventeenth century, where the first fully fledged architect was Inigo Jones (1573–1652). The next major English architect, however, achieved something which no architect had done before. This was to design and complete a great cathedral in just thirty-five years.

The cathedral was St Paul's, in the City of London, and the architect, Sir Christopher Wren (1632–1723). Wren first had a career as a scientist. Self-taught in architecture, he did not design a

Wren planned a church in the form of a Greek cross (equal arms), but the clergy wanted a long nave for their processions. The result is a compromise.

building before he was thirty, but apart from his masterwork of St Paul's, Wren produced no less than fifty-two other London churches and many important public buildings. He also produced a famous plan for rebuilding London after the Great Fire of 1666 which, if it had been carried out, would have made London into one of Europe's most elegant cities.

Built between 1675 and 1710, St Paul's replaced the old medieval cathedral which had been destroyed in the Great Fire. Its most famous feature is the great dome, which Wren intended to dominate the skyline of the surrounding City of London. Supported on a colonnaded drum which rests on eight massive piers and crowned by a stone cupola or lantern carrying a ball and cross, the dome rises 366 feet (111.5 metres) and is nearly 131 feet (40 metres) in diameter. Its beautiful proportions make it possibly Europe's finest dome, excelling even the dome designed by Michelangelo for St Peter's in Rome.

In designing the dome Wren achieved a brilliant solution to several problems. Seen from the outside, the dome had to be tall enough to dominate its surroundings. But seen from the inside, such a tall dome would have been uncomfortably like looking up a tall chimney. Supporting the great weight of the stone lantern was another problem. The answer was to build three domes, one inside the other. The inner, semicircular, dome is high enough to be impressive, but not too high. The next 'dome', hidden from view, is actually a great brickwork cone. It carries the weight of the lantern and supports the outer dome, which is built of timber and covered with lead.

The ground plan in Wren's first design for St Paul's was for a centralized church based on a Greek cross. This idea was rejected by the clergy, who wanted a long, traditional nave, so the final plan was a Latin cross. As with medieval cathedrals, this made flying buttresses necessary above the side aisles to take the outward thrust of the nave vault. These Wren concealed and counterweighted by extending the walls of the façade upwards as screens, so that from the outside St Paul's seems to have two storeys. This stratagem also brought the height of the building into proportion with its great dome.

The main entrance at the west end of St Paul's has a two-storeyed portico with two sets of columns, arranged in pairs to balance the height of the portico. A triangular pediment, sculpted with the conversion of St Paul, crowns the portico. On either side of the portico is a beautifully

proportioned campanile. Together with the dome, these two towers are considered to be Wren's finest achievement. The north campanile contains the cathedral bells; the south one is a clocktower.

Entering from the west door, the interior of St Paul's seems radiant with light; the great central space beneath the dome has an overwhelming impact. The decoration in wood, stone and iron work was by some of the finest craftsmen of the period. The fine choir stalls and organ case are by the great woodcarver Grinling Gibbons and the richly patterned wrought-iron grilles and gates are by the Frenchman Jean Tijon.

Wren himself lies buried under the south aisle of the choir. On the wall above his grave is an inscription placed there by his son, ending with one of the best-known and most appropriate of epitaphs: '. . . si monumentum requiris, circum-spice' (. . . if you seek a monument, look around you).

St Paul's (below) is essentially London's church (the 'national' church is Westminster Abbey). The cathedral was severely damaged by bombs in 1940 but lovingly restored according to Wren's plans. It no longer dominates the skyline, however.

Opposite: Seen from the inside, the dome and the Whispering Gallery.

The Sistine Chapel

Michelangelo Buonarroti (1475–1564), who was equally gifted as a painter, sculptor and architect, is generally believed to have been not only the greatest artist of the Italian Renaissance, but one of the greatest of all times. His contemporary Giorgio Vasari, in surveying every important Italian artist from the thirteenth to the sixteenth centuries in his famous book *Lives of the Artists*, saved Michelangelo until last as one who was 'certainly sent by God as an example of what an artist could be'. Even if Michelangelo had done no other work than his paintings for the Sistine Chapel in Rome this would have been no idle claim.

Built by Pope Sixtus IV in about 1475, the Sistine Chapel stands next to the Vatican Palace, and houses the conclave of cardinals which elects a new pope. It is a large hall without side aisles, covered by a shallow barrel vault, and the chapel's dimensions, 132 feet by 44 feet (40.23 by 13.41 metres), follow the proportions of Solomon's Temple as stated in the Bible: the length being twice the height and three times the width. Pope Sixtus hired a group of artists, including Perugino, Signorelli and Botticelli, to decorate the chapel walls with painted scenes: episodes from the life of Christ on the north side and scenes from the life of Moses on the south. The vaulted ceiling, however, was left as a simple starred design.

In 1508 Sixtus's nephew, Pope Julius II (1503–1513), commissioned Michelangelo to redecorate the ceiling of the Sistine Chapel.

At first Michelangelo was not keen to do it complaining that he was a sculptor rather than a painter. But Julius was insistent and Michelangelo, seeing that there was no way out, threw himself into the task. He worked almost constantly for more than four years, so absorbed in what he was doing that he even spent his nights on the scaffolding. The medium he used was true fresco: watercolour painted into freshly applied, damp plaster. Michelangelo worked under great discomfort, having to look upwards all the time, so that his paint brush dripped in his face.

Left: The Libyan Sibyl, detail from Michelangelo's vault frescoes. The sibyls were female prophets in antiquity, who were adopted by monks in the Middle Ages and given an appropriately Christian prophecy. The Libyan Sibyl's was, 'The day shall come when men shall see the King of all living things.' As with all his figures, Michelangelo used a male model, giving the sibyl a distinctly androgynous appearance.

Right: General view of the Sistine Chapel, with Michelangelo's Last Judgement *on the wall behind the altar. Michelangelo accepted commissions for large frescoes with reluctance, yet they were the projects which, despite the fantastic demands made on the artist, he carried through to the end.*

While Michelangelo was painting, the pope pestered him continually to see how the work was going, and when it was only half finished he insisted on a public viewing. Finally Julius became so impatient that he threatened to have Italy's greatest artist thrown off the scaffolding unless he finished the ceiling. So Michelangelo left it without carrying out the final retouching he had planned. But when the Sistine ceiling was at last revealed to the public, it had a shattering effect – not least on the great artist Raphael, who immediately changed his style.

Down the centre of the ceiling Michelangelo had painted the Biblical history of the world, in nine scenes: God separating Light from Darkness; the Creation of the Stars, the Separation of Earth and Water; the Creation of Adam; the Creation of Eve; the Fall and Expulsion from Paradise; the Sacrifice of Noah; the Flood; and the Drunkenness of Noah. Five of these scenes are placed in a framework, each incorporating four nude youths holding oak garlands which are twined around a medallion containing a biblical scene. Beneath each pair of nudes is a throne; these thrones are occupied by the prophets and sybils who foretold the coming of Christ. Below the prophets and sybils on each side are the ancestors of Christ.

The whole composition of the Sistine ceiling is a vast narrative scheme which amounts to one of man's greatest achievements. It reaches a peak of intensity in its most famous and dramatic image, the Creation of Adam, in which God, having made Adam from clay, reaches out and brings him to life.

The Sistine ceiling was not Michelangelo's last contribution to the chapel. In 1535 he returned, at the request of Pope Paul III, to replace the frescoes on the end wall with a scene of the Last Judgement. Now aging, Michelangelo worked at this picture for six years.

In his Last Judgement, Michelangelo achieved a quite different impact from the Sistine Chapel ceiling. As the angels of the Apocalypse blow the last trumpet, hundreds of figures swirl around the wrathful figure of Christ the Judge. As a reference to his own suffering, Michelangelo painted his own portrait on the flayed skin of St Bartholomew. The Last Judgement had a more mixed reception than the Sistine ceiling, but its awesome character never fails to have a dramatically sombre effect.

The Deluge – the second of the nine history paintings on the vault of the chapel which progress chronologically from the entrance to the altar. The chapel was divided by a screen between clergy and laity. Paintings in which the Creator appeared were all in the clergy's section.

Neuschwanstein Castle

The last European ruler to lavish a fortune on his own building projects was Ludwig II (1845–86), the 'Mad King' of Bavaria. Dreamy, passionate, romantic and finally insane, Ludwig was a king born in the wrong century. His great heroes were the composer Richard Wagner, whose operas evoked Germany's legendary past, and Louis XIV of France, who had shown what it was for 'a king to be a king'.

As a thirteen-year old, Ludwig secretly read the score of Wagner's *Lohengrin* and learned it by heart. At eighteen, he summoned the composer to Munich and a close friendship grew between them. But Wagner's politics and private life had scandalized public opinion and Ludwig was forced to send him into exile. To this and other disappointments in Ludwig's personal life was to be added the political humiliation of having to accept second place when Germany was unified under the leadership of Bismarck and Prussia. Finally Ludwig took refuge from reality by throwing all his energies into building a never-neverland of fantastic castles, in which he might find the solitude he increasingly craved.

Of the three Bavarian castles created by Ludwig, it is the second, Neuschwanstein, which comes closest to the fairytale idea of a castle. Based on the thirteenth-century Rhine strongholds of the German knights, Neuschwanstein is the distilled essence of a medieval castle, with turrets, watch-towers, drawbridges, interior courtyards and massive ramparts at the top of a precipice – all features which, in the nineteenth century, had long ceased to have anything but romantic significance. Following Ludwig's detailed instructions, the castle was designed by the architect Riedel in 1867, and construction began in 1869. After the work was taken over by Georg von Dollman, who designed Ludwig's other two castles, the exterior was finished by 1881, though much of the decoration was completed later.

As striking as Neuschwanstein is from the outside, particularly with its precarious position on a forested mountainside, it is the interior which gave full reign to Ludwig's imagination. The corridors, staircases and windows were carved with thirteenth-century decorations. Paintings and frescoes on the walls depict old legends, including that of Sigurd and Gudrun from the Old Norse Edda.

Ludwig believed that the legend of Lohengrin, in which the hero appeared in a boat drawn by swans, was connected with the village of Neuschwanstein ('New Swan Stone'). Swan symbols are repeated on doors, coats of arms and porcelain throughout the castle. On the large drawing room wall Lohengrin, Elsa, Tristan and Isolde and other Wagnerian characters are illustrated.

The king was not destined to enjoy his fantasy castle for very long. Ludwig's behaviour became increasingly eccentric, and while he was building his third castle, Herrenchiemsee, his ministers voted to cut off his funds and arrest him for insanity.

While at Neuschwanstein, Ludwig was warned

by the villagers that a commission was on its way to arrest him, and he barricaded himself into the castle. The government of Bavaria then officially deposed him, and a second commission managed to reach Neuschwanstein. Ludwig asked for the key to the highest tower so that he could leap to his death, but he was seized and taken to the castle of Berg, which was turned into a guarded asylum. Next day, Ludwig seemed calm and his doctor took him out for a walk. That evening, their drowned bodies were found in the lake.

Had he tried to escape? Had his doctor tried to stop him? The mystery was never solved. But Neuschwanstein Castle remains as one of Bavaria's most famous sights and a fabulous memorial to a tragically unbalanced king.

Of Ludwig's three phoney but desirable castles, Linderhof is a charming Rococo villa which seems quite habitable, Herrenchiemsee a vast palace modelled on Versailles, and Neuschwanstein (below) his favourite, the ultimate German romantic dream.

Lapland

Lapland, at the top of the Finnish-Scandinavian peninsula, reaches across the borders of four nations – Norway, Sweden, Finland and the Soviet Union. With an area of 150011 square miles (388500 square kilometres), this large, sparsely peopled region lies almost entirely inside the Arctic Circle. It is famous as the homeland of the reindeer-herding Lapps and for its scenery of mountains, forests and lakes, its summers of never-setting sun and its dark winters of northern lights.

Lapland's mountains, called fells, are the remains of one of the world's oldest mountain ranges, eroded to gentle, undulating shapes without sharp peaks. Mostly no higher than 1968 feet (600 metres), they are covered by a treeless tundra of lichens, mosses and heathers. In the summer, the heathers form carpets of tiny, beautiful flowers, interspersed with arctic pinks. The fells are the home of the lemming, the little rodent which is famous for its mass migrations.

Below the open fells, the hills and valleys of Lapland are covered by blue-grey evergreen forest and woodland of birch, aspen and rowan. Lush meadows and swamps border the many streams, rivers and lakes. In the spring and summer, the river and lake sides are thick with flowers such as marsh marigold, globeflower and goldenrod. Lying in wait for the unsuspecting tourist during the summer are swarms of mosquitoes, gnats and gadflies.

The Lapland spring, summer and autumn are packed into four months at the most, but their intensity makes up for their shortness. During summer, the magically soft light of the midnight sun can be seen north of the sixty-sixth parallel. It is visible for twenty days on the Arctic Circle and for seventy days on the seventieth parallel. During this time the sun drops close to the horizon, at 'night', but never actually sets, and it is almost as light as it is by day. At midnight the sun very often appears as a large, faintly red sphere above the horizon, so weak that its light throws no shadow and is softened in the hazy air.

As if to balance matters, the sun disappears altogether for two months in the middle of winter, from December to January. This dark time in Lapland is called the *kaamos*. However, the darkness is not complete. As the sun is not far below the horizon, its light, on a clear day, can be

All of Lapland lies above the Arctic Circle, though in the summer it can be surprisingly warm in spots. The Lapps were originally nomadic herdsmen.

refracted to produce an effect known as 'light-dusk', which lasts for about four hours and produces a beautiful play of colours in the sky.

Even more striking are the northern lights, which can be seen on frosty, cloudless nights during the winter. After their first, flickering appearance as thin, yellowish-green veils on the north or north-west horizon, the lights move higher up the sky, forming a large arc from which pointed darts move towards the zenith. As the yellowish-green light becomes brighter, a red and blue glow appears on the edges of the flashing darts, which can reach and even encircle the zenith. This immense electrical display in the upper atmosphere, with its constantly changing forms, is perhaps the most eerily impressive of nature's phenomena.

Before the long winter snows, which last from October to May, comes the *ruska* or autumn, Lapland's most poignantly beautiful season. For a short time in September, after the first frosts, the deciduous birch, aspen, rowan and bog-whortle-berry take on intense, flaming shades of red and yellow before the first autumn storms strip them of their leaves.

Until recently the Lapps were Europe's most isolated and little-known peoples. Their origins are uncertain but it is thought that they migrated to Lapland from central Asia more than two thousand years ago. The Lapp language is probably descended from the same root as modern Finnish. It is as reindeer-herders that the Lapps are best known, though strictly speaking only one of the three main groups of Lapps, the Mountain Lapps, still lead a nomadic life, living in collapsible tents and following the migrations of their reindeer herds. The reindeer provide them with almost all their needs: meat and milk for food, hides for clothing and shelter and bone for tools. The other main groups of Lapps, the Coast Lapps and River Lapps, do not rely on reindeer to the same extent, and are more settled, living along the coast and river banks in wood and turfed huts. Both groups are hunters and fishermen; the River Lapps keep some domesticated reindeer for transport and as decoys for wild reindeer.

Although southern Lapland's rivers have been dammed for hydro-electricity and its forests cut down for timber and paper, much of Lapland remains undisturbed as Western Europe's last great wilderness. It is the peace and solitude of this wilderness, as well as its beauty, which give Lapland its fascination.

Above: 'The Aurora Borealis shakes over the vault of heaven its veil of glittering silver – changing now to yellow, now to green, now to red. It spreads, it contracts again, in restless change . . .; and then the glory vanishes'.
(Fridtjhof Nansen).

The reindeer is the one member of the deer family which can be domesticated – a fact of great benefit to the Lapps among others.

Left: Lapp herdsmen in traditional dress.

232

Mount Etna

For the people of the lovely Mediterranean island of Sicily, the brooding outline of Mount Etna is an ever-present reminder of the threat posed to their age-old civilization by the earth's pent-up subterranean power. Its asymmetrical cone mantled in snow for most of the year, looms over the eastern part of the island and is visible for great distances in every direction. From its summit billows a constant plume of smoke that hints at the awesome forces ready to be unleashed at any moment. For Etna is an active volcano and its unpredictable behaviour has since time immemorial gripped men's imagination and been the inspiration for both superstition and legend.

In ancient times the Greeks, whose complex mythology ascribed all natural phenomena to the moods and activities of the gods, regarded Etna as one of the forges of Hephaistos, their god of fire. And it was an awareness of Etna's divine associations that prompted the philosopher and scientist Empedocles of Akragas to throw himself into its boiling crater in the belief that in that way he would achieve immortality, and in one sense he has.

In recent times scientific investigation has unravelled much of the mystery surrounding the behaviour of volcanoes and compiled much basic factual data. We now know that Etna was formed at a time when great upheavals below the earth's surface caused the seabed in this part of the Mediterranean to rise and create what is now the Plain of Catania on Sicily's east coast and the volcano of Etna. Over many centuries constant eruptions built up the cone on the northern edge of the plain as it spewed out great masses of molten lava and clouds of cinders and ash. Today, the main crater rises to about 12598 feet (3840 metres), its exact height continually changing as fresh deposits are added by each eruption and then worn away by the wind, rain and other agents of erosion.

Of the 135 eruptions recorded since ancient times the most dramatic occurred in 1669, when a great fissure opened in the side of the mountain and a tremendous river of molten lava swept down to the sea and devastated the port city of Catania to the south. There have also been regular eruptions during the present century, the worst in 1928 when lava destroyed the little town of Mascali. Between these bursts of activity the permanent stream of smoke from the summit and the red glow in the sky above the crater at night are reminders that Etna is merely taking a pause in its violence.

Yet despite its reputation, Etna is not without beauty. Magnificent views of its irregular cone can be enjoyed from the countryside on all sides, particularly from the coastal city of Taormina to the north-east or across the Gulf of Catania from the road near Augusta to the south. From Taormina the sight of the mountain silhouetted against the red glow of sunset is especially memorable. And, of course, the volcano itself has many lookout points offering breathtaking panoramas on all sides of the countryside below.

There is a road that completely encircles the volcano as it winds for 86 miles (138 kilometres) from Catania through a string of quiet villages nestling on the fertile lower slopes. Among them are the inland communities of Paternò, Adrana, Bronte, Randazzo and Linguaglossa and, along the coast, Fiumefreddo, Giarre and Acireale, each with its own special points of interest. Paternò, for example, has its restored Norman castle and Randazzo its medieval streets and thirteenth-century cathedral, while on the coast near Acireale there are the curious volcanic rock formations known as the Cyclops' Reefs (Scogli dei Ciclopi) at Aci Trezza and the rock castle at Aci Castello.

Along the route the road is flanked by lush growths of umbrella pines, eucalyptus and palm trees, and spiny agaves, interspersed with cultivated fields of vegetables and corn, citrus fruit orchards, vineyards and groves of gnarled olive trees. At various points there are fine views of the surrounding country, the stretch between Adrana and Randazzo offering outstanding panoramas of the Simeto Valley.

From Linguaglossa, on the north-eastern side of the mountain, a side road climbs through the pinewoods to the village of Mareneve, where a minibus waits to take visitors up the slopes to within 656 feet (200 metres) of the central crater. An alternative route to the summit leaves the village of Nicolosi, about 3281 feet (1000 metres) up the southern slopes, and climbs through woods of chestnut, beech and pine trees to the Sapienza Refuge, where there are restaurant and parking facilities at an altitude of about 6266 feet (1910 metres). From here a cable-car takes visitors up to a height of 8202 feet (2500 metres), swinging high above the desolate landscapes of the upper slopes. This undulating wasteland of dark-coloured volcanic rocks and contrasting patches of glaring white snow is devoid of vegetation, except for sparse clumps of vetch and broom bushes.

The last stage of the ascent is by sturdy all-purpose vehicles that climb to within 328 feet (100 metres) of the central crater. Along the route there are marvellous views of the countryside far below, but the most awesome spectacle of all is of the gaping crater. Its walls are shrouded in clouds of

233

steam and pungent, sulphurous gases, while from the central cone explosions of red-hot lava come shooting out amid fearsome rumblings and splash with strange cracks on the surrounding rocks.

The ascent of Etna today is a much less onerous and dangerous affair than it was when such adventurous travellers as Patrick Brydone rode to the summit on a mule in 1770 in order to see the sunrise. Since Brydone stood there transfixed 'in a silent contemplation of the sublime objects of nature', an observatory, two hotels, a cable-car lift

and winter sports facilities have brought twentieth-century civilization to these wild landscapes.
Yet, despite that, Etna remains one of the world's
most impressive natural wonders.

*Mount Etna is the highest volcano in Europe and the highest
peak in Italy south of the Alps. It covers an area of about 500
square miles (1,295 sq km) and is about 90 miles (144 km)
around the base. Left: Red-hot lava flows from the
mountain. Below: Warning signal from the summit.*

Leningrad

One of the advantages of being a Russian tsar was
that you could achieve the impossible. That is what
Peter the Great, the most extraordinarily energetic
of tsars, did in 1703 when he ordered the construction of St Petersburg – the city which ranks as
one of the world's most beautiful, and which was
Russia's capital from 1712 to 1918 (receiving its
present name of Leningrad in 1924).

During the seventeenth century Russia was the
most backward of European nations, but western
influences were already at work when Peter the
Great became tsar in 1689. He was the first Russian
sovereign to travel abroad, and his incognito trip
to France, England and Holland in 1697–8 made
him determined to modernize Russia. One of the
most important parts of his programme was to
strengthen Russia's navy by building a great dockyard and a new city to go with it – which would
not only support the dockyard with its revenues,
but would rival any European capital in splendour.

It was the naval consideration which prompted
the choice of what otherwise seemed an unprom-
ising site for St Petersburg: the inhospitable marsh-
lands of the Neva delta on the Gulf of Finland.
The decision to make this city the capital came
later, in 1712, and to many of Russia's ruling class
it seemed perverse to govern Russia from its north-
western extremity. Yet St Petersburg's position
made it into a 'window into Europe', a clearing
house for Western cultural influences, so that its
importance as an intellectual and artistic centre
became second to none.

Having decided the site, Tsar Peter then had to
decide what kind of city to build. He knew that if
he hired Russian architects he would get a copy of
Moscow, which he wanted to avoid: St Petersburg
was to be like no other Russian city. So he sent
abroad for the best European architects who could
be tempted to Russia: men like the Italians Trezzini
and Fontana and the German Schädel. Though
Russian architects were in fact to make important
contributions to St Petersburg, it continued to be
foreigners who had the greatest impact on the style
of the city during the eighteenth and nineteenth
centuries.

By Peter's death in 1725 a solid start had been
made on St Petersburg, with such impressive
buildings as the Peter-Paul fortress and cathedral,
the Menshikov Palace, Summer Palace and first
Winter Palace, and the pace and style were set for
the city's future development. St Petersburg was
built by the efforts of people from all over Russia
and many from abroad. Noblemen, merchants and
skilled craftsmen were compelled to take up resi-

dence there and build their own houses. As there was no stone in the region, every wagon entering the city had to bring three stones, every boat ten and every ship at least thirty. But as much as any one individual can be said to have 'built' a city, St Petersburg was the personal creation of Peter the Great. Not only did he oversee every detail of the city plan, he often plunged into the labouring work as well – to the alarm of visiting nobles, whom he expected to join him.

Though many styles can be seen in St Petersburg – so much so that the city has been called 'a symphony of architecture' – two great styles predominate: the Baroque, combining the European Baroque with Russian decorative features; and the Russian classical style. The Baroque reached its height in the middle of the eighteenth century with the work of Bartolommeo Rastrelli (1700–1771), who designed, or redesigned, the Winter Palace, Peterhof, Smolny Cathedral and Convent, the Vorontsov and Strogonov Palaces, and other notable buildings; and S. I. Chevakinsky whose masterpiece was the Nikolsky Cathedral. A trend towards more spacious monumental buildings, with greater simplicity and clarity, marked the appearance of the classical style in the later eighteenth century, reaching its peak in the first half of the nineteenth century. The leading classical architects of St Petersburg included Carlo Rossi (1775–1849), Giacomo Quarenghi (1744–1817) and Andrey Voronikhin (1769–1814). Examples of their work include the Yelagin and Mikhaylovsky Palaces (Rossi); the Hermitage Theatre and Smolny Institute (Quarenghi); and the Kazan Cathedral (Voronikhin).

Just as important as the magnificent architecture of St Petersburg's individual buildings was the city's spacious layout. This is best seen in the Nevsky Prospekt, one of the world's great thoroughfares, which runs through the centre of St Petersburg from the Admiralty near the Neva River eastwards for more than 2.5 miles (four kilometres) to the Alexander Nevsky Abbey. The Prospekt has a special beauty, with its majestic and graceful buildings including the Strogonov and Arichkov Palaces, the Shuvalov Estate and its finest feature, the Kazan Cathedral.

If any one building sums up almost the whole history of St Petersburg, it is the famous Winter Palace. From the first version which was commenced in 1711, it went through five more versions until the Sixth Winter Palace, designed by Rastrelli, was completed in 1760. The Palace, with its grand proportions, was intended to be viewed from all four sides. The two great superimposed ranges of columns of the façade, running

The Russian Baroque palaces of Leningrad help to make it one of Europe's most beautiful cities. Right: The elaborate façade of the Winter Palace. Below: Peterhof.

from ground to roof, add to the impression of height. A balustrade runs right round the roof; above it stand large bronze figures interspersed with classical urns. In all, the Palace has fifteen hundred rooms in its three storeys: the ground floor housed the palace services; on the first floor were the state rooms; and above were the bedrooms and courtiers' apartments. In 1837 the Winter Palace was gutted by a disastrous fire, but it was rapidly restored by the architect V.I. Stasov.

In the Revolution of 1917 it was the storming of the Winter Palace which brought down the final curtain on tsarist Russia. In World War II the Palace was severely damaged during the nine-hundred-day German siege of Leningrad, but since then it has been carefully restored, like many other of the city's great buildings. Today, most of the Winter Palace has been given over to the great Hermitage art collection, which was founded by Catherine the Great in 1764.

From 1912 to 1924 St Petersburg was known as Petrograd; then, on the death of Lenin, it was renamed Leningrad in honour of the architect of the Russian Revolution. There was no irony in naming the city which was a monument to tsardom after the man who destroyed it. The political heritage of tsardom was one thing; its cultural heritage quite another, as the loving restoration of Leningrad's great palaces under the Soviet government has shown.

The Fjords of Norway

The fjords of Norway, great, sea-drowned valleys slicing their way inland from Norway's rugged coast, are some of northern Europe's most dramatically impressive scenery. Hundreds of millions of years ago, from the Cambrian to the Silurian periods, most of Norway lay below sea level. Then the earth folded and buckled to create a mountain system that is a continuation of the Caledonian mountains of Scotland. Later, in the Tertiary period beginning sixty-five million years ago, more folding took place in a vast process which lifted the Norwegian mountains, especially along the west coast, at the same time as creating the rest of the world's great mountain systems.

In Norway, many westward flowing rivers developed tremendous powers of erosion. Following lines of weakness in the mountains, they dug out vee-shaped gorges and canyons which cut deep into the coast. Then, less than two and a half million years ago, during the Quaternary Ice Age, the rivers formed mighty glaciers which scoured out the gorges and canyons into great U-shaped valleys. The glaciers were so heavy they they eroded the bottoms to depths of hundreds of metres below sea level before finally breaking up to form icebergs. When the glaciers finally melted, the sea flowed in to form the fjords which are Norway's most famous feature.

Often, the rocky walls of the fjords may rise vertically from the water for hundreds of metres, with not even a narrow strip of land for settlement. But at the head of the fjord the river which formed the original valley re-established itself after the ice melted and built a delta land. Often, such deltas may be the only places in fjords where villages and farms can exist.

Norway's fjord coastline has had a shaping influence on the country's history. Along the shores of the fjords, wherever there is land, peasant communities survive, many of them farming in ways which have changed little since the Middle Ages. The people of each fjord always tended to act as an independent unit. In the ninth century, when King Harald Haarfarge first tried to unify Norway, it was the chieftains of the western fjords who put up the greatest resistance.

But if the fjords, with their dividing mountains, made Norway hard to unite, they pointed the Norwegians out to sea and encouraged them to become one of the most adventurous of seafaring peoples. Rather than submit to royal authority, many of the Viking warlords and farmers sailed out of the fjords and emigrated to Shetland, Orkney, Ireland, the Isle of Man and Iceland.

Each of the great fjords is a self-contained region. Even within a single fjord there are great differences between the outer seaward parts and the deep, sheltered inner reaches. In the populated parts, the gentle, cultivated delta slopes, with their orchards and rich fields, are starkly contrasted by the barren, rocky cliffs plunging straight into the inky depths of the fjord.

To the south of Bergen, two of the largest fjords

are Hardanger and Bokn, both running south-west to north-east. These are wide fjords with many complex branches, peninsulas and islands. Their lower parts contain some of Norway's richest farmland; Hardangerfjord is particularly famous for its lush, emerald green fields.

The great fjords to the north of Bergen, Sognefjord and Nordfjord, bite deeply into the plateau of western Norway, running west to east.

Sognefjord is one of the most spectacular features of the Norwegian landscape. Stretching more than 124 miles (two hundred kilometres) inland, it lies almost 4003 feet (1220 metres) below the surrounding plateau and its floor is more than 2953 feet (nine hundred metres) below sea level.

The town of Geiranger, at the end of a series of winding fjords, about 80 miles (130 km) from the sea.

The Alhambra

The year 1492 was a watershed in history, not only because it was then that Columbus discovered the New World, but also because it marked the final defeat of Arab rule in Spain after almost 800 years. At its height, from the eighth to the eleventh centuries, the Arabs' Spanish empire, with its capital at Cordoba, was the most advanced society in Europe. Under the tolerant rule of the Umayyad caliphs, Jews and Christians as well as Muslims shared in the literature, art and science of Islam. From Spain, Arab learning seeped through to medieval Europe, providing the intellectual stimulus which was to lead to the Renaissance.

However, Moorish Spain's cultural richness was not matched by political unity. In 1031 the Cordoba caliphate collapsed and broke up into a series of petty kingdoms, and the Christian kingdoms in the north were able to begin their slow reconquest of Spain. By the beginning of the thirteenth century, only the kingdom of Granada remained in Arab hands. Here, however, Muslim rule lasted for another two and a half centuries, until 1492, when Boabdil, the last sultan of Granada, was forced to surrender to the Roman Catholic sovereigns Ferdinand and Isabella. And it was in Granada, its last stronghold, that Moorish Spain's greatest monument was built, the Alhambra Palace – a glorious swansong to the age of Islam in Europe.

The city of Granada (whose name is derived from 'pomegranate') lies on the north-western edge of the Sierra Nevada range in southern Spain, overlooking the rich plain of La Vega. The Alhambra stands on a plateau formed by a spur of the Sierra Nevada, its northern side protected by the gorge of the Darro River and its southern side facing the plain. The building was begun in 1238 by Ibn-al-Ahmar, the first Nasrid sultan of Granada, and completed in the fourteenth century by Yusuf III and Muhammad V.

From the outside the massive walls and towers of the Alhambra are impressive but plain; its architectural and decorative delights are all within. The enclosure formed by the walls is divided into three parts: the fortified citadel of the Alcazaba to the west; in the centre, the Alhambra proper, the palace which housed the sultan and his harem; and to the east, the royal city (of which nothing remains). The entrance to the complex is the horseshoe-arched Gate of Justice in the south wall, over which is an open hand symbolizing the five rules of Islam: belief in the oneness of God, prayer, fasting during the month of Ramadan, giving alms, and pilgrimage to Mecca.

The Gate of Justice leads into a wide esplanade, the Place of Cisterns, where there are great rock-cut cisterns which were used to store rain water in case the aqueduct which supplied the citadel was cut during a siege. Here, in front of the Alhambra Palace, lies an incongruous square Renaissance palace begun by Charles V in 1524, but never completed.

Entering the Alhambra itself, through a simple doorway, the visitor finds himself in a world of enchantment. The American writer Washington Irving described the transition as '. . . almost magical. It seemed as if we were at once transported into other times and another realm, and were treading the scenes of Arabian story'. The

entrance leads into the large, oblong Court of Myrtles, with a large pool in the centre between two myrtle borders. At the north end of this court a colonnaded portico leads to the Hall of the Blessing. This was the antechamber to the magnificently decorated Hall of Ambassadors, the throne room where the Nasrid sultans met important visitors. Here, as in other parts of the Alhambra, the doors, beams and ceilings are carved cedar wood; the floors and wainscoting are patterned earthenware mosaics in purple, green and orange; and the rest of the ornamental surfaces are carved stucco painted in red, blue and yellow.

In the south-east of the palace is the famous Court of the Lions, surrounded by porticos and pavilions, with beautifully ornamented interiors, held up by over one hundred slender marble columns. In the centre of the court is an alabaster fountain resting on the backs of twelve roughly-carved stone lions. Other halls and rooms of the Alhambra include the Queen's Dressing Room, the Royal Baths, the Hall of Two Sisters, the Hall of the Kings and the Hall of the Abencerrages. There is also the Garden of Daraxa, with its summer house, one of whose chambers is a whispering gallery called the Hall of Secrets. Its acoustics enable one to hear from one corner what is whis-

On the hillside above the Alhambra, the Generalife's gardens are a delightful retreat in the heat of summer.

pered in the opposite corner.

Apart from its delicately proportioned architecture, the Alhambra is remarkable for its decoration, which is of three basic types: stylized foliage carved in stucco, geometrical patterns in mosaic tiles, and Arab calligraphy. Because Islamic art avoided representations of people or animals as sacrilegious, these three forms of pattern were developed to extraordinary heights. The geometrical patterns of the Alhambra represent a complete statement of Islamic philosophy, while the calligraphic designs, consisting of Koranic verses, traditional religious sayings and verses in praise of the builders of the palace, literally make the Alhambra a fusion of architecture and poetry.

The intricate delicacy of the abstract and calligraphic ornament dispels the solidity of stone (below). The famous Lion Court (right: freestanding animal figures are rare in Islamic art) was the centre of the area reserved for the harem. The use of alternate single and double columns in the arcades is typical of the highly sophisticated elegance deployed by the Alhambra's builders.

El Escorial

In 1556, when the Holy Roman Emperor Charles V (Charles I of Spain) retired to a monastery, his son Philip II began his forty-two year reign. Next year, the Spanish won a decisive victory over the French at the battle of St Quentin on 10 August, the feast day of the Spanish martyr St Lawrence (who had been roasted to death on a gridiron in the third century AD). Philip vowed to build a great monument to St Lawrence, which would also serve as a tomb for the Spanish Hapsburgs, a monastery for the Hieronymite order (to which his father had retired) and a royal palace.

The chosen spot lay high in the foothills of the Guadarrama Mountains 30 miles (48 kilometres) north-west of Madrid. The nearby village of Escorial took its name from the heaps of scoria, or slag, left by some deserted iron mines. The basic structure was built between 1563 and 1584. The Spanish architects Juan Bautista de Toledo and Juan de Herrera were responsible for the building, but Philip was closely involved in the design and the details of construction.

Built mainly in local grey granite, El Escorial is a huge rectangle of about 680 feet (207 metres) by 499 feet (152 metres); it is built on a grid plan of

halls and courtyards (possibly symbolizing the grid on which St Lawrence was martyred). Rising from the building are four spired towers at the corners, and the graceful dome and twin belfries of the church of San Lorenzo (St Lawrence) in the centre of the complex. On the east side the royal apartments jut out of the building, as if to form a 'handle' for the grid.

The main entrance, in the middle of the west façade, is surmounted by Philip II's shield, and a granite and marble statue of St Lawrence carved by Juan Bautista Monegro. The entrance leads into the large courtyard, the Patio of Kings. Directly opposite the entrance, statues of the six kings of Judah, also by Monegro, adorn the façade of the church of San Lorenzo. On the left of the patio is a college, and to the right is the monastery.

The church of San Lorenzo is built to a Greek cross plan; it was inspired by St Peter's in Rome, but its ornamentation is far more austere. The great granite dome rises more than 299 feet (91 metres) above the church floor, resting on plain stone arches connecting four massive piers, on which are fluted Doric pilasters. The nave and aisle vaulting, originally covered in plain stucco, was later decorated with frescoes by the Italian artist Luca Giordano.

Underneath the high altar of the church is the octagonal vault in which almost every Spanish monarch from Charles V onwards is buried. A stairway connects this vault to a crypt which contains the remains of lesser royalty.

The Royal Palace, which Philip II actually never occupied, takes up the north-east quadrant of El Escorial. In contrast to the austerity of the rest of the building, the palace was richly decorated by the Spanish Bourbon monarchs, who sometimes used it as a summer residence.

Philip II's sparate private apartments were far more modest than the Royal Palace of the Bourbons. They included the family quarters, the throne room and the king's personal suite, consisting only of an antechamber, a study and a bedroom connected to a small prayer room. From the prayer room a small opening overlooks the high altar of the church of San Lorenzo. Through this, Philip was able to hear mass during his final illness before his death in 1598.

Although the overwhelming impression of El Escorial is of a grand austerity, it contains many great works of art. Some of the painters whose works are in the Escorial Picture Gallery are the German and Flemish masters Dürer, Bosch, van der Weyden, Vandyke and Rubens; the Italians Tintoretto and Titian; the Spaniards Velázquez and El Greco. Another great treasure of El Escorial is the library in the west front of the monastery, which contains one of the world's finest collections of rare manuscripts.

On its completion, El Escorial was hailed by the Spanish as the 'eighth wonder of the world'. Ever since then, Philip II's massive, sombre building has aroused respect, if not affection, for it expresses both the intolerant piety and splendour of Spain's greatest age.

In an age of visual flamboyance, the external aspect of the Escorial is notably severe, reflecting the temperament of its builder. There are splendours enough inside.

245

The superbly vaulted library in the Escorial, with frescoes based on a medieval educative scheme, is a tribute to the learning of the Middle Ages. In the foreground, an armillary sphere.

Fingal's Cave

Because we are accustomed to irregular natural forms (take, for example, the Grand Canyon, the Great Barrier Reef, Mount Everest), the occurrence of 'natural architecture', where nature assumes an apparently man-made regularity, always has a striking impact. Fingal's Cave, the basalt sea cave on the Hebridean islet of Staffa off the west coast of Scotland, is a famous example of natural architecture. Here, by a geological fluke, the basalt cliff which plunges vertically down to the sea has been shaped into myriad black and brown columns, forming a double colonnade which recedes gracefully into the vast cavern in the side of the cliff. The columns are topped first with a sponge-like basalt mass and then with a layer of springy turf. Each column is outlined by what the cave's eighteenth-century visitors called 'yellow Stalagmitic matter' which exuded between pillar and pillar. The effect is as if nature had decided to imitate a Greek temple.

Fingal's Cave became famous throughout Europe towards the end of the eighteenth century as the result of a visit by Sir Joseph Banks, President of the Royal Society, in 1772. Banks and his friends, who were on their way to Iceland, were amazed by the cave, which seemed to show nature's own classical ruins. Enquiring its name, they were told by their guide that it was the Cave of Fiuhn. Fiuhn, it seemed, was Fingal, or Finn, a legendary chief who was a hero of the poems attributed to the Gaelic bard Ossian, who was supposed to have lived in the third century AD.

The linking of the natural phenomenon of Fingal's Cave with so-called bardic literature (even though the poems of Ossian turned out to be forgeries) had great romantic appeal, and the cave attracted a procession of visitors – poets, painters and musicians, Turner, Wordsworth, Scott, Sir Robert Peel (who called it 'the temple not made with hands'), Mendelssohn, Queen Victoria and Prince Albert, and thousands of travellers from all over Europe. Depending on how it was looked at, Fingal's Cave seemed to be Gothic as well as classical architecture – a cave-cathedral 'placed far amid the melancholy main'. It is not often that a natural spectacle can be said to have inspired a new style of musical composition, but this was the case with Mendelssohn's *Fingal's Cave* overture.

Below: Fingal's Cave; a feature of some basalt lava flows is the formation of hexagonal 'prisms' perpendicular to the surface.

The Dolomites

The Dolomites, a mountain group in the North Italian Alps, close to the Austrian border, are famous for their magnificent sunrises and sunsets, and for their jagged, fantastic outline. The mountains are named for their dolomite rock, or magnesium limestone. The rock is mainly composed of hard, crystalline dolomite, a mineral first described by the eighteenth-century French geologist Dolomieu, whose name it bears. Touch the rock, and a salty powder comes off on the fingers, a reminder that the Dolomites originated aeons ago as coral reefs beneath the ocean. The highest peak, Marmolada, rises to 10958 feet (3340 metres) and seventeen other peaks rise to more than 9842 feet (3000 metres).

The Dolomites are as wild and beautiful a mountain landscape as anyone could wish. But they are far from inhospitable. The lower, gentler slopes are covered with hay meadows and dark green pine forests. In the spring, fruit trees and fields of flowers are in full bloom in the valleys; the hillsides are green with vineyards, while wild alpine flowers carpet the fantastically-formed rocky heights. Mountain streams teem with speckled trout whilst pike and perch swim in the mirror-smooth lakes scattered over the high valleys. In the autumn, the mountain basins – Belluno, Trento, Bolzano, Bressanone, Merano – remain surprisingly warm. The deep, crisp snow which settles over the Dolomites in winter provides some of Europe's best skiing.

In two valleys of the Dolomites, Val Gardena and Val Badia, live about 16000 Ladini. They are the descendants of Roman soldiers sent by the emperor Tiberius to conquer the original Celtic peoples of the area. Having carried out their orders, the legionaries sent for their families, settled – and were forgotten. Living in isolation until comparatively recent times, their original Latin evolved separately from Italian to become Ladin or Romansch.

Cortina d'Ampezzo, in its sunny valley, is surrounded by five towering Dolomite peaks, each different: Sorapis, with its tongue-like subsidiary ridges; the cathedral-shaped Cristallis; Cinque Torri, like five towers with crenellated battlements; Pelmo and Civetta, like soldiers standing to attention; and Antelao, with its distinctive glacier and buttresses.

The Dolomites are celebrated not for their height but for their grotesque yet beautiful forms. In the setting sun they glow red, mauve and purple against the darkening sky.

The Eiffel Tower

The mass production of iron and steel which accompanied the Industrial Revolution offered, for the first time in history, an alternative to stone which promised the possibility of building to previously unattainable heights.

In Britain and the United States of America, the industrial leaders of the nineteenth century, the idea of building a 1000-foot (305-metre) iron tower became popular with engineers. Such a tower, which would dwarf any structure in history, would be a fitting symbol of the new industrial age. But it was France which first seriously took up the challenge of such a tower, to be the centre-piece of the 1889 Paris Exhibition. Not only was the Exhibition to be held on the centenary of the French Revolution, it was to show the world the dramatic recovery France had made from its humiliating defeat by Germany in the war of 1870. What better way to signal French prestige than by building the world's tallest tower?

The man chosen for the job was Gustave Eiffel (1832–1923), France's most brilliant engineer, whose work in designing railway bridges made him uniquely experienced in building in iron and steel. When he signed the contract in 1887, Eiffel had just two years to construct a completely new kind of project – a wrought-iron tower which would soar to 984 feet (300 metres) [the nearest round metric equivalent to the international target of 1000 feet (305 metres)].

The result was the flawlessly-planned master-piece which immediately became world famous as the symbol of Paris. Rising from the corners of its 410-foot (125-metre) square base by the Seine, the Eiffel Tower's lattice-work piers curve gracefully towards each other until they unite to form a single structure. In all the tower is constructed of 15000 pieces of wrought iron, each separately designed because of the tower's changing curve, engineered to a tolerance of one-tenth of a millimetre and joined together with two and a half million rivets.

The open lattice-work of the Eiffel Tower means that the wind pressure on its surface is much less than it would be on a similar building with a closed surface. Even in the highest wind the tower's maximum sway is 5 inches (12 centimetres).

The Eiffel Tower's three platforms are at 187 feet (57 metres), 377 feet (115 metres) and 899 feet (274 metres). On a clear day the view from the third platform is 42 miles (67 kilometres) and Paris and its suburbs spread out like a giant map. Very energetic visitors can climb up the 1652 steps to the top; most take the lifts, which had to be specially designed to cope with the varying angle of ascent.

With the general public the Eiffel Tower was an instant hit, and has remained Paris's most popular and famous landmark. Its reign as the world's tallest man-made edifice lasted exactly forty years, until 1929 when it was topped by New York's 1046-foot (319-metre) Chrysler Building, followed by the Empire State Building at 1250 feet (381 metres) in 1931. When its flagpole was replaced by a television mast in the 1950s the Eiffel Tower gained another 68 feet (20.75 metres) making it 1052 feet (320.75 metres) tall. Today, taller buildings are commonplace. But every taller structure built since the Eiffel Tower has served a purpose, either as shelter or for communications. The Eiffel Tower is still the world's largest 'pure' tower, built for no other reason than to excel.

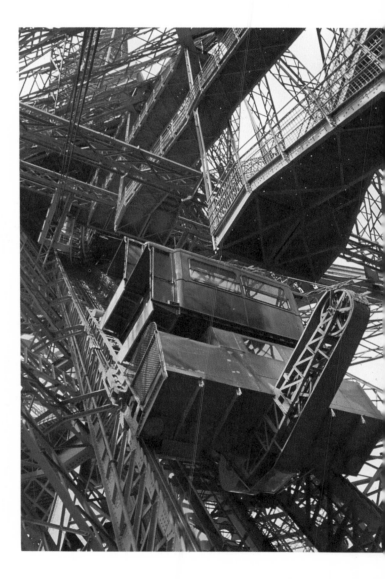

The Eiffel Tower may be regarded (perhaps not by the French) as the world's greatest 'folly' – a building without practical purpose. One of the 19th century's most prolific engineers, Eiffel had long experience of building iron railway bridges. Above: Seen from below. Opposite: Seen from the Trocadéro Gardens.

Hadrian's Wall

Stretching across northern Britain from the Tyne to the Solway, Hadrian's Wall was by far the most impressive and elaborate of the fortifications built by the Romans to protect the land frontiers of their far-flung empire. As a man-made wonder, it may be dwarfed by the Great Wall of China, just as the Great Pyramid dwarfs Stonehenge, but as the northernmost frontier of Europe's first great empire, Hadrian's Wall ranks as an astonishing undertaking in its own right.

After the emperor Claudius invaded Britain in AD 43, the Romans conquered the north of England during the governorship of Agricola (78–84). But they established no definite frontier against the tribes of lowland Scotland, who seriously defeated them in 117. So it was decided to build a great fortified line from the Tyne estuary in the east to Solway Firth in the west; the emperor Hadrian probably confirmed this plan when he visited Britain in 122, and the wall was complete by about 136.

Hadrian's Wall was, of course, not merely a wall but a complete offensive/defensive system, with forts, 'milecastles' and turrets built into it; there was a great ditch on the northern side and a road and an elaborate earthworks to the south of the wall. The forts, from 3 to 5 acres (1.2 to 2.2 hectares) in size, housed garrisons of up to 1000 infantry or 500 cavalry, and included barracks, headquarters, granaries and workshops. Outside the forts villages grew up to house the soldiers' families and various camp followers.

The milecastles quartered the soldiers who did sentry duty along the walkway on top of the wall. Most of them are a Roman mile (4859 feet/1481 metres) apart, and at equal distances between each milecastle are two square turrets built into the wall's south side. Each turret housed a sentry group, consisting of two men on duty on top of the wall and two resting.

The wall itself is 73 miles (118 kilometres) long, from Wallsend in the east to Bowness-on-Solway in the west. Its core is mostly rubble and mortar and it is faced with stones of fairly regular size, small enough to be carried and handled by one man. The average thickness of the wall is 7 feet (2.28 metres) and the height 15 feet (4.5 metres).

The spacing of milecastles and turrets, all within view of each other, made it easy to keep the entire length of the wall under observation, and to signal up and down its length. When attackers appeared before the wall at any point, the sentries could alert the troops in the nearest forts or milecastles

on either side. The troops would sally forth in an encircling movement, drive the enemy against the wall and tackle them in hand-to-hand combat. Thus, the wall was not a defensive fortification in the strict sense. The Romans did not line the wall and wait to be attacked, but emerged and fought in the open, according to their normal tactics.

About 20 feet (6 metres) to the north of the wall runs a ditch shaped like a shallow vee, about 27 feet (8.2 metres) wide and 9 feet (2.7 metres) deep. This can still be seen in places where the wall has been destroyed. Close behind the wall, on the southern side, is a road, the Military Way, which links the forts and so provided for rapid troop movements along the wall. The road was added by the third century AD, after the wall itself had been built. Behind the Military Way is a curious earthwork called the Vallum, which was modified several times. Initially, the Vallum was a flat-bottomed ditch, with two continuous mounds

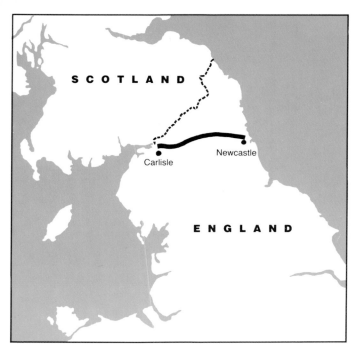

heaped up at about 30 feet (9 metres) distance from either side. Before the Military Way was built, the space between the south mound and the ditch provided a line of communication along the wall. The combination of all these features must have presented an alarming prospect to any would-be attackers.

However, by the end of the fourth century the Roman armies had permanently abandoned the wall. By that time, anyway, it had outlived its purpose; the real danger to Roman Britain was no longer from the lowland north but from sea attacks by the Saxons, Highland Picts and the Scots of Ireland (who had not yet migrated to Scotland).

Today, Hadrian's Wall remains only in short stretches, but its appeal as a unique memorial of Roman Britain survives intact.

Hadrian's Wall is the largest single structure ever undertaken by those fine engineers, the Romans.

254

Acknowledgements

Ace Photo Agency, London 149 bottom; Stephen Benson, London 73; BPCC/Aldus, London – Mount Everest Foundation 108 top left; The British Architectural Library – RIBA, London 24 top; Camerapix Hutchison, London 20–21, 28, 32, 36–7, 37 top, 38, 39, 40, 41, 74, 82–3, 88, 105, 107, 108–9, 116–17, 118 bottom, 122, 125, 131 top, 140, 142, 144–5, 147 top, 160, 161 top, 161 bottom, Mohamed Amin, Timothy Beddow 83 top, S. Burman 148, T. E. Clark 136, John Downman 52, 80 top, 80 bottom, 242, Melanie Friend 53, Patricia Goycolea 126, René-Nicolas Guidicelli 121 top, Maurice Harvey 120 top, Lesley McIntyre 34–5, 35, Michael McIntyre 116 top left, 116 bottom left, 132 left, 132–3, Jenny Pate 29, 76, 77 top, 77 bottom, 153, Sarah Errington 122–123 top, J. Reditt 128, Bernard Regent 22–3, 66 bottom, 68, 78–9, 82, 84, 184–5, 200 bottom, David Simpson 31, V. Southwell 154, Liba Taylor 12–13, 54, 54–5, 55 top, Von Puttkamer 95 top, Val and Alan Wilkinson 33; J. Allan Cash, London 178 left; China Tourist Service Company, Beijing 159 bottom; Bruce Coleman, Uxbridge 89, 181, 232 bottom, Melina Berge 218 bottom, Chris Bonnington 108 bottom left, Gerald Cubitt 124, Jessica Ehlers 141 top, Francisco Erize 74–5, 101 bottom, M. P. L. Fogden 64, 65, Michael Freeman 86 left, Jennifer Fry 137, 144, David Goulton 147 bottom, Charles Henneghien 157 top, David C. Houston 92, 131 bottom, Dr. H. Jungius, 75, L. C. Marigo 58–9, M. Timothy O'Keefe 178 top, Jaroslav Poncar 130, Prato 143, Leonard Lee Rue III 56 bottom, W. E. Ruth 172–3, Eugene Schuhmacher 100, William

E. Townsend Junior 78, Bill Wood 178–9, Jonathan T. Wright 62 top; John Dayton, London 139; Michael Dent, Twickenham 61; Department of the Environment, London (Crown Copyright) 214–15, 216, 217; C. M. Dixon, Canterbury 155, 156, 157 bottom, 185 top, 251; Charles Fowkes, Dunsfold 18, 19; John Green, London 106, 194–5, 200 top, 206; David Halford, London 46 top, 129, 211; Hamlyn Group Picture Library, Twickenham 224, 225, 226–7; Eric Inglefield, London 9 bottom, 51, 63; Jarrolds, Norwich 221; A. F. Kersting, London 228–9; Mansell Collection, London 14–15, 16 top, 17, 23, 25 top; Newnes Books, Feltham 16 bottom, 24 bottom, 25 bottom, 45, 104, 190–91, 191 top, 191 bottom, 192, 193, 219; Pana-Vue 90 left; The Photographers Library, London 6–7; The Photo Source/Colour Library International, London 2–3, 26–7, 42–3, 44, 49, 50–51, 57, 60–61, 62 bottom, 66–7, 67 bottom, 69, 70–71, 71, 90–91, 95 bottom, 112–13, 114, 127, 141 bottom, 166–7, 168–9, 169, 177, 186, 188–9, 195 top, 196–7, 236, 240–41; Rapho, Paris 115; Scottish Tourist Board, Edinburgh 247; Spectrum Colour Library, London 9 top, 30, 48, 56 top, 86–7, 93, 96–7, 98–9, 101 top, 102–3, 120–21, 138, 146, 149 top, 150–51, 152, 170–71, 174, 175, 187, 198, 223, 232 top, 234 top, 237, 246, 250; Syndication International, London 47 top; Judy Todd, London 15, 81, 94 top, 110, 111, 158, 172, 205, 218 top, 220; ZEFA (U.K.), London 165, 222, Armstrong 46–7, Klaus Benser 11, Braeanhage 230–31, Bramaz 94 bottom, F. Breig 248–9, Camera Hawaii 162–3, Damm 182–3, 199, 234–5, W. F. Davidson 252–3, R. Everts 10–11, 202–3, 244–5, Hackenberg 242–3, Havlicek 212 bottom, Konrad Helbig 207, M. Hoch 1, Messerschus 238–9, Orion Press 134–5, Photri 212 top, T. Schneiders 208–9, H. Schumacher 201, Starfoto 159 top, W. Stoy 176.